The Basics of
AMERICAN
POLITICS

The Basics of AMERICAN POLITICS

Gary Wasserman

Eighth Edition

LONGMAN

An imprint of Addison Wesley Longman, Inc.

New York • Reading, Massachusetts • Menlo Park, California • Harlow, England
Don Mills, Ontario • Sydney • Mexico City • Madrid • Amsterdam

Acquisitions Editor: Margaret Loftus
Project Coordination and Text Design: York Production Services
Cover Design: Kay Petronio
Art Coordination: York Production Services
Electronic Production Manager: Valerie Zaborski
Manufacturing Manager: Helene G. Landers
Electronic Page Makeup: York Production Services
Printer and Binder: R. R. Donnelley & Sons Company
Cover Printer: Phoenix Color Corp.

Library of Congress Cataloging-in-Publication Data

Wasserman, Gary
    The basics of American politics/Gary Wasserman. —8th ed.
        p.   cm.
    Includes index.
    ISBN 0-673-52506-6 (pbk.)
    1. United States—Politics and government. I. Title.
JK274.W249   1996
320.973—dc20   96-5102
                                                                 CIP

ISBN 0-673-52506-6

4567890—DOC—9998

Contents

Preface

Throughout its twenty-year career *The Basics of American Politics* has had modest aims: to be an engaging "nuts and bolts" text; a short, readable introduction to American politics. It seems to have worked. As one student remarked when asked if he liked the book, "Well, it gets to the point." High praise indeed.

The basics of American politics remain the same. And so this Eighth Edition holds to the focus on eight major players, both inside and outside of government, in the American game of politics. The "rules" are largely found in the chapters on the Constitution and civil liberties. The book opens by discussing American political ideas ("What Is Politics?") and closes similarly ("Who Wins, Who Loses: Pluralism Versus Elitism").

But much in our political life has changed and this edition adds more than previous editions to reflect those changes. New Republican majorities in Congress boldly question the country's political consensus. President Clinton responds to this rare challenge to a president's power to set the nation's agenda. A resurgent Supreme Court raises its voice on a series of issues from civil rights to term limits. Third parties and independent voters organize against two-party dominance; computer technologies, alternative media, and corporate mergers shake the dominant media in uncertain ways. Traditional figures in modern dress—federalism, religion in politics, balanced budgets—stride to center stage. And within political science new analysts try to make sense of these remarkable changes. To all this, *Basics* provides an introduction and, perhaps, encouragement to go further.

Thanks for help on this edition go to Mike Toppa for his research and drafting skills; to David Cingranelli, State University of New York-Binghamton; Jane Elza, Valdosta State College; Frederick Harris, Northwestern University; Meredith Heiser-Duron, Foothill College; Jack Meek, University of LaVerne; Morton Sipress,

University of Wisconsin-Eau-Claire; Stuart Susnick, Washtenaw Community College; and M. Elliot Vittes, University of Central Florida for reading and commenting on this edition and earlier versions; to Leo Wiegman and Margaret Loftus of Addison Wesley Longman for their customary helpful professionalism. To Ann, Daniel, and Laura, just for being there (often when I was trying to write). And to the students and teachers who have supported this text by buying, reading, and improving it with their comments, a respectful thanks. To my family—all of them.

Gary Wasserman

CHAPTER ONE

What Is Politics?

THE FIRST DAY OF CLASS

Man, they have some strange dudes teaching here this year. The first day of my American government class, the prof comes in and asks us to sit in alphabetical order. Is this believable? Of course all the freshman sheep do it forthwith. But since I am sitting next to the door to allow for a quiet exit, I am very put out by this. So I ask him whether he might not want us to wear Power Rangers shirts to his next class. A bit too cute, perhaps, because he asks me if I think politics goes on in the classroom.

I reply, "No, we are alleged to study politics, but very few of us actually indulge."

"Incorrect," the dude responds, and would I mind removing myself from his class.

"Yes, I would very much mind," I say, "considering the costs of my first seven years at college."

"Will you *please* leave?" he says.

Seeing no gain from further dialogue, I start to exit. He then stops me and asks why I am departing. I remind the gentleman that while he may have missed it, he has just requested my absence. But he insists, inquiring why I'm doing what he asked. I am beginning to think I have missed something and I retort that he is *the head honcho* here, the teach, while I am but a lowly student.

"In other words," he says, "my position as the teacher of this class influenced you to do something you didn't want to do. In fact, it influenced everyone's behavior by getting the class to sit in alphabetical order. So we just saw a process of influence in this classroom that affected a group of people. That's politics. Now you may sit down, and I'm sorry I put you through all that."

"Not at all," I graciously respond, "it was a pleasure to assist in instructing my fellow students."

This story reveals a process of influence between the teacher and the students. This relationship is not only an educational one, but a political one as well. It is political in the sense of political scientist Harold Lasswell's famous definition of *politics* as *the process of who gets what, when, and how.* The teacher (who) gets the student to leave the class (what) immediately (when) by using his authority to persuade and threaten him (how). This indeed is politics.

Our definition of politics centers on actions among a number of people involving influence. How do people get others to do what they wish? How does our society or any society (like that classroom) distribute its valued things, such as wealth, prestige, and security? Who gets these valued things, which political scientists call *values,* and how? The dialogue hints at an answer to these questions. That answer lies in the concepts of *power* and *authority.*

POLITICS AND POWER

Notice in the story that the teacher influenced the student to do something the student didn't want to do (leave the class). The teacher demonstrated that he had power over the student. *Power* is simply the *ability to influence another's behavior.* Power is getting someone to do something they wouldn't otherwise do. Power may involve force (often called *coercion*), or persuasion, or rewards. But its essence is the ability to change another's actions in some way. The more power one has over another, the greater the change, or the easier the change is to accomplish. Having more power could also mean influencing more people to change.

Power always involves a relationship between people and groups. When someone says that a person has a lot of power, one should ask: Power to influence whom to do what? What is the power relationship being discussed? Take the statement "The United States is the most powerful nation in the world today." If this sentence means that because of its huge wealth, large army, and educated population, the United States can influence any other country however it wishes, the statement is wrong. These resources (wealth, army, and population) can give only a *capacity* for power. Whether this capacity is converted into effective influence will depend on the relationship in which it is applied. Certainly the United States had greater wealth, population, and troops than Somalia. Yet in attempting to bring order to that chaotic African country with American troops in 1993, the United States had very limited power to change the behavior of the warlords who ruled there. America's unwillingness to see more casualites or commit more troops was also an unwillingness to bear the costs of power. Eventually all the troops were withdrawn.

People generally do not seek power for its own sake alone. They usually want it for other values it can get them—for the fame or wealth or even affection they think it will bring. Power, like money, is a means to other ends. Most people seek money for what it can buy, whether possessions, prestige, or security. Just as some people go after money more intently than others, so too some people seek power more than others. Of course, power, like money, does not come to everyone who seeks it.

Elites

Those who do gain power are often called a political *elite*. Elites are those who get most of the values society has available (such as wealth and respect). We could answer the "who" part of the question "who gets what, when, and how?" by saying the elite are those who get the most.

There may be different elites depending on what value is being considered. In a small town, the owner of the largest business may be getting most of the wealth in the community, whereas the poor but honest mayor may have most of the respect. In most cases, however, the values overlap. The wealthy businessperson will get plenty of respect, and the mayor will use people's respect for him or her to make income-producing contacts and investments.

To see the difference between an elite and the rest of us, we can look at one value (wealth) in one society (the United States). Clearly, wealth is not distributed equally among the population—some (the elite) get more than others. The top fifth of the American population has an income nine times that of the bottom fifth. The top 1 percent of the nation owns 33 percent of the wealth. Federal government figures show that more than 34 million Americans live below the official poverty line. Further, inequality seems to be growing. One study of the auto industry showed that in a recent five-year period, the income of production workers rose 33 percent while the income of chief executive officers rose 246 percent. These differences show the division between an elite and the bulk of the population in the way our society's value of wealth is distributed. (See "Guess Who's Coming to Dinner.")

Guess Who's Coming to Dinner

Imagine one hundred people at the banquet seated at six tables. At the far right is a table set with English china and real silver, where five people sit comfortably. Next to them is another table, nicely set but nowhere near as fancy, where fifteen people sit. At each of the four remaining tables twenty people sit—the one on the far left has a stained paper tablecloth and plastic knives and forks. This arrangement is analogous to the spread of income groups—from the richest 5 percent at the right to the poorest 20 percent at the left.

Twenty waiters and waitresses come in, carrying 100 delicious-looking dinners, just enough, one would suppose, for each of the one hundred guests. But, amazingly, four of the waiters bring 20 dinners to the five people at the fancy table on the right. There's hardly room for all the food. (If you go over and look a little closer, you will notice that two of the waiters are obsequiously fussing and trying to arrange 10 dinners in front of just one of those five.) At the next-fanciest table, with the fifteen people, five waiters bring another 25 dinners. The twenty people at the third table get 25 dinners, 15 go to the fourth table, and 10 to the fifth. To the twenty people at the last table (the one with the paper tablecloth) a rude and clumsy waiter brings only 5 dinners. At the top table there are 4 dinners for each person; at the bottom table, four persons for each dinner. That's approximately the way income is distributed in America—fewer than half the people get even one dinner apiece.

Source: From Equality by William Ryan. Copyright © 1981 by William Ryan. Reprinted by permission of Pantheon Books, a division of Random House, Inc.

Authority: Legitimate Power

Often, members of an elite reinforce their position by gaining authority. *Authority* is legitimate power. By *legitimate* we mean even more than *"legal"*: The word implies something *accepted as right.* This *correctness* or legitimacy is connected in people's minds to both the position and the wishes of the authority. People may also think something is legitimate if it was chosen using an agreed-upon procedure, such as an election. People generally recognize certain others as having the right to influence their behavior in certain ways. Most people feel that a vice president *should* follow the wishes of the president; students *should* listen to their teacher; children *should* obey their parents. All these influences have a personal moral quality. Other reasons that people have for obeying authorities include habit, the authority figure's personal appeal, desire to be accepted by the group, and self-interest. But although they may not always follow it, people widely recognize authority as deserving obedience, and that is what gives it legitimacy.

Thus authority is an efficient form of power. If people feel they *should* follow the wishes of an authority, then there is no need to force or even to persuade them to do so. The cost of influence is lowered for the authority. If, however, people do not respect the authority's legitimacy, its power can quickly disappear. For example, in April 1992, Los Angeles, California, saw riots by black youths enraged at a jury decision declaring four policemen not guilty in the beating of Rodney King. The three days of rioting left dozens dead and almost $1 billion in damage. Because the police had lost their legitimacy in the eyes of many in the black community, the cost to the police of influencing their behavior went up. The police could still force people off the street; an element of force lies behind most authority. But anyone can clear a street with a gun. Only an accepted authority can do it with just a word.

Power and authority, then, are central to politics. They are also central to many other aspects of life—almost all human interactions involve people trying to influence others. In a political science course, we could study the politics of a school or a hospital or a family—who influences, who is influenced, and what is the process of influence. But most students of politics are interested in a bigger question: How does our whole society decide who gets what, when, and how? To find out, we need to study the most important organization that decides who is to get the valued things of our society—government.

THE NEED FOR GOVERNMENT

Government is one of humanity's oldest and most universal institutions. History records very few societies that have existed with no government. *Anarchy* (a society without government) may be an interesting theory, but it seldom has been applied for long. Instead, people have lived under forms of government that vary from the tribal council of a Native American village to the complex dictatorship of Communist China. Why is government so common?

One answer is that government is as common in society as is *political conflict*—the dispute over distribution of a society's valued things. These values (such as wealth) are limited, but people's demands for them are pretty unlimited. This imbalance means conflict. Whenever people have lived together, they have needed a way to regulate the conflicts among them. The question is not *whether* there will be conflict, but *how* the conflict will be handled. Who will decide on the rules that determine who wins and loses? And how does one get the loser to accept the decision? The usual way to channel political conflict, and thus preserve society, is to have some form of government.

Most governments in the world today claim to be democratic. A *democracy* is a form of government in which all people effectively participate. Because it is generally impractical for all the people to take part in their government directly, their participation is usually through representatives whom they choose in free elections. (What many countries call "free elections," however, without competing political parties and an independent press, would not impress Americans.) Hence, the people rule themselves indirectly, through their representatives, and the government is often called a *representative democracy.*

Yet establishing governments, even democratic ones, to settle conflicts creates new problems. Government allows some people to have their way by coercing others even more effectively than they could if government didn't exist. And to control government is to have great power over many others. As the mass murders of Jews by Nazi Germany illustrated, having control of government may even mean having the power to kill millions of people.

In Chapter 2, we will see that the politicians who wrote the United States Constitution recognized this problem. They set up a number of checks and divisions of power to limit the future leaders of the United States government. Of course, these checks may not always

work. In the late 1980s, the press learned that government officials had transferred money from arms sales to Iran to the Contra forces fighting the Nicaraguan government. This had been done by advisers to the president in violation of the law. It had been kept secret from Congress, the public and, apparently, President Reagan.

What Is Government?

Government is a political association that does two things:

1. **It makes rules determining who will get the valued things of a society.**
2. **It alone regulates the use of legitimate force in society.**

The first part of the definition deals with how society distributes the values it has available—wealth, respect, safety, and so on. The second part deals with how these decisions are enforced. Government, then, has the final word over who gets what and the ultimate say over how it will be done.

The government does not always *directly* determine who will get the valued things in a society. The United States is a capitalist system, based on the private ownership of the economy. This means that the government doesn't directly decide on what jobs people will do, what products they will make or who will get the income from the sale of the products. Instead, in theory, the United States government only protects and legitimates the private distribution of most of society's values. Our government is set up to allow people to get what they can without government interference.

But this noninterference also can be viewed as a decision supporting the status quo or existing distribution of values in American society. The government not only refuses to interfere but also prevents others from interfering in the status quo. For example, it enforces laws such as those supporting repayment of debt and punishment of robbery. In practice, these and other government functions, such as providing a sound currency, protecting from domestic unrest, and safeguarding private property, do mean government intervention. Most groups, whatever their political leanings, favor intervention if it favors them.

At the same time, the government sets limits on the private distribution of values. While allowing people to accumulate wealth, the government puts higher taxes on those with higher incomes. It also supports welfare programs to help the people who are getting the least of society's wealth. Both taxes and welfare illustrate the government's use of its legitimate power (authority) to place limits on the private distribution of this value of wealth.

Making and Supporting Decisions

The government may also intervene more directly in disputes among its citizens. Citizens of a town near a river may not be able to swim there because a paper mill dumps sewage into it. The citizens of the town or the owners of the mill may ask the government to settle the dispute. The appropriate part of the government may respond by passing a law, or by a ruling of an administrative agency such as the Environmental Protection Agency, or by a court decision on whether the town or the paper mill will get the use of the river (the "valued thing").

How the government supports its decision brings us to the second aspect of government—its exclusive regulation of legitimate force. In enforcing its decisions, the government may employ, allow, or prevent the use of force. Either the paper mill or the town's swimmers may be ordered not to use the river. If they try to, they may be fined or arrested. The government alone is allowed to regulate what kind of force is used, and how.

The government is not the only group in society that can legitimately use force. Parents may spank their children to keep them from swimming, or the paper mill may employ guards to keep people off their property. But only the government can set limits on this force. Most governments, although permitting parents to spank their kids, forbid physical abuse of children. The paper mill's guards may be forbidden to use guns to keep swimmers out. Government does not *monopolize* the use of legitimate force, but it alone *regulates* its use.

THE STUDY OF POLITICS

What is the study of politics? One thing you will notice about political science is that it's a lot like other *social sciences* such as history, economics, sociology, and psychology. Each studies aspects of the relations among people. In any large group of people, many social interactions are going on. Each of these disciplines may look at the same group and ask different questions about the relationships that are occurring. This division of labor is partly traditional and partly a way of separating complicated human relations into more easily understood parts. *Political science* fits in by studying one type of interaction between people—that involving power and authority. An example will make the approaches of the other disciplines clearer and distinguish them from political science.

Political Science and Microsoft

What questions would an economist, a psychologist, and a historian ask about the operations of a "society" like the giant computer software company Microsoft? An *economist* might ask questions about the production and distribution of the various Microsoft operating systems and other programs. In designing its Microsoft Network, how did the company attract subscribers and content providers? How were Windows 95 buyers encouraged to use the Network? A *psychologist* might concentrate on the motives and goals of Bill Gates, the founder of Microsoft and probably the richest man in America. What is the psychological makeup of this successful entrepreneur? How does he deal with subordinates and competitors? A *historian* might look at the origins and development of Microsoft. What factors within the industry explain why in a few years its operating systems ran more than four-fifths of the world's computers. Why did it become a $5 billion corporation while competitors fell by the wayside?

Of course, these different fields of study overlap. Members of one discipline are often interested in the findings of another. The economist may find answers to her questions about how focused and innovative the company is in a psychological study of Bill Gates. The historian might ask the economist about Microsoft's mergers with potential competitors to determine the logic behind its expansion. Certainly the economist and the psychologist would want to know about the history of the corporation before studying their particular parts of it.

A political scientist, although interested in the other disciplines' findings, would most likely focus on our central question: *Who is getting what, when, and how?* If Bill Gates runs Microsoft, how does he do it? How do he and his executives reach decisions, and implement them? How has the government influenced their decisions and why did the Justice Department raise and then drop its antitrust suit against Microsoft? How did Microsoft gain preeminence in its industry and how do its leaders keep it, and themselves, on top? Political science focuses on the study of power and authority—on the powerful, the ways in which they exercise their authority, and the effects they produce.

As Lasswell wrote, "The study of politics is the study of influence and the influential."[*] That is the core of what a political scientist would want to find out about Microsoft.

Why Give a Damn About Politics?

After looking at what politics is and what government and political scientists do, you could still be asking one basic question: Who cares? Why give a damn about politics? Often students say: "Politics is just an ego thing. I don't want to get involved in it." But you *are* involved. Apathy is as much a political position as is activism. Either position will influence who gets what in our society. Safe streets, good schools, clean food are political deci-

---

[*]Harold Lasswell, *Politics: Who Gets What, When, How* (New York: World, 1936, 1958), p. 13.

sions influenced by who participates in making them, who is prevented from participating, and who chooses not to participate.

Our lives are webs of politics. From the moment we wake up in the morning, we are affected by someone's political choices. Think of what you've done today and how politics has influenced you. What you had (or didn't have) for breakfast was probably influenced by the price and availability of the food. The quality of the food you ate was regulated by a government agency that made sure those Grade A eggs were Grade A and that the milk was indeed pasteurized. The cost of that milk or those eggs was affected by the decisions of government to aid farmers, as well as the ability of farmers' groups to influence the government (through campaign contributions, for instance). The news you heard on the radio of what the government was doing for the economy was conditioned by what officials felt they should tell the public, and what media editors felt was newsworthy. The lack of good public transportation to take

Who Needs Government?

Senator Ernest Hollings (D-S. Car.) tells this story:

A veteran returning from Korea went to college on the GI Bill; bought his house with an FHA loan; saw his kids born in a VA hospital; started a business with an SBA loan; got electricity from TVA and, then, water from a project funded by the EPA. His kids participated in the school-lunch program and made it through college courtesy of government-guaranteed student loans. His parents retired to a farm on their social security, getting electricity from the REA and the soil tested by the USDA. When the father became ill, his life was saved with a drug developed through NIH; the family was saved from financial ruin by Medicare. Our veteran drove to work on the interstate; moored his boat in a channel dredged by Army engineers; and when floods hit, took Amtrak to Washington to apply for disaster relief. He also spent some of his time there enjoying the exhibits in the Smithsonian museums.

Then one day he wrote his congressman an angry letter complaining about paying taxes for all those programs created for ungrateful people. In effect, he said, the government should get off his back.

Source: Jonathan Yates, "Reality on Capitol Hill," *Newsweek,* November 28, 1988, p. 12.

you to school may have been a result of government decisions to put money into highways rather than buses or trains. The college you attend, the tuition you pay, the student loans or other aid you may or may not receive, are all the results of someone's choices in the political game. (See "Who Needs Government?")

Let's take a personal example. Studies of American government have often pointed out that federal regulatory commissions have not effectively regulated the businesses they oversee. These commissions have tended to be closely tied to the powerful economic interests they supervise. The lesson was brought home to me in graduate school.

In July 1972, the cargo door blew off an American Airlines DC-10 flying over Windsor, Canada, causing violent decompression. The pilot managed to land the empty jumbo jet safely. The government's independent National Transportation Safety Board investigated the near disaster. Their recommendations went to the Federal Aviation Administration (FAA), the government regulatory commission in charge of airline safety. The safety board recommended that the FAA order that all cargo doors have modified locking devices and that McDonnell Douglas, the plane's builder, be required to strengthen the cabin floor.

The FAA, headed by a political appointee, was operating under a policy of "gentlemen's agreements" with the industries it was regulating. After discussions with the plane's manufacturers (who were large contributors to President Nixon's reelection campaign), they allowed McDonnell Douglas to modify the door on its own instead of under FAA supervision and simply to issue advisory service bulletins for the 130 or so DC-10s already in operation. McDonnell Douglas was allowed to reject as "impractical" the idea of strengthening the floor.

Somehow the changes were not made on the door of a DC-10 flown by Turkish Airlines. The plane, flying from Paris to London in March 1974, crashed, killing all 346 people aboard. It was at the time the world's worst air disaster. The cargo door had blown off. This loss produced explosive decompression, collapse of the cabin floor, and loss of control. Passengers still strapped in their seats were sucked from the plane. A subcommittee of the House of Representatives, in a report on the crash, attacked the FAA for its "indifference to public safety" and for attempting to "balance dollars against lives."

A teacher and friend of mine, Professor Wayne Wilcox of Columbia University, was on the plane. With him were his wife and two children.

We have no choice over *whether* to be involved in the political game. But we can choose *how* to be involved. We can choose whether to be a *subject* in the political game or an *object of* that game. The question is not whether politics affects us—it does, and will. The question is whether we will affect politics. The first step in this decision is choosing how aware we wish to be of the game. This book may, with luck, be a start of your awareness.

WHAT IS THIS BOOK ABOUT?

This book is, in a way, a scorecard covering the major players in the game of national politics. This first chapter introduces some of the terms and substance of politics—the means (power and authority) and goals (values) of the game. Chapters 2 and 6 cover the formal constitutional rules and the civil liberties and rights under which the competition proceeds. Chapters 3, 4, and 5 deal with the governmental players—the president and bureaucracy, Congress, and the federal courts—their history and structure, their strengths and weaknesses. Chapters 7 and 8 are about four important nongovernmental players—voters, political parties, interest groups, and media. Though they are not official parts of the government, they have great influence over the outcome of political conflicts. Finally, the last chapter goes into different theories of who wins and loses, who plays and doesn't play the game.

Let's be clear about this "game"; it is not "Monday Night Football." It is important, complex, ever changing, never ending, and serious. Actually, many games are going on at the same time with overlapping players and objectives. They are games in which the participants seldom agree, even on the goals. For the goals (unlike the touchdown in football) vary with the objectives of the players. A business group may seek higher profits from its involvement in a political issue, a consumer organization may want a lower-priced product, and a labor union may demand higher wages for its workers. They may all compete for their differing objectives over the same issue. They all seek to use power to obtain the values they consider important. We can analyze objectively how they play the game, but which side we root for depends on our own interests and ideals.

Another problem is that the players we've grouped together may not see themselves as being on the same team. Each participant, whether the bureaucracy, Congress, or the media, is hardly one player seeking a single goal. They are not only players but also *arenas* in which competition goes on. We may read of Congress opposing the president on an issue, but a closer look will find the president's congressional supporters and opponents fighting it out in the committees of Congress. Some of the media may oppose a certain interest group, while allowing or limiting the use of television news and radio talk shows as arenas for the group's views.

Finally, in this brief introductory text all the political players are not discussed. State and local governments are certainly important in national politics. Ethnic groups and foreign governments may have a role in the outcome of the competition. An even more fundamental omission, as one student remarked, are the people. What ever happened to the people in this game? Are they players or spectators?

For the most part, politics today is a spectator sport. The people are in the audience. To be sure, people do influence the players. The president and Congress are selected by election, interest groups depend on their members' support, and political parties need popular backing for their activities. But though it is played for the crowd and paid for by them, the game generally doesn't include them directly. Whether it will depends on the players, the rules and nature of the competition, and the people watching.

Thought Questions

1. In the opening dialogue of this chapter, we discovered politics in a place that may seem unlikely—a classroom. Describe some other common situations in which politics goes on.
2. How do authorities gain legitimacy? How do they lose it? Can you think of recent examples of both?
3. Why do you think many people are apathetic about national politics? Is apathy encouraged? If so, how? By whom?
4. In what ways has your life been affected by governmental action? Did you have anything to say about those actions? If you didn't, do you know who did?

Suggested Readings

Anonymous. *Primary Colors: A Novel of Politics.* New York: Random House, 1996.
    A *Newsweek* columnist's fictional account of the nitty gritty of President Clinton's 1992 Campaign.

Golding, William G. *Lord of the Flies.* New York: Capricorn Books, 1959. Pb.
    A somewhat pessimistic novel (also a movie) on what happens to a group of British children on a deserted island without adults or government, but with lots of politics.

Mathews, Christopher. *Hardball: How Politics Is Played.* New York: Summit Books, 1988. Pb.
    A collection of short "rules" and stories that half-seriously tell how the Washington, D.C., game goes.

O'Rourke, P. J. *Parliament of Whores.* New York: Vintage Books, 1991.
    Funny, cynical, and, on occasion, insightful O'Rourke is a conservative humorist who attempts to describe and explain this "ongoing behemoth," the U.S. government.

Warren, Robert Penn. *All the King's Men.* New York: Harcourt Brace Jovanovich, 1946.
    A terrific novel about a terrifically manipulative politician modeled on Louisiana's Huey Long.

CHAPTER TWO

The Constitution: Rules of the Game

THE SECOND DAY OF CLASS

Man, the second day was worse than the first. This time the dude wants to play word games. He says to us let's do word associations—what words come to mind when he says "politician"?

Well, this one I know the answer to. My hand shoots up. "How about 'Slime balls'?"

High fives all around.

Someone else shouts, "Crooks." then, "Mediocre." "Ego-tripping." Boy did we let him have it.

Then he says, "What about 'politics'?"

Not too difficult—"Dirty." "Corrupt." "Games." "Boring." "A Waste."

So then he says, "Well what about when I say 'Founding Fathers' or 'Framers of the Constitution'?"

This also wasn't too hard—"Patriots." "Freedom." "George Washington." "Independence."

"How about 'The Constitution'?" he says.

"Liberty." "Equality." "National values." "Bill of Rights.". . .

Well, some of us are beginning to catch on.

Then he lets us have it. "Didn't the Framers of the Constitution have to run for election, make promises and win peoples' votes? And not all of them were the most honest or principled in their own lives. Didn't they represent conflicting interests and cut secret deals with each other? And the Constitution they wrote—didn't that come from their wheeling and dealing? And I believe you'll find that many people at the time were unhappy with the results and with their leaders.

"Sounds like our Founding Fathers were a bunch of politicians."

I dunno. . . . It is possible I might learn something in this class.

The Constitution did not fall from the sky. It was created by political leaders trying to form a government while dealing with immediate problems and conflicts, all within the understandings of their day. It has lasted because the politicians into whose care it was put proved flexible enough to adapt it to different times, and because it commanded loyalty as a symbol of a nation's traditions and ideals. But the Constitution has never been "above politics." Its words cannot be understood apart from the politics in which they were written, and in which they are applied.

So far we have discussed what the game of politics is about, what winning means, and why one plays. This chapter deals with the principles and procedures of the competition. It first discusses the politicians who wrote the Constitution, their debates, the interests they represented and the compromises they reached. The Constitution itself contains the official rules of the American political game; it also establishes three major players and their powers—the president, Congress, and the Supreme Court. Further, it places limits on the game, providing protection for the players. And by creating a central government that shares power with state governments, the Constitution establishes the playing field of federalism. What led to the adoption of the Constitution, its meaning, how it has changed, and its influence today are the central concerns of this chapter.

BACKGROUND TO THE CONSTITUTION

On July 4, 1776, the Declaration of Independence proclaimed the American colonies "Free and Independent States." This symbolized the beginning not only of a bitter fight for independence from Great Britain, but also of a struggle to unify the separate and often conflicting interests, regions, and states of America. Only after a decade of trial and error was the Constitution written and accepted as the legal foundation for the new United States of America.

The politicians who gathered in Philadelphia in May 1787 to write the Constitution were not starting from scratch. They were able to draw on (1) an English legal heritage, (2) American models of colonial and state governments, and (3) their experience with the Articles of Confederation.

The English political heritage that the framers were part of included the *Magna Carta,* which in the year 1215 had declared that the power of the king was not absolute. It also included the idea of natural rights, expressed by English philosophers, most notably John Locke, who wrote that people were "born free" and formed society to protect their rights. Many colonists felt that they were fighting a revolution to secure their traditional rights as Englishmen, which they had been denied by an abusive colonial government.

During their 150 years as colonies, the states had learned much about self-government, which they used to create the Constitution. Even the earliest settlers had been determined to live under written rules of law resting on the consent of the community: The *Mayflower Compact* was signed by the Pilgrims shortly before they landed at Plymouth in 1620. Similar documents had been written in other colonies, most of which had their own constitutions. Other aspects of colonial governments, such as two-house legislatures, also were later to appear in the Constitution. After the Revolution, in reaction to the authority of the royal governor, the colonists established the legislature as the most important branch in their state governments.

Most of the colonies had a governor, a legislature, and a judiciary, a pattern that would evolve into the constitutional separation of powers. Most had regular elections, though generally only white males who owned property could vote. There was even an uneasy basis for the federal system of local and national governments in the sharing of powers between the American colonies and a central government in England. Perhaps most important was the idea of limited government and individual rights written into the state constitutions after the Revolution.

But unity among the colonies was evolving slowly. Attempts to tighten their ties during the Revolution were a limited success. The First Continental Congress in September 1774 had established regular lines of communication among the colonies and gave a focus to anti-British sentiment. The Second Continental Congress, beginning in Philadelphia in May 1775, created the Declaration of Independence. At the same time a plan for confederation—a loose union among the states—was proposed. The *Articles of Confederation* were ratified by the states by March 1781 and went into effect even before the formal end of the American Revolution in February 1783.

The Articles of Confederation (1781–1789)

Pointing out the shortcomings of the Articles of Confederation is not difficult. No real national government was set up in the articles. Rather, they established a "league of friendship" among the states, which didn't have much more authority than the United Nations does today. The center of the federation was a *unicameral* (one-house) legislature, called the Confederation Congress. Each state had one vote, regardless of its size. Most serious actions required approval by nine states, and amendments to the articles needed approval by all thirteen.

The confederation had no executive branch and no national system of courts. Perhaps most important, the congress had no ability to impose taxes; it could only *request* funds from the states. Each state retained its "sovereignty, freedom, and independence." Nor did the congress have any direct authority over citizens, who were subject only to the government of their states. In short, the congress had no ability to enforce its will on either states or citizens.

The confederation did have many strengths, however. Unlike the United Nations, it had the power to declare war, conduct foreign policy, coin money, manage a postal system, and oversee an army made up of the state militias. The articles were also anti-elite in requiring compulsory rotation in office, what we would today call a type of *term limits*—no member of the congress could serve more than three years in any six. Finally, real accomplishments were made under the articles, such as the start of a national bureaucracy and the passing of the *Northwest Ordinance,* which established the procedure for admitting new states into the union.

But by 1787, the inadequacies of the articles were more apparent than the strengths. Too little power had been granted to the central authority. Many people worried that Britain, France, or Spain would attack America because of its weak central government. The confederation was in deep financial difficulty: Not enough funds were coming from the states, the currency was being devalued, and the states were locked in trade wars, putting up tariff barriers against each other. Shays' Rebellion in late 1786, an angry protest by Massachusetts farmers unable to pay their mortgages and taxes, reinforced the fears of many among the property-owning elite that strong government was needed to avoid "mob rule" and economic disruption.

The Constitutional Convention

Against this background, the convention met in Philadelphia from May 25 to September 17, 1787. The weather was hot and muggy, making tempers short. All the meetings were held in strict secrecy. One reason was that the congress had reluctantly called the convention together "for the sole purpose of revising the Articles of Confederation." Yet within five days of its organization, the convention had adopted a Virginia delegate's resolution "that a national government ought to be established consisting of a *supreme* legislative, executive, and judiciary." In other words, the convention violated the authority under which it had been established and proceeded to write a completely new United States constitution in a single summer.

The Constitution was a product of a series of compromises. The most important compromise, because it was the most divisive issue, was the question of how the states would be represented in the national legislature. The large states proposed a legislature with representation based either on the taxes paid by each state to the national government or on the number of people in each state. The small states wanted one vote for each state no matter what its size. After a long deadlock, an agreement called the *Great Compromise* established the present structure of Congress—representation based on population in the lower house (House of Representatives) and equal representation for all states in the upper one (Senate).

Other compromises came a bit more easily. Southern delegates feared the national government would impose an export tax on their agricultural goods and interfere with slavery. A compromise was reached that gave Congress the power to regulate commerce, but not to put a tax on exports. In addition, the slave trade could not be banned before 1808. The slave issue was also central in the weirdest agreement—the Three-Fifths Compromise. Here the debate was over whether slaves should be counted as people for purposes of representation and taxation. The South, which did not want to treat slaves as people, did however want to count them that way. It was finally agreed that a slave should be counted as three-fifths of a person for both. (This provision was later removed by the Thirteenth and Fourteenth Amendments.) Another main issue, the right of a state to withdraw or *secede* from the union, was simply avoided. The questions of secession and slavery had to wait for a later generation to resolve in a bloody civil war.

The Framers

Given the importance of the Constitution, it is a bit surprising how quickly and relatively painlessly it was drafted. No doubt the writing went so smoothly partly because of the wisdom of the men in Philadelphia. The universally respected General Washington chaired the meetings; the political brilliance of Alexander Hamilton and James Madison illuminated the debates; and 82-year-old Benjamin Franklin added the moderation of age. The delegates themselves possessed a blend of experience and learning. (See "Colonial Drinking and Voting.") Of the 55 delegates, 42 had served in the Continental Congress. More than half were college educated and had studied political philosophy. As a relatively young group, the average age being 40, they may have reflected a generation gap of their own time. Having politically matured during the revolutionary period, they were less tied to state loyalties than were older men whose outlook was formed before the war. They were nationalists building a nation, not merely defending the interests of their states.

But there was more to the consensus. The framers were not exactly a representative sample of the population of America at the time. They were wealthy planters, merchants, and lawyers. Fifteen of them were slaveholders, fourteen were land speculators. The small farmers and workers of the country, many of whom were suffering from an economic downturn, were not represented at Philadelphia. Nor did leaders who might speak for this poorer majority, such as Thomas Jefferson (who was in Paris as ambassador) or Patrick Henry (who stayed away because he "smelt a rat"), attend the convention. Only 6 of the 56 men who signed the Declaration of Independence were at the convention. The delegates were a conservative, propertied elite, worried that

---

Colonial Drinking and Voting

[James] Madison . . . believed deeply in a government based on the consent of the people, *as long as the direct involvement of the people was strictly limited.* Early in his political career he had seen the ways of popular politics, and the experience made him uncomfortable. In Madison's Virginia, men got elected to office by plying the freeholders with bumbo—in the vernacular of the day. Rum punch was preferred, accompanied by cookies and ginger cake and occasionally a barbecued bullock or a hog. For one election, in 1758, George Washington supplied 160 gallons of liquor to 391 voters—a stiff one and a half quarts per voter.

That was the way it was done. Though good enough for the likes of Washington, Jefferson, Henry, Mason, and the rest, to young Madison it was a "corrupting influence," inconsistent with the "purity of moral and republic principles." During his second run for the Virginia House of Delegates, in 1777, he decided to set an example. He refused to supply the bumbo.

Madison lost that election—to a tavernkeeper.

Source: Fred Barbash, *The Founding* (New York: Simon & Schuster, 1987), p. 131.

continuing the weak confederation would only encourage more and larger Shays' Rebellions. Thus the debates at the convention were not between the "haves"
and the "have-nots," but between the "haves" and the
"haves" over their regional interests.

Motives Behind the Constitution

Much scholarly debate has gone on about the motives
of the framers since Charles Beard published his book
*An Economic Interpretation of the Constitution of the
United States* in 1913. Beard argued that the convention was a counterrevolution engineered by the delegates to protect and improve their own property holdings by transferring power from the states to an
unrepresentative central government. Certainly the 40
delegates who held nearly worthless confederation securities stood to profit from a new government committed to honoring these debts. Certainly their interests as
creditors and property holders would be better protected by a strong central government. Nor did the delegates particularly favor democracy. Most thought that
liberty had to be protected *from* democracy (which they
thought of as "mob rule") and agreed with Madison's
statement in *The Federalist Papers* (No. 10) that "those
who hold and those who are without property have ever
formed distinct interests in society."

Critics of Beard's theory argue that the framers' motives were more varied. They reason that the delegates
sought to build a new nation, to reduce the country's
numerous political disputes, and to promote economic
development that would benefit all. They point out that
having a central government able to raise an army to
protect the states from foreign attack appeared to be
the most important reason that George Washington,
among others, backed the Constitution.

But the arguments of the two sides don't necessarily
cancel each other. The framers' *public* interest of building a strong nation and their *private* interest of protecting their property could work together. Like most people, they believed that what was good for themselves
was good for society. That most of the population

(workers, the poor, blacks, women) was not represented at Philadelphia was not surprising by the standards of the day. Nor should it be surprising that the delegates' ideas for a government did not work against their own economic interests, and in many cases, aided them. (See "Is the Constitution Anti-democratic?")

Federalists Versus Anti-Federalists

This is not to say that there were not divisions within the elite. Many of the debates during the writing and ratification of the Constitution divided the political elite into two camps: the Federalists and the Anti-Federalists.

The *Federalists* generally favored a strong federal (national) government, with protection of private property rights and limits on popular participation in government. (Alexander Hamilton, a leader of the Federalists, described the people as "a great beast.") In the debates over the Constitution, the Federalists pushed

"Is the Constitution Anti-democratic?"

There is an argument that the Constitution was an antidemocratic attempt to limit popular participation in government. Many of the framers saw liberty and democracy as very separate, with peoples' liberties often needing constitutional protections from democratic pressures. Certainly the selection of the president, the senate, and the Supreme Court, as well as many constitutional procedures, like the veto, were seen as restraints on democracy. Critics often quote an antidemocratic framer like Roger Sherman of Connecticut who wrote that the people "should have as little to do as may be about the government. They . . . are constantly liable to be misled."

Thurgood Marshall, the Supreme Court's first black justice who died in 1993, pointed out that the Constitution's preamble that begins "we the people," did not include the majority of America's citizens—women and blacks. He called the Constitution "defective from the start" because it required tremendous social upheaval "to attain the system of constitutional government, and its respect for the individual freedoms and human rights, we hold as fundamental today." He warned against a complacent belief in the original vision of the founders. Instead, Marshall praised those who through the Civil War created virtually a new constitution using the Fourteenth Amendment to ensure the rights of all Americans.

for high property qualifications for voting, an indirectly elected Senate modeled after the English aristocratic House of Lords, a lofty indirectly elected president, and a strong nonelected judiciary. The Federalists, being more pessimistic about human nature (including the nature of the rulers), wanted these "cooling-off" devices in the government to filter down the popular will and create guardians of the people's real interests.

The *Anti-Federalists* were more optimistic about human nature, though just as suspicious about the nature of those in power. Led by men like Patrick Henry and George Mason, they favored strong state governments because they felt the states would be closer to the popular will than a strong central government. They wanted fewer limits on popular participation and pushed for the legislative branch to have more power than the executive and judicial branches. Believing that the majority was responsible, though agreeing that it might need cooling off, they wanted government to be accountable to elected officials.

The Constitution is a compromise between these two positions. It was designed to prevent tyranny both from the bottom—the people (whom the Federalists feared), and from the top—the rulers (whom the Anti-Federalists feared). Both sides generally believed that the government that governed best governed least.

Ratification and the Bill of Rights

The struggle for ratification of the Constitution focused the debate between the Federalists and Anti-Federalists. Conventions in nine states had to approve the Constitution before it could go into effect. Because a majority of the people were against the Constitution, the fight for ratification wasn't easy. The Anti-Federalists wanted a more rigid system of separation of power and more effective checks and balances. Fearing that the president and Senate would act together as an aristocratic clique, they proposed compulsory rotation in office (as under the Articles of Confederation).

The Federalists criticized the Anti-Federalists for their lack of faith in popular elections and for ignoring the advantages of national union. Through a propaganda campaign in the newspapers, they discussed the failures of the confederation, reassured people that the proposed president would be more like a governor than a king, and dismissed charges that the judiciary would be a threat to individual liberties. A series of these essays in a New York newspaper written by Madison, Hamilton, and John Jay was later republished as *The Federalist Papers.* The book stands today as the most famous commentary on the framers' thinking regarding their Constitution.

The debate over including the *Bill of Rights,* the first ten amendments, in the Constitution became a key issue in the struggle over ratification. The Philadelphia convention, dominated by Federalists, had failed to include a bill of rights in the original document, not so much because of opposition to the ideals of the bill, but from a feeling that such a statement was irrelevant. (A proposed bill of rights was voted down unanimously near the end of the convention partly because everyone was worn out and wanted to go home.) The Federalists, from their conservative viewpoint, believed that liberty was best protected by the *procedures,* such as federalism and checks and balances, established by their constitutional government. No matter what ideals were written down, such as freedoms of speech, press, and religion, the Federalists argued that support for them would depend on the "tolerance of the age" and the balance of forces established by the Constitution.

For the Anti-Federalists, the Bill of Rights was a proclamation of fundamental truths—natural rights due to all people. No matter that another generation might ignore them, these rights were sacred. Any government resting on the consent of its people must honor them in its constitution. Although the Anti-Federalists had lost the battle in Philadelphia, they eventually won the war over the Bill of Rights. Massachusetts and Virginia agreed to accept the Constitution with the recommendation that such a proclamation be the first order of business of the new Congress. It was, and the Bill of Rights became the first ten amendments to the Constitution on December 15, 1791.

FOUR MAJOR CONSTITUTIONAL PRINCIPLES

In establishing a system of government, the United States Constitution did three things. First, it *established the structure* of government. In setting up three branches of government within a federal system, it gave the country a political framework that has existed down to the present. Second, the Constitution *distributed certain powers* to this government. Article I gave legislative powers, such as the power to raise and spend money, to Congress. Article II gave executive powers to the president, including command over the armed forces and wide authority over foreign policy. And Article III gave judicial power, the right to judge disputes arising under the Constitution, to the United States Supreme Court. Third, the Constitution *restrained the government* in exercising these powers. Government was limited, by the Bill of Rights for example, so that certain individual rights would be preserved.

The Constitution, then, both *grants* and *limits* governmental power. This point can be most clearly illustrated by looking closely at four major constitutional principles: *separation of powers and checks and balances, federalism, limited government,* and *judicial review.*

Separation of Powers and Checks and Balances

The first major constitutional principle is actually two: separation of powers, and checks and balances. But the two principles can't be understood apart from each other, and they operate together.

Separation of powers is the principle that the powers of government should be separated and put in the care of different parts of the government. Although never exactly stated in the Constitution, this principle had a long history in political philosophy and was in practice in the governments of the colonies. (See "Madison on Separation of Powers and Government.") The writers of the Constitution divided the federal government into three branches to carry out what they saw as the three major functions of government. The *legislative function*—passing the laws—was given to Congress; the *executive function*—carrying out or executing the laws—was given to the president; and the *judicial function*—interpreting the laws—was given to the Supreme Court.

Though it is nice and neat, the principle is probably unworkable. The purpose of separation of powers was to allow ambition to counter ambition, to prevent any one authority from monopolizing power. Yet simply dividing the powers of government into these three branches would probably make the legislature supreme—as it had been in the colonies. As the starter of the governmental process, the legislature could determine how, or even if, the other branches played their roles. Something else was needed to curb legislative power. That something was checks and balances.

Checks and balances create a mixture of powers that permits the three branches of government to limit one another. A *check* is a control one branch has over another's functions, creating a *balance* of power. The principle gives the branches constitutional means for guarding their functions from interference by another branch. Checks and balances blends together the legislative, executive, and judicial powers, giving some

---

Madison on Separation of Powers and Government

But the great security against a gradual concentration of the several powers in the same department consists in giving to those who administer each department the necessary constitutional means and personal motives to resist encroachments of the others. . . . Ambition must be made to counteract ambition. The interest of the man must be connected with the constitutional rights of the place. . . . If men were angels, no government would be necessary. If angels were to govern men, neither external or internal controls on government would be necessary. In framing a government, which is to be administered by men over men, the great difficulty lies in this: You must first enable the government to control the governed; and in the next place, oblige it to control itself.

Source: James Madison, *The Federalist Papers* (No. 51).

legislative powers to the executive, some executive powers to the legislative branch, and so on, to keep any branch from dominating another.

There are a number of examples of checks and balances in the Constitution. The president is given legislative power to recommend measures to Congress and to call Congress into special session, and some judicial power like the right to pardon. The presidential veto gives the chief executive a primarily legislative power to prevent bills he dislikes from being passed into law. Congress can check this power by its right to override the veto by a two-thirds vote. The Senate is given an executive power in its role of confirming presidential nominations for major executive and judicial posts. Further, Congress can refuse to appropriate funds for any executive agency, thereby preventing the agency from carrying out the laws.

But the system of separation of powers and checks and balances is even more elaborate. The way each branch of government is set up and chosen also checks and balances its power. For example, Congress is divided into two houses, and both must approve legislation before it becomes law. Limited terms of office and varied methods of selection help keep any one person or branch from becoming too strong. The House of Representatives was to be popularly elected for two-year terms; Senators were elected for six years, originally by their state legislatures (changed by the Seventeenth Amendment to popular election); the president was elected for four years by an electoral college; and federal judges were to be appointed by the president, confirmed by the Senate, and to serve for life during good behavior. All these procedures were designed to give government officials different interests to defend, varied bases of support, and protection from too much interference by other officials.

The institutions that result from this separating and mixing of powers are separate bodies that in practice *share* the overall power of government. Each needs the others to make the government work, yet each has an interest in checking and balancing the powers of the others. This elaborate scheme of separation of powers and checks and balances was certainly not designed as the most efficient form of government. Rather, it was established "to control the abuses of government"—to oblige the government to control itself. It set up a structure that historian Richard Hofstadter has called "a harmonious system of mutual frustration."

Federalism

Federalism, calls for political authority to be distributed between a central government and the governments of the states. Both the federal and state governments may act directly on the people, and each has some exclusive powers. Federalism, like separation of powers, spreads out political authority to prevent power from being concentrated in any one group. It is a constitutional principle around which major political arguments continue down to the present day.

Actually, the men who wrote the Constitution had little choice. The loose confederation of states hadn't operated well, in their eyes, and centralizing all government powers would have been unacceptable to the major governments of the day—those of the individual states. Federalism, then, was more than just a reasonable principle for governing a large country divided by regional differences and slow communications. It was also the only realistic way to get the states to ratify the Constitution.

American federalism has always involved two somewhat contradictory ideas. The first, expressed in Article VI, is that the Constitution and the laws of the central government are supreme. This condition was necessary to establish an effective government, able to pass laws and rule directly over all the people. The second principle ensures the independence of the state governments: The Tenth Amendment *reserved powers* to the states or the people not delegated to the central government. These substantial reserved powers include control of local and city governments, regulation of business within a state, supervision of education, and exercise of the general "police power" over the safety of the people. (See Figure 2.1.)

Figure 2.1   Federalism.

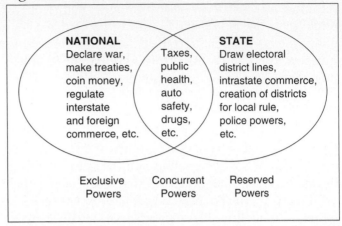

Source: Reprinted with permission of Macmillan Publishing Company from *An Introduction to American Government,* 2nd ed., by Erwin L. Levine & Elmer E. Cornwell, Jr. Copyright © 1972 by Macmillan Publishing Company.

The conflict between the two principles—national supremacy and states' rights—came to a head in the Civil War, which established the predominance of the national government. That is not to say that the question was settled once and for all. Even today, in issues such as gun control and immigration, state governments often clash with the federal government. Such conflicts can be expected from a Constitution that not only divided the powers of government into a federal system, but also clearly set up the basis for national union.

As political issues—whether regulating the economy or protecting the environment—became national, so too did solutions center in the national government. In practice today, there are few domestic programs that are solely run by the federal government. Almost all require cooperation by the states and often the cities. In the best cases, this arrangement helps adjust the programs to local conditions; in the worst, it may delay needed changes. Either way, federalism now exists far less as separate boxes of powers than as a mix of overlapping relations between the states and the federal government, sometimes called a *marblecake.*

This mix of relations can be seen in looking more closely at public education. Public high schools in this country are overseen by local school boards. The boards set teachers' salaries and make the basic decisions concerning day-to-day operations of a public school system. Local taxes on property in the school district are usually the basic source of public school funds.

Public education in America is not, however, solely a local government responsibility. State governments provide a large part of the funds for local education. These funds, from state taxes, are partly supplied to school districts according to financial need. This equalizes local revenues from property taxes, which vary widely from poorer to wealthier school districts. In addition, state governments usually control teacher qualifications, set educational standards in public schools, and approve the textbooks to be used.

The federal government is also involved in public education. Federal aid programs help equalize state funding, just as state funds are used to reduce the differences among local school districts. Some "strings" are attached to these federal funds. For example, no school district that receives federal funds may discriminate on the basis of race in hiring teachers. This same kind of overlap that exists in the funding and regulation of public education is found in government activities ranging from pollution control to public roads.

THE DEBATE OVER MODERN FEDERALISM   At first glance modern federalism appears far different from the original creation. While the Constitution remains an important limit on centralized power, the federal government has grown much stronger. Yet most of the nonmilitary services provided by government are supplied by state and local governments in complex, overlapping relationships with Washington. In some ways federalism makes it easier for citizens to participate in decisions because they occur closer to home. In other ways it's more difficult because people need to keep track of separate decisions being made in a variety of places. (See Figure 2.2.)

36

Figure 2.2 Fridley Federalism: Layers of Government, Fridley, Minnesota.

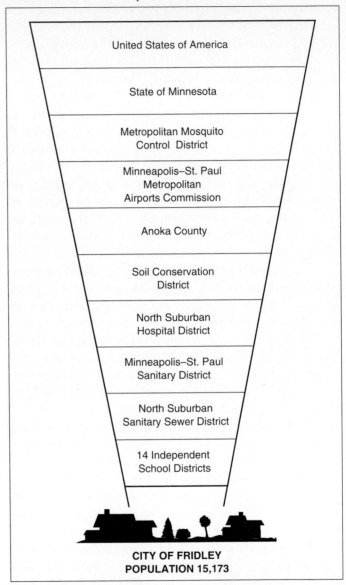

Source: Committee for Economic Development, Modernizing Local Government (Washington, D.C., 1971.)

Is local/state government better than national government because it is closer to the people? Historically, the answer to this question has depended on how satisfied people have been with what government does. The growth of government has been fueled by economic problems and popular demands for their solution. As the economy became national, problems like regulating large corporations, urban decay and worker protection seemed beyond the states' capacities to solve. By responding to these challenges the national government appeared both efficient and representative; certainly more so than state and local governments.

These activist programs produced opponents. Business opposed expensive regulations, environmental restrictions and consumer protection efforts that curtailed the marketplace. Wealthy and middle-class families disliked paying taxes for programs that benefited others. Elected officials worried about ever-expanding government spending causing budget deficits. And political opinion, always lukewarm on big government, concluded that despite some real accomplishments (such as lifting half the people who were poor in 1965 above the poverty line by 1972), there were too many badly run programs wasting money on people unwilling to improve themselves. The federal government seemed part of the problem, not part of the solution.

Most of these domestic programs were the product of Democratic congresses. Conservatives, who had generally opposed federal government actions, rode the rising antigovernment tide to power. The Republican control of Congress in 1995 produced a bipartisan consensus for reducing federal programs and shifting more responsibility to state and local governments. This effort, labeled *New Federalism* (echoing President Reagan's policies of the same name) had some common themes: smaller, more efficient government; less federal management of programs; and greater flexibility for states and localities. However, this agreement on theory and direction didn't make the actual practice any clearer. (See Case Study: Federalism at 55 MPII.)

Even conservatives' political agenda may conflict with their notions of federalism. Former senator Robert

Dole accidentally illustrated this in a speech on crime when he said "Republicans . . . believe that our country's increasingly desperate fight against crime is an area where more freedom is needed at the state level." Then, in the next breath, he said, "Our crime bill will impose mandatory minimum sentences on those who use guns in the commission of a crime, and make sure the jails are there to lock them up." Note that these mandatory sentences are imposed by the federal government.

In 1908, Woodrow Wilson, a political scientist as well as a president, wrote that the relations of the states and federal government cannot be settled "by one generation, because it is a question of growth, and every new successive stage of our political and economic development, gives it a new aspect, makes it a new question." To see federalism as a flexible system for representing the varied interests of a large, diverse country is not far from what we have today. Actually it's not far from what the framers of the Constitution had in mind.

Limited Government

The principle of *limited government* means that the powers of government are limited by the rights and liberties of the governed. This principle is basic to the very idea of constitutional government: The people give the government listed powers and duties through a constitution, while reserving the rest to themselves. This *political compact* means that government actions must rest on the *rule of law,* approved, however indirectly, by the consent of the governed. Furthermore, the Constitution sets up procedures, such as separation of powers and federalism, to ensure that the government remains limited to its proper duties and powers. For example, the president may not exercise powers given by the Constitution exclusively to Congress.

Limited government guarantees citizens their *rights against* the government as well as *access to* the government. Civil liberties and rights guarantee the openness and competitiveness of the political process, which means not only the right to vote, but also the freedom to dissent, demonstrate, and organize to produce alternatives, in order to make the right to vote meaningful. Civil liberties are supposed to protect the citizen from arbitrary governmental power. Under civil liberties would fall a citizen's right to a fair and speedy trial, to have legal defense, and to be judged by an impartial jury of his or her peers. Further, government cannot take life, liberty, or property without due process of law, nor interfere with a citizen's right to practice religion, nor invade his or her privacy. In short, the people who make the laws are subject to them. (See Chapter 6 on civil liberties and rights.)

Judicial Review

An important means of keeping government limited and of maintaining civil rights and liberties is the power of judicial review vested in the Supreme Court. *Judicial review*, the last constitutional principle, is the judicial branch's authority to decide on the constitutionality of the acts of the various parts of the government (local, state, and federal).

Although judicial review has become an accepted constitutional practice, it is not actually mentioned in the document. There was some debate in the first years of the Constitution over whether the Court had the power merely to give nonbinding opinions or whether it had supremacy over acts of the government. Most people at that time agreed that the Court did have the power to nullify unconstitutional acts of the state governments, but opinion was divided over whether this power extended to the acts of the federal government. In 1803, in the case of *Marbury* v. *Madison*, the Supreme Court first struck down an act of Congress (see p. 150). Since then, this power has become a firmly entrenched principle of the Constitution.

Judicial review has put the Court in the position of watchdog over the limits of the central government's actions and made it the guardian of federalism. The latter function, reviewing the acts of state and local governments, has historically been the Court's most important use of judicial review. Though relatively few federal laws have been struck down by the Court, hundreds of state and local laws have been held to violate the Constitution. As Justice Oliver Wendell Holmes said more than 75 years ago, "The United States would not come to an end if we lost our power to declare an act of Congress void. I do think the Union would be imperiled if we could not make that declaration as to the laws of the several states." (See Chapter 5 on the judicial branch.)

HOW IS THE CONSTITUTION CHANGED?

To say that the Constitution has lasted over 200 years is not to say it is the same document that was adopted in 1789. The Constitution has changed vastly; in practical ways, it bears little resemblance to the original. Most of the framers would scarcely recognize the political process that operates today under their constitution. Changes in the Constitution have been made by four major methods: formal amendment, judicial interpretation, legislation, and custom.

Amendments

Although the amendment process is the first way we usually think of for changing the Constitution, it is actually the least common method. Only 27 amendments (including the first ten amendments, which can practically be considered part of the original document) have been adopted. (The Equal Rights Amendment and the Washington, D.C., Voting Rights Amendment were proposed by Congress but not ratified by the needed three-fourths of the state legislatures.) The process of adopting amendments is meant to be difficult. Though the Constitution's framers recognized the need for change in any such document, no matter how far-sighted, they wanted to protect it from temporary popular pressure. Hence, they required unusually large majorities for adopting amendments. (See the Case Study: The Balanced Budget Amendment in Chapter 4.)

Article V of the Constitution provides a number of methods for adopting amendments. (See Figure 2.3.) Amendments may be *proposed* by a two-thirds vote of each house of Congress or (if requested by two-thirds of

Figure 2.3   Amending the Constitution.

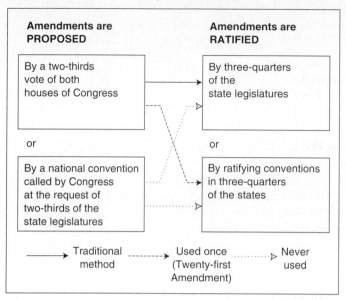

Amendments are PROPOSED	Amendments are RATIFIED
By a two-thirds vote of both houses of Congress	By three-quarters of the state legislatures
or	or
By a national convention called by Congress at the request of two-thirds of the state legislatures	By ratifying conventions in three-quarters of the states

Traditional method ┈┈➤ Used once (Twenty-first Amendment) ┈┈➤ Never used

the state legislatures) by a national convention called by Congress. They must be *ratified* by conventions in three-fourths of the states, or by three-fourths of the state legislatures (the choice is up to Congress).

The national convention has never been used; all amendments have been proposed by Congress. The most recent attempt occurred in the late 1980s, when 32 states of the needed 34 passed resolutions calling for a constitutional convention to draft a new amendment requiring a balanced budget. Only the Twenty-first Amendment, repealing Prohibition, was ratified by state conventions. The idea behind this one use of state conventions was that the state legislatures were still full of the same representatives who had passed Prohibition in the first place, and conventions seemed likely to be the fastest way to change it. A major reason that the national convention method has never been used to propose amendments is Congress's jealousy toward another body trespassing on its powers. Another is worry over how many other amendments might be proposed by such a convention. After all, the Constitution was written by an

The Long and Winding Road of the Twenty-seventh Amendment

"No law varying the compensation for the services of the Senators and Representatives, shall take effect, until an election of Representatives shall have intervened."

—The Twenty-seventh Amendment

The Twenty-seventh Amendment to the Constitution took over two hundred years to be ratified. Referred to as the Madison Pay Raise Amendment, it began its journey as one of the original twelve amendments to the Constitution, the first ten of which became the Bill of Rights. Initially, only six states ratified the Madison Amendment. No further action was taken from 1789 to the late 1970s, with the exception of Ohio's ratification in 1873. Since 1978, thirty-three states ratified the amendment with the vote by Michigan on May 7, 1992, pushing it over the three-fourths of the states needed to ratify.

Most recent amendments to the Constitution have had deadlines of seven years for passage, but the Madison Amendment was not given any time limits. Some in Congress cited a Supreme Court decision that ratification must reflect "a contemporaneous consensus," arguing that the states that approved the amendment prior to 1978 would have to vote again. However, Congress did not have the political stomach to formally confront the issue due to members' defensiveness about their own recent pay raises. Thus the Amendment became part of the Constitution on May 18, 1992.

earlier runaway convention set up only to amend the Articles of Confederation. (See "The Long and Winding Road of the Twenty-seventh Amendment.")

Judicial Interpretation

If the amendment process is the least-used method of changing the Constitution, interpretations by the Supreme Court are probably the most common. Practically every part of the Constitution has been before the Supreme Court at some time or another. The Court has shaped and reshaped the document. Modern Court decisions have allowed Congress great scope in regulating the economy, prohibited legal segregation of races, allowed local communities to determine the limits of obscenity, and established "one man, one vote" as a constitutional principle governing election to the House of Representatives. The Supreme Court has also given practical meaning to general constitutional phrases such as "necessary and proper" (Article I, Section 8), "due process of law" (Amendments 5 and 14), and "unreasonable searches and seizures" (Amendment 4). No wonder the Supreme Court is sometimes called "a permanent constitutional convention."

Legislation

Although legislation is passed under the Constitution and does not change the basic document, Congress has been responsible for filling in most of the framework of government outlined by the Constitution. Congress has established all the federal courts below the Supreme Court. It has determined the size of the House of Representatives as well as of the Supreme Court. The cabinet and most of the boards and commissions in the executive branch have been created by congressional legislation. And most of the regulations and services we now take for granted, such as social security, have come from measures passed by Congress.

Custom

Custom is the most imprecise way in which the Constitution has changed, yet one of the most widespread. Many practices that have been accepted as constitutional are not actually mentioned in the document. The growth of political parties and their role in congress and the executive branch, the presidential nominating conventions, the breakdown of the electoral college, and the committee system in Congress are just a few customary practices not foreseen by the Constitution.

Custom has also changed some practices that, at least on the surface, seem to have been clearly intended by the framers. The Eighth Amendment, forbidding "excessive bail," has not prevented courts from setting bail for serious offenses that is too high for the accused to raise. Although Congress has the right to declare war (Article II, Section 8), presidents have entered conflicts that looked very much like wars (Korea, Vietnam) without such a declaration. Customs also have been broken and reestablished by law. The custom that a president serves only two terms was started by Washington and cemented by Jefferson. Broken with much debate by Franklin D. Roosevelt in 1940, the custom was made law in the Twenty-second Amendment, adopted in 1951 to keep FDR's example from being followed in the future.

WHY HAS THE CONSTITUTION SURVIVED?

How the Constitution has been changed does not entirely explain why it has survived. Indeed, many of the framers saw the Constitution as an experiment not likely to last more than a generation. Various explanations have been offered for why the Constitution has endured to become the oldest written constitution of any country.

The major reason it has lasted probably lies not in the Constitution itself, but in the stability of American society. Upheavals like the Civil War, the Indian campaigns and massacres, and foreign wars all have been handled within the same constitutional structure. The Constitution has been made more democratic to include potentially disruptive groups, such as immigrants, former slaves, women, and the poor, that were originally excluded from political participation. The Constitution's emphasis on procedures has served it well through the wars and depressions as well as the peace and prosperity of various ages.

Other explanations for the Constitution's durability focus on the document itself. One maintains that it is a work of genius. William Gladstone, the nineteenth-century British prime minister, described it as "the most wonderful work ever struck off at a given time by the brain and purpose of man." Incorporating centuries of English political traditions as well as the framers' own experience, the Constitution set out the principles and framework of government in concise, well-written phrases. (See "A British View on the Constitution's Survival.")

A British View on the Constitution's Survival

The American Constitution is no exception to the rule that everything which has the power to win the obedience and respect of men must have its roots deep in the past and that the more slowly every institution has grown, so much the more enduring it is likely to prove. There is little in the Constitution that is absolutely new. There is much that is as old as Magna Carta.

Source: James Bryce, *The American Commonwealth* (New York: Macmillan, 1910), vol. 1, p. 28.

The *shortness* of the document (only some 7,000 words with all its amendments) is another major reason for its durability. Although it sets out the basic principles and structures of a government, the Constitution leaves much only generally stated or not mentioned at all. In a word, the Constitution is *vague.* Many of the most enduring constitutional phrases ("freedom of speech," "due process of law," "all laws which shall be necessary and proper," "privileges or immunities of citizens") have been applied differently at various times in our history. Other principles, such as majority rule and individual liberties, sometimes seem contradictory. It is left to the political players of each age to resolve the conflicts among groups claiming constitutional support. This flexibility has been one of the Constitution's major strengths in adapting to new political pressures and allowing people to reach compromises under competing principles.

Case Study

FEDERALISM AT 55 MPH

The Senate vote to repeal the 55-mile-an-hour speed limit for automobiles was widely hailed as a victory for states' rights and federalism. By scrapping the national speed limit (55 mph in urban areas and 65 mph in rural regions) the Senate left it up to the states to pass their own legislation. But a closer look at the issue shows both the inconsistencies

and the politics that surround the practice of modern federalism.

Highways, Safety, and the Federal Government

In June of 1995 the Senate began debate on spending $13 billion to upgrade highways across the country and establish a National Highway System. Attention quickly centered on proposals dealing with various federal laws that had been enacted to conserve fuel and to protect the public safety, especially the 55 mph speed limit. The new Republican majority focused on federal government involvement with issues that they felt should be left to the states.

Twenty-one years earlier the public concerns had been much different. In 1974 following the Arab oil embargo and in the middle of the "energy crisis," Congress passed a national speed limit of 55 mph. (While, under federalism, Congress couldn't directly legislate a speed limit, it accomplished the same thing by threatening to withhold highway money from states that did not comply with the federally set speed limits.) Conservation of gasoline was the major motivation, although safety was also mentioned. It quickly became one of the nation's most ignored laws; anyone traveling 55 mph on an interstate risked getting run over by one of the 90 percent of the drivers rocketing past. It was especially unpopular in western states where people drove long distances with few cars on the road.

In 1987 Congress allowed states to raise the federal limit to 65 mph in rural areas. The federal speed limits were kept largely because they were seen as a safety measure that saved an estimated 4,750 lives a year and prevented countless injuries. In addition many environmental laws to reduce air pollution, particularly ozone, required lower automobile speeds.

Driving for Federalism

The 1995 Senate debate focused on Washington's role in enforcing highway safety. One freshman senator denounced speed limits, seat belt and helmet laws as representing a "paternalistic . . . Washington knows best" attitude that had been rejected by voters who elected a Republican majority the previous November. Another freshman Republican called the laws "fiscal blackmail," because the legislation allowed the federal government to withhold highway money from states that did not obey the speed limits.

Defenders of federal involvement argued that it was needed to force reluctant states to impose safety rules that saved lives and billions of dollars in medical costs. "People will die," said freshman Senator Mike DeWine, (R-Oh.) whose 22-year-old daughter was killed in an auto accident the year before.

But by 65 to 35 the Senate voted to repeal the speed limits. Oklahoma Senator Don Nickles's question on safety seemed more convincing, "Are we taking a position that we need to have the national government mandate speed limits because states do not care about safety, states do not care about fatalities?" The regional pressure from western states and from Republicans, claiming a mandate to return power to the states on issues from the environment to welfare reform, helped to carry the day.

Muddying the Federal Role

This strong endorsement of federalism was not the whole story of the Senate's actions on the Highway bill. Indeed, its other actions muddied up the seemingly clear sense of direction on speed limits and illustrated that positions on federalism must exist in a political setting.

On the same day that the speed limit for cars was repealed, the Senate voted to *keep* the current federal government limits for big trucks and buses, which were viewed as more dangerous. The next day, the Senate voted to repeal federal penalties forcing states to require motorcyclists to wear helmets. Senator Ben Nighthorse Campbell (R-Co.)—who regularly roars around Washington on a Harley-Davidson—argued that the federal government should not tell people "how to dress for recreational pursuit."

But later in the session the Senate rejected an effort to repeal more popular federal requirements that people use seat belts. And when Senator Robert Byrd of West Virginia proposed requiring tough new state laws against drinking and driving by minors, it passed 64–36. The proposal would withhold 10 percent of a state's federal highway funds if it did not adopt "zero tolerance" policies banning any drinking by drivers under age 21. Public support for seat belt use and concern over deaths from drunk driving were cited by newspapers as overwhelming the drive to roll back the federal government's role in highway safety. Federalism took a backseat to safety.

By November the "Bill Ending Speed Limits" (as the newspapers called it) overwhelmingly passed both houses of

Congress in substantially the same form that the Senate had approved in June. President Clinton, while objecting to changes in the speed limit and helmet laws, signed it into law.

Conclusion

After the Senate action, the conservative columnist George Will wrote, "The speed limit issue, having been an energy issue and then a safety issue, now is a federalism-10th Amendment-states rights issue, with anti-paternalism in the bargain." He was partly right. Federalism, the proper division of power between the states and central government, was an important concern in the debate over repealing federal highway speed limits. But the other issues of safety and protecting the environment had not disappeared. They were still in the political arena because they were still public concerns. And they influenced the federal role on highway safety.

Federalism in real life is not just an abstract Constitutional principle. In whatever issue packaging it appears, federalism must compete with other policy choices. This will make the modern practice of federalism at times appear hesitant and uncertain. But as the Senate actions on highway safety illustrate, the application of federalism can only be as consistent as the politics swirling around it.

Sources: The Washington Post, June 21, 22, 25, 1995; *The Dallas Morning News,* June 26, 1995, *Congressional Quarterly,* June 24, 1995.

WRAP-UP

We have covered quite a bit in this chapter. In looking at the writing of the Constitution, we saw how the colonists drew from the tradition of English political thought, the models of colonial government, and experience with the Articles of Confederation in shaping the Constitution. But the framers were also influenced by who they were. As a wealthy elite, they sought to establish a government that would further both the interests of the nation and their own economic concerns. They divided into Federalists and Anti-Federalists over how strong the government should be and how personal rights would be best protected. Ratification and the addition of the Bill of Rights forged an uneasy agreement between the two groups.

The Constitution, as it has developed, centers on four major principles: separation of powers, and checks and balances; federalism; limited government; and judicial review. Although these principles remain fundamental to the document, the Constitution has been changed vastly by four main methods: formal amendment, judicial interpretation, legislation, and custom. The changes it has undergone have enabled the Constitution to endure. Perhaps more important to its survival, however, have been the stability of American society and the ambiguity of the document itself. The flexibility of the document can be seen in the modern example of the principle of federalism being applied in the case of the 55 mph speed limit.

But does the flexibility and vagueness of the document mean that the Constitution as a body of rules governing the American political game is meaningless? That essentially it serves the interests of those in power and its interpretations change only as those interests change? Perhaps. Certainly any document that has legitimized a political system that imported and enslaved most of its black residents, placed its citizens of Japanese descent in detention camps, allowed sweatshops and child labor, ignored great wealth alongside extreme poverty, has much to answer for. Is the Constitution a grab bag of obsolete principles used to rationalize domination by the few?

As we said in Chapter 1, politics is not primarily about words; it is about power and ideals. Can we blame a body of principles and procedures for the power or lack of power, for the ideals or lack of ideals, of the players in the game? All great historical documents, from the Bible to the Constitution, have been differently applied at different times.

More than the rules of the game, then, the Constitution stands as a symbol of the ideals of a people. But this symbol does influence behavior. That a president violates the law does affect whether he remains in power. That people have a constitutional right to elect representatives can immediately change what laws are passed and the direction the government takes. That the press has the right to publish government documents (and the courts, not the administration, make the decision) does place limits on the bureaucracy. Even the hypocrisy of politicians in bowing to ideals they may wish to ignore shows the strength of the symbol.

Yet the substance of the principles in the Constitution must ultimately rest on the political relationships of the players. The *right* to vote is meaningless without the *will* to vote. Freedom of speech means nothing if no one has any informed criticism to make. Freedom of the press, or judicial safeguards, or rights to privacy could be lost without anyone necessarily changing a word of the Constitution. Power without principle may be blind, but principle without power is impotent.

The rules of this game, then, are not fixed or unchanging. Though written in the traditions of the past, they exist in the politics of the present. They are not only guidelines but goals as well. Therefore they remain unfinished, as must any constitution setting out to "secure the Blessings of Liberty to ourselves and our Posterity."

Thought Questions

1. Was the Constitution as written by the framers antidemocratic? Give examples from each branch of government.
2. What were some of the issues that the framers of the Constitution agreed on almost from the beginning? On which did they have to compromise, and what have been the historical effects of those compromises?
3. How important was the principle of federalism to the senators voting on the speed limit? Were the senators voting against the principle "unprincipled"?
4. How efficient are the political structures set up by the Constitution in dealing with contemporary problems? Do the goals of efficiency and democracy in the Constitution work against each other?

Suggested Readings

Beard, Charles A. *An Economic Interpretation of the Constitution of the United States.* New York: Macmillan, 1935. Pb.
The famous criticism of the framers' economic motivations in writing the Constitution.

Bowen, Catherine Drinker. *Miracle at Philadelphia.* Boston: Little, Brown, 1986. Pb.
Written a while ago, this is a bit worshipful ("Miracle"), but still a good read of the personalities and issues behind the writing of the Constitution.

Currie, David P. *The Constitution of the United States: A Primer for the People.* Chicago: University of Chicago Press, 1988. Pb.
A scholar's review of how the meanings of the Constitution have changed.

Hamilton, Alexander, James Madison, and John Jay. *The Federalist Papers.* New York: New American Library, 1961.
The classic work on what the framers thought about their Constitution.

Kammen, Michael. *A Machine That Would Go of Itself.* New York: Vintage Books, 1986. Pb.
A challenging study of the cultural history of the Constitution.

CHAPTER THREE

The Executive Branch: The Presidency and the Bureaucracy

Although the head of just one of the three branches of the United States government, the president is the superstar of the American political game. As the only official (along with the vice president) elected by the entire nation, he stands as the symbol not only of the federal government but, at times, of the country as well.

Historically Americans have frequently idolized their presidents. (See "The Death of a President.") Often he has been elevated to a democratic priest-king. As a priest, he represents the country's belief in its religious mission as "the last best hope of mankind." Like a king, the president is expected to act on his own for the good of the nation and explain the actions afterwards in words usually reserved for royalty. Yet he is also democratic, elected by the entire population while personally remaining one of the people. These roles create impossible expectations. Political scientist Thomas Langston points to the "childish" relationship between the public and the president, mixing despair, hope, and unreasonable demands. The results, when these fantasies clash with reality, are presidents who leave office as disappointments.

Not surprisingly Americans have swung back and forth in how powerful they want their presidents. At times they demand strong leaders, yet they soon worry about the consequences of that strength. At other times they call for less activity from the executive branch, yet they dismiss inactivity from the chief executive as weakness. Presidents have walked a thin line between too much and too little power in the White House.

The experiences of modern presidents illustrate this dilemma. Underlying Richard Nixon's resignation in 1974 was the public's fear of the president's growing—and illegal—use of his authority, underlined by the Watergate scandal. Distancing himself from Nixon, a more open Jimmy Carter fell victim to the popular view that the president was too weak to solve the country's major problems. Later, Ronald Reagan vigorously attempted to extend the powers of the office in order to limit the growth of the federal government. Inheriting the public relations successes of the Reagan years, George Bush's low-key concentration on governing proved popular in the first part of his presidency and less so later on. President Bill Clinton brought his populist campaigning style to an administration that emphasized youth and change, but often seemed inexperienced and indecisive. Each of these presidents seemed to contrast himself with his predecessor.

This chapter is about the executive branch of government and its chief executive, the president. We will trace the history of the growth of the presidency from the limited powers granted to the office in the Constitution. We will discuss different approaches to being president and the various roles of the office. The departments of the federal bureaucracy under the president, and the problems of controlling the bureaucracy, will take up another part of the chapter. Finally, we will look at a case of the uses of presidential power in the war with Iraq.

THE PRESIDENT AND THE CONSTITUTION

Article II of the Constitution lists the president's powers. It grants a president far less power and far fewer duties than it gives Congress in Article I. Yet the opening sentence of the article ("The executive Power shall be vested in a President of the United States of America") and other vague phrases ("he shall take Care that the Laws be faithfully executed") have been used by presidents to justify enlarging their powers. As we will see, presidential practice has vastly expanded the Constitution's ideas of executive powers.

In setting requirements for the office, the Constitution states that the president must be at least 35 years old, a resident of the United States for 14 years, and a native-born citizen. The president is immune from arrest while in office and can be removed by impeachment or, because of the Twenty-fifth Amendment, if he is disabled. His term of office is fixed at four years. Under the Twenty-second Amendment, passed in 1951, presidents are limited to two terms.

During the last months of his final term the president is often called a *lame duck:* Because he cannot be reelected, his influence—and his accountability—are lessened. For political reasons, the term is often expanded to label presidents in their last term as powerless. When Republicans captured control of both houses of Congress in 1994 some of them labeled President Clinton a lame duck, even though he had only completed half of his term and could still run for reelection. More appropriately, after his defeat in November 1992 and his successor's inauguration in January 1993, President Bush was a lame duck.

Presidents are not chosen by direct popular elections. All the votes across the United States are not added up on election day with the candidate receiving the most declared the winner. Rather, presidents are chosen through the *electoral college.* Each state is granted as many *electors,* members of the electoral college, as it has senators and representatives combined (the District of Columbia gets three votes). On election day, the votes *within each state* are added up, and the candidate with the most votes receives *all* that state's votes in the electoral college, except for Maine and Nebraska which don't use this "winner take all" system. When the counting has been done in each state, the number of electoral college votes for each candidate is added up. If any candidate has a majority (270 votes, which is 50 percent plus 1), he becomes president. If no candidate wins a majority (because several candidates have split the votes), the Constitution then provides that the election will be decided by a majority vote in the House of Representatives with each state delegation casting one vote.

During the 1992 elections, when it was thought that three presidential candidates might split the vote, concern was expressed as to how congressional representatives would vote if the election went to the House. Would they follow the majority of their district? Or of their state? Would they support their party's candidate no matter what the vote? Or would they endorse the person with the most popular vote nationwide? These questions were never answered, nor did they have to be, when Ross Perot's candidacy, while gaining 19 percent of the popular vote, did not win any electoral votes.

The electoral college was created by the authors of the Constitution as another way of filtering what they feared might be the passions and prejudices of the mass of voters. It was hoped that the members of the electoral college would be cautious, sober people who would make a wise choice. The development of political parties (see Chapter 7) has undercut the purpose of the electoral college, for electors are now pledged to one party's candidate at the time of the elections. Although there have often been calls for replacing the "outmoded" electoral college with direct popular election (which would require a constitutional amendment), they have so far been unsuccessful.

Vice President

The major constitutional duties of the *vice president* are to preside over the Senate and to succeed the president if the office should become vacant. (The Speaker of the House of Representatives and the president pro tem of the Senate are next in line.) Traditionally the vice presidency has been seen as a limited, frustrating office. John Nance Garner, Franklin Roosevelt's vice president, commented that his position was "not worth a pitcher of warm spit." But the fact that thirteen vice presidents have become president, and that four of our last seven presidents were vice presidents at some time, has increased the political importance of the office.

Today scholars speak of a "new vice presidency." In recent years, vice presidents such as George Bush and Al Gore have been delegated power by the president and have played key roles in their administrations. They have represented the chief executive in diplomatic visits overseas, lobbied for him in Congress, campaigned in midterm elections, and served as a top presidential adviser. When Al Gore was selected, he was considered, and treated, almost as a partner of President Clinton. His leadership on government reform and in dealing with Congress strengthened the role of the vice president. Provided he keeps the confidence of the president and gives him the credit, Gore is likely to continue in the modern pattern of being used as a "deputy president."

HISTORY OF THE PRESIDENCY

Forty-two men have been president of the United States, from George Washington, who took office in 1789, to Bill Clinton, who began his term in 1993. (See Table 3.1 and Table 3.2 on pp. 58–59.) Between Washington and Clinton, the influence and powers of the office of the presidency have expanded considerably.

Most members of the Constitutional Convention in 1787 did not see a *political* role for the president. They pictured the president as a gentleman-aristocrat, who would stand above politics as a symbol of national unity. He would be selected by an electoral college chosen by the states, to ensure that he wasn't dependent on party or popular support. Congress, not the

---

The Death of a President

The public's reaction to the deaths of presidents has revealed deep emotional ties. Political scientists studying the response to John F. Kennedy's assassination on November 22, 1963, reported classic symptoms of grief that usually appear only at the death of a close friend or family member. People said that they "didn't feel like eating" and "felt dazed and numb." One college student reflected this personal attachment in his response: ". . . It was not so much that Kennedy was dead, but that I was without a friend and a leader, and so was the whole country. It had become sort of queer. Well, my mother's been in the hospital recently, you know, and kind of ill. In a kind of a way I felt that it would be better if she had died rather than Kennedy."

Source: Fred I. Greenstein, "College Students' Reactions to the Assassination," in Bradley S. Greenberg and Edwin B. Parker, eds., *The Kennedy Assassination and the American Public* (Stanford: Stanford University Press, 1965), pp. 220–39.

Table 3.1 Presidents of the United States

Year	President	Party	Year	President	Party
1789	George Washington		1896	William McKinley	Republican
1792	George Washington		1900	William McKinley	Republican
1796	John Adams	Federalist	1901	Theodore Roosevelt[a]	Republican
1800	Thomas Jefferson	Democratic-Republican	1904	Theodore Roosevelt	Republican
1804	Thomas Jefferson	Democratic-Republican	1908	William H. Taft	Republican
1808	James Madison	Democratic-Republican	1912	Woodrow Wilson	Democratic
1812	James Madison	Democratic-Republican	1916	Woodrow Wilson	Democratic
1816	James Monroe	Democratic-Republican	1920	Warren G. Harding	Republican
1820	James Monroe	Democratic-Republican	1923	Calvin Coolidge[a]	Republican
1824	John Quincy Adams	Democratic-Republican	1924	Calvin Coolidge	Republican
1828	Andrew Jackson	Democratic	1928	Herbert C. Hoover	Republican
1832	Andrew Jackson	Democratic	1932	Franklin D. Roosevelt	Democratic
1836	Martin Van Buren	Democratic	1936	Franklin D. Roosevelt	Democratic
1840	William H. Harrison	Whig	1940	Franklin D. Roosevelt	Democratic
1841	John Tyler[a]	Whig	1944	Franklin D. Roosevelt	Democratic
1844	James K. Polk	Democratic	1945	Harry S Truman[a]	Democratic
1848	Zachary Taylor	Whig	1948	Harry S Truman	Democratic
1850	Millard Fillmore[a]	Whig	1952	Dwight D. Eisenhower	Republican
1852	Franklin Pierce	Democratic	1956	Dwight D. Eisenhower	Republican
1856	James Buchanan	Democratic	1960	John F. Kennedy	Democratic
1860	Abraham Lincoln	Republican	1963	Lyndon B. Johnson[a]	Democratic
1864	Abraham Lincoln	Republican	1964	Lyndon B. Johnson	Democratic
1865	Andrew Johnson[a]	Democratic (Union)	1968	Richard M. Nixon	Republican
1868	Ulysses S. Grant	Republican	1972	Richard M. Nixon	Republican
1872	Ulysses S. Grant	Republican	1974	Gerald R. Ford[a]	Republican
1876	Rutherford B. Hayes	Republican	1976	James E. Carter	Democratic
1880	James A. Garfield	Republican	1980	Ronald W. Reagan	Republican
1881	Chester A. Arthur[a]	Republican	1984	Ronald W. Reagan	Republican
1884	Grover Cleveland	Democratic	1988	George H. Bush	Republican
1888	Benjamin Harrison	Republican	1992	William J. Clinton	Democratic
1892	Grover Cleveland	Democratic			

[a]Not elected to office but succeeding to it through the death or resignation of predecessor.

Table 3.2 Vice Presidents of the United States

Year	Vice President	Party	Year	Vice President	Party
1789	John Adams	Federalist	1896	Garrett A. Hobart	Republican
1792	John Adams		1900	Theodore Roosevelt	Republican
1796	Thomas Jefferson	Democratic-Republican	1904	Charles W. Fairbanks	Republican
1800	Aaron Burr	Democratic-Republican	1908	James S. Sherman	Republican
1804	George Clinton	Democratic-Republican	1912	Thomas R. Marshall	Democratic
1808	George Clinton	Democratic-Republican	1916	Thomas R. Marshall	Democratic
1812	Elbridge Gerry	Democratic-Republican	1920	Calvin Coolidge	Republican
1816	Daniel D. Tompkins	Democratic-Republican	1924	Charles G. Dawes	Republican
1820	Daniel D. Tompkins	Democratic-Republican	1928	Charles Curtis	Republican
1824	John C. Calhoun	Democratic-Republican	1932	John N. Garner	Democratic
1828	John C. Calhoun	Democratic-Republican	1936	John N. Garner	Democratic
1832	Martin Van Buren	Democratic	1940	Henry A. Wallace	Democratic
1836	Richard M. Johnson	Democratic	1944	Harry S Truman	Democratic
1840	John Tyler	Whig	1948	Alben W. Barkley	Democratic
1844	George M. Dallas	Democratic	1952	Richard M. Nixon	Republican
1848	Millard Fillmore	Whig	1956	Richard M. Nixon	Republican
1852	William R. King	Democratic	1960	Lyndon B. Johnson	Democratic
1856	John C. Breckinridge	Democratic	1964	Hubert H. Humphrey	Democratic
1860	Hannibal Hamlin	Republican	1968	Spiro T. Agnew	Republican
1864	Andrew Johnson	Democratic (Union)	1972	Spiro T. Agnew[a]	Republican
1868	Schuyler Colfax	Republican	1973	Gerald R. Ford[a]	Republican
1872	Henry Wilson	Republican	1974	Nelson A. Rockefeller[a]	Republican
1876	William A. Wheeler	Republican	1976	Walter F. Mondale	Democratic
1880	Chester A. Arthur	Republican	1980	George H. Bush	Republican
1884	Thomas A. Hendricks	Democratic	1984	George H. Bush	Republican
1888	Levi P. Morton	Republican	1988	Dan Quayle	Republican
1892	Adlai E. Stevenson	Democratic	1992	Albert Gore, Jr.	Democratic

[a]Nonelected vice presidents nominated by the president and confirmed by Congress.

president, was to be supreme. Yet strong presidents overcoming national problems soon increased these powers, although at times, weak presidents and popular sentiment have reduced executive power. In the twentieth century, presidential power has irregularly expanded as a result of wars and domestic crises, such as economic depression.

George Washington sent troops to put down a rebellion among farmers in western Pennsylvania who were angered by a tax placed on whiskey. Washington's action in the Whiskey Rebellion was later claimed as the precedent for a president's *residual power* (also called inherent power)—powers not spelled out in the Constitution but necessary for the president to be able to carry out other responsibilities. The third president, Thomas Jefferson, had, as leader of the liberals, fought against establishing a strong executive in the Constitution. Yet as president, he expanded the powers of the office. By negotiating and signing the Louisiana Purchase, gaining the approval of Congress only after the fact (perhaps inevitable in an age of slow communication), Jefferson weakened the principle of checks and balances. Congress not only played a minor role in doubling the size of the country, but couldn't easily reverse the president's action once it had been taken.

Abraham Lincoln, the sixteenth president, disregarded a number of constitutional provisions when he led the North into the Civil War. Lincoln raised armies, spent money that Congress had not appropriated, blockaded the South, suspended certain civil rights, and generally did what he felt was necessary to help preserve the Union. He even sent money and troops to Virginia and helped create West Virginia, all without participation by Congress. Congress later approved these actions, but the initiative was clearly with the president.

This pattern of *crisis leadership* continued into the twentieth century. Included in this pattern were strong presidents like Theodore Roosevelt, pushing his pro-environment and anti-monopoly policies, and Woodrow Wilson, who led the country into World War I. They were followed, however, by a series of weak presidents in the 1920s (Harding, Coolidge, Hoover), who arguably were responding to a mood in the country that favored inactivity from the chief executive.

Franklin D. Roosevelt's coming into office in 1933 in the midst of the Depression resulted in the president's taking virtually full responsibility for the continual shaping of both domestic and foreign policy. His programs in response to the Depression (called the New Deal), and his leadership of the United States into the international role it would play during and after World War II, firmly established the strong leadership patterns we find today in the presidency. Roosevelt thus is often called the first modern president. He probably influenced the shape of that office more than anyone else in this century.

TYPES OF PRESIDENTS

This growth of the presidency should not be seen as a straight line expansion of presidential powers between Washington and Clinton. There have been cycles in which the power of the office has waxed and waned reflecting many factors of personality and politics. To simplify matters, we will talk about three general approaches that various presidents have adopted toward the office and see which chief executives fit into each category.

Buchanan Presidents

The first category has been called *Buchanan presidents*, after James Buchanan, who is known mainly for his refusal to end southern secession by force in 1860. Presidents in this group view their office as purely administrative: The president should be aloof from politics and depend on leadership from Congress. Buchanan presidents adopt a *custodial* view of presidential powers: The president is limited to those powers expressly granted to him in the Constitution. Otherwise, they argue, there would be no limits on presidential power. Presidents who have followed this approach generally have been less active chief executives. They include Warren Harding, Calvin Coolidge, and Herbert Hoover, all Republican presidents in the 1920s and early 1930s.

Lincoln Presidents

Second, there are the *Lincoln presidents.* In this approach, the president is an active politician, often rallying the country in a crisis. Abraham Lincoln did so in the Civil War; Theodore Roosevelt did it later when he moved against the large business monopolies called trusts. In this century, the Lincoln president also originates much of the legislation Congress considers, he leads public opinion, and he is the major source of the country's political goals.

Lincoln presidents do not interpret the Constitution as narrowly as do Buchanan presidents. In their view the presidency is a *stewardship;* its only limits are those explicitly mentioned in the Constitution. The president's powers, then, are as large as his political talents. Following this approach have been activist presidents such as Andrew Jackson, Theodore Roosevelt, Franklin Roosevelt, Harry Truman, Lyndon Johnson, and Ronald Reagan.

Eisenhower Presidents

The two previous approaches to the presidency were outlined by Theodore Roosevelt, who as the twenty-fifth president did much to expand the influence of the office. Another style of presidential leadership is a combination of the other two just discussed, which can be called the *Eisenhower president.* While Eisenhower was a skilled politician, he concealed his own involvement in political business. He delegated responsibility widely, which allowed others to take the blame for policy failures while he preserved his own reputation of being "above" politics. This *hidden-hand leadership* hurt Eisenhower's ability to transfer his personal popularity to his party or his chosen successor. Some observers saw parallels to Eisenhower in George Bush's style of leadership.

Modern Presidents

While presidents never fall into exact categories, modern presidents have all leaned toward the activist end of the scale. Lyndon Johnson sought not only to represent a national consensus but also to create and guide this coalition as well. President Johnson, a master politician, was well known for his midnight phone calls and political arm twisting to gain support for his proposals. (See "A Presidential Politician.") Richard Nixon tried to create an image of the presidency being above politics while using his own powers as president for partisan and, sometimes, unconstitutional ends. After Nixon's resignation as president, Gerald Ford's brief presidency began as the nation's first nonpopularly elected vice president (he was selected by Nixon and confirmed by Congress). His calm tenure of low activity was marked by his issuing more vetoes of congressional legislation in a shorter time than had any other president in history.

A Presidential Politician

All of our modern presidents have been politicians, skilled at persuading others. None was more totally political than Lyndon B. Johnson. Here is a description of the "Johnson Treatment" as delivered when he was a senator:

The Treatment could last ten minutes or four hours. It came, enveloping its target, at the LBJ Ranch swimming pool, in one of LBJ's offices, in the Senate cloakroom, on the floor of the Senate itself—wherever Johnson might find a fellow Senator within his reach. Its tone could be supplication, accusation, cajolery, exuberance, scorn, tears, complaint, the hint of threat. Its velocity was breathtaking, and it was all in one direction.

Interjections from the target were rare. Johnson anticipated them before they could be spoken. He moved in close, his face a scant millimeter from his target, his eyes widening and narrowing, his eyebrows rising and falling. From his pockets poured clippings, memos, statistics, mimicry, humor, and the genius of analogy that made The Treatment an almost hypnotic experience and rendered the target stunned and helpless.

Source: As quoted by Robert Donovan, Nemesis: Truman and Johnson in the Coils of War in Asia (New York: St. Martin's Press, 1984), pp. 10–11.

Jimmy Carter, though gaining high marks as a hard-working honest manager, was criticized for his lack of political leadership. Trained as an engineer, Carter thoroughly (and often privately) surrounded himself with the details of policy decisions. By the end of his term a widespread feeling that the country's problems—inflation at home and Soviet advances abroad—were not being competently handled led to the Democrat's defeat for reelection in 1980.

Ronald Reagan came to the presidency with a career as an actor and two terms as a conservative Republican governor of California behind him. He excelled in the ability to communicate through the media, while delegating broad powers to his subordinates. His relaxed, optimistic attitude toward the office and his advanced age (76 when he left office) led critics to accuse him of being a "nine-to-five" president. Yet his media and political skills helped to get decreases in social programs, increases in defense spending, large tax cuts, and his vice president elected as his successor.

George Bush's presidency had two faces. The one looking out to foreign affairs seemed filled with successes; the domestic view revealed far fewer achievements. Foreign policy gave Bush notable victories, some of his own doing (Iraq), some by the actions of others (Eastern Europe), and some through a mixture of his own and others' efforts (the end of the Cold War). His claims in domestic fields of being the "education president" and the "environmental president" just added to critics' complaints that he neglected these national concerns. A stalled economy drastically lowered his popular support and he lost his 1992 bid for reelection.

Bill Clinton brought youth, a commitment to change, and his twelve years' experience as Democratic governor of Arkansas to the White House. His zest for campaigning combined with his party's control of both houses of Congress in his first two years in office led to many of his proposals becoming law, including deficit reduction, a national service program, a crime bill, and the North American Free Trade Agreement (NAFTA). The defeat of healthcare reform in the fall of 1994 stalled his own aggressive legislative program. The Republican takeover of Congress that year shifted much of the national agenda from the White House to Capitol Hill. Policies were now begun by Congress and the president had to react to them. Clinton tried to compromise with Republicans by sounding like them on issues of welfare and balancing the budget, while denouncing their cuts in social programs like medicare. His fight with Congress led to a government shutdown in late 1995. By using his office as a pulpit to address values like race, religion, and family, Clinton regained his political footing in time to face Robert Dole in a battle for reelection. (See "Popular Opinion Overwhelms Washington.")

A Psychological Approach

A well-known modern attempt to categorize presidents has concentrated on their psychological makeup. Political scientist James D. Barber uses this personality approach to focus on the style and character of various chief executives.* A president's *style* refers to his ability to act and to the habits of work and personal relations by which he adapts to his surroundings. A style is either *active* or *passive*. *Character* refers to the way a president feels about himself (his self-esteem). Character is either *positive* or *negative*. Putting style and character together, Barber comes up with four categories of personalities in which he places some of our recent presidents (Active-Positive, Active-Negative, Passive-Positive, Passive-Negative).

And so, for example, because of their activism in office, as well as their ability to gain satisfaction from their accomplishments, John Kennedy, Harry Truman, and Jimmy Carter are labeled Active-Positive. Not so fortunate are Active-Negative types like presidents Johnson and Nixon, who, though intensely active, suffered from a low opinion of themselves and gained little personal satisfaction from their efforts. Passive-Positive presi-

---

*James David Barber, *The Presidential Character*, 3rd ed. (Englewood Cliffs, N.J.: Prentice-Hall, 1985).

Popular Opinion Overwhelms Washington

Zoë Baird was on track to become the first woman attorney general. Although not well known in political Washington, the 40-year-old head lawyer for Aetna Insurance Company had the backing of women's groups and the popular new president who nominated her.

A January 14, 1993, newspaper article had revealed that she had hired an illegal immigrant for child care services and then had not paid taxes or social security for her. But most of the senators on the Judiciary Committee that had to vote on her nomination did not think this violation would disqualify her. Others in Washington agreed. *The Washington Post* headline the next day read, "Baird's Hiring Disclosure Not Seen as Major Block."

But her illegal hiring struck a raw nerve in public opinion. When it was revealed that Baird's annual salary was over $500,000, it became a personal issue for many people: a woman of privilege skirting the law and dodging taxes. Radio talk shows around the country picked up the issue and the call-ins ran heavily against the nominee. Mail and phone calls to Senate offices condemned her appointment as the government's chief law officer.

Despite her apology, waves of popular outrage soon overwhelmed her support. Senators withdrew their backing. President Clinton's aides gave clear signals that he was not going to fight for her nomination. On January 22, eight days after the news article, Zoë Baird asked the president to withdraw her name. The voters' opinion had been heard, and a president had to listen.

dents (one of whom, Barber believes, was Ronald Reagan) are easily influenced men searching for affection as a reward for being agreeable rather than for being assertive. President Eisenhower fits into the final category, Passive-Negative, combining a tendency to withdraw from conflict with a sense of his own uselessness. Only his sense of duty leads the Passive-Negative type into the presidency.

This last category gives us a clue to some of the shortcomings of Barber's personality approach. Having been Supreme Allied Commander during World War II, Eisenhower may have seemed Passive-Negative compared with other presidents, but could hardly have achieved what he did if these characteristics had dominated his entire career. The strength of his party, the interests he represented, and the political mood of the country are just some of the factors needed to understand the Eisenhower presidency. Studying a president's personality will provide interesting insights into how and why he acts. It does not, as Barber would agree, give us the full picture of the staff, institutions, and political and economic interests that shape the presidency. Perhaps that is why Barber has been reluctant to place Bush or Clinton in one of these categories. (See "Presidential Mama's Boys.")

PRESIDENTIAL ROLES

The reasons the presidency has expanded lie not only in the history of the office and the personality of the occupant, but also in the increasing expectations focused on the president. When a specific national problem arises, whether it is rising crime rates, illegal immigration, or a stalled economy, the president is usually called on to re-

---

Presidential Mama's Boys

One overlooked part of recent presidents' emotional makeup has been their extraordinarily close relationship with their mothers. Harry Truman had a portrait of his mom hung in the White House, and Calvin Coolidge died carrying a picture of his. In Richard Nixon's Watergate farewell address, he called his mother a "saint." Lyndon Johnson declared his mother "the strongest person I ever knew," and used to break off Senate meetings to call home to "see what Mama thinks." Sara Roosevelt rented an apartment in Cambridge to be near Franklin at college. Years later when some New York political bosses asked him to run for office, he responded, "I'd like to talk with my mother about it first."

It's no accident that most of our presidents were their mother's first boy.

These mothers were strong, religious women who dominated the raising of their favorite sons. They single-mindedly pushed their sons to overcome the image of failure frequently found in their husbands' careers. Alas, our presidents' fathers were not great role models: Truman's lost his farm in speculation; both Eisenhower's and Nixon's dads were unsuccessful store-keepers; Lyndon Johnson's failed at farming and politics; and Reagan's dad had a drinking problem. Bill Clinton's father died before he was born and his stepfather was an alcoholic.

But the sons of these laid-back fathers and strong mothers were hardly sissies. Rather, they became self-confident men who took their mothers' belief in them and turned it into real success.

spond. Even the current battle for control of domestic legislation between the President and Congress has underlined the importance of the presidency for ultimately enacting and implementing these policies. The president is also required by law to handle a number of important duties, such as drawing up and presenting the federal government's annual budget. In fulfilling these responsibilities, the president plays six somewhat different roles that often overlap and blend into one another.

Chief of State

The president is the symbolic head of *state* as well as the head of *government*. (In England, the two positions are separate: The monarch is head of state, a visible symbol of the nation, and the prime minister is head of government, exercising the real power.) As chief of state, the president has many ceremonial functions, ranging from declaring National Codfish Week to visiting foreign countries (often in an election year). Because of this role, many people see the president as a symbol of the nation, blessed with extraordinary powers. This perception raises public expectations, often unrealistically, but also gives him a political advantage. The difficulty in separating his ceremonial from his political actions is evident when, after President Clinton speaks on television, the Republicans ask for equal time. Is he speaking in his role as a nonpolitical chief of state, or as the head of the Democratic party?

Chief Diplomat

One has only to look at the Administration's efforts to bring peace to Bosnia—with much of the resulting attention, blame and credit focused on President Clinton—to see the importance of the president's second role: chief diplomat. The president has the power to establish relations with foreign governments, to appoint United States ambassadors, and to sign treaties that take effect with the consent of two-thirds of the Senate. Over the years, the president has become the chief maker and executor of American foreign policy. Despite the Senate's power to approve treaties and Congress's power to appropriate money for foreign aid and to declare wars, the checks on the president's power over foreign affairs are fewer than those on his conduct in domestic matters.

After World War II, in an age of cold war when the United States and the Soviet Union seemed to be competing in every sphere, this authority over foreign policy elevated the president's standing to ever greater heights. Often presidents went so far as to argue that the health of the economy, the effectiveness of the educational system, and even racial discrimination affected our standing abroad and thus involved the president in how they should be resolved.

The Senate's power to approve or reject treaties also has been changed by practice. Since its refusal in 1920 to approve United States membership in the League of Nations, the Senate has seldom refused to ratify a treaty. However, most international agreements involving the United States never reach the Senate. Because *executive agreements* do not require the approval of the Senate, their use has increased to the point where a president may sign hundreds of them in a single year. Presidents argue that these agreements usually concern only minor matters, and that important issues, such as the 1993 START II Treaty reducing nuclear weapons, are still submitted to the Senate. However, many agreements that involve matters of far-reaching importance are kept secret from the public and Congress. Both Wilson and Franklin D. Roosevelt used executive agreements to aid the Allies in the two world wars and, by doing so, involved the country in those conflicts before war was formally declared. Attempts by Congress to limit the president's use of executive agreements have all failed, although Congress can refuse to appropriate funds to carry out the agreements.

Commander-in-Chief

As illustrated by former President Bush mobilizing armed forces in response to Iraq's invasion of Kuwait, the president's role as commander-in-chief is closely tied to his role as chief diplomat. The principle behind this is *civilian supremacy* over the military: An elected civilian official, the president, is in charge of the armed forces. In practice, this authority is given to the secretary of defense, who normally delegates his command to members of the military. This role is not limited to actions abroad, as shown by President Bush's use of federal troops in Florida in 1992 to help victims of Hurricane Andrew, or President Clinton's order dealing with gays in the military. Its political importance is further reflected by the fact that national defense controls almost $300 billion, one-fifth of the government's budget.

Although the Constitution gives Congress the power to declare war, Congress has not done so since December 1941, when the United States entered World War II. Presidents, in their role as commander-in-chief, initiated the country's involvement in the Korean and Vietnam Wars. Congress supported both actions by appropriating money for the armed forces. Criticism of the president's role in Vietnam led to the *War Powers Act* of 1973 to restrict the president's war-making powers. The law, passed over President Nixon's veto, limited the president's committing of troops abroad to a period of 60 days, or 90 at most, if needed for a successful withdrawal. If Congress does not authorize a longer period, the troops must be removed.

The effectiveness of the War Powers Act is now questionable. In signing a law in 1983 that allowed American Marines to remain in Beirut, Lebanon, President Reagan stated that the War Powers Act did not apply because the troops were not involved in hostilities. The argument became hard to justify after several hundred were killed, and the peacekeeping force was withdrawn in early 1984. In the invasion of Panama, President Bush basically ignored the act. Congress tolerated this, leading some journalists to conclude that by 1990 the War Powers Act was "a dead letter." But in the war with Iraq (1991) Congress frequently referred to the act while the president cited it as unconstitutional. His seeking a congressional resolution of approval was seen by many as reinforcing the intent of the act. In his 1994 use of troops in Haiti, President Clinton avoided seeking congressional approval for his actions. Basically Congress and modern presidents have agreed to disagree on the War Powers Act. (See Case Study: President Bush, Congress, and the War with Iraq.)

Chief Executive

The president is, at least in theory, in complete charge of the huge federal bureaucracy in the executive branch. His authority comes from Article II of the Constitution, which states: "The executive Power shall be vested in a President of the United States of America." Executive power in this instance means the ability to carry out or execute the laws. By 1995, this had led to the president heading a bureaucracy spending $1.5 trillion a year, employing 2.8 million civilians on a payroll of around $113 billion. The federal government, with revenues larger than those of the top 40 United States corporations combined, ranks as the largest administrative organization in the world. Criticism of the bureaucracy is widespread, including a long tradition of presidential candidates promising to get the government "off the backs of the American people." We will take a closer look at the federal bureaucracy later in this chapter.

Chief Legislator

Although the Constitution gives the president the right to recommend measures to Congress, it was not until the twentieth century that presidents regularly and actively participated in the legislative process. The president delivers his *State of the Union address* to a joint session of Congress at the beginning of every year to present the administration's annual legislative program. He also gives an annual budget message, an economic message and report, and frequently sends special messages to Congress supporting specific legislation. Historically, most bills passed by Congress originate in the executive branch.

After 1994 it was more difficult to consider President Clinton the chief legislator. With Republican control of Congress in an election interpreted as a rejection of the Democratic party, the President lost much of his ability to initiate major legislation. This situation left the president attempting to modify congressional policies, veto those he couldn't change, and when all else failed suffer through stalemate as shown by the government shutdowns in late 1995. With special interest money and media attention focused on Republican leaders, it became difficult for Clinton to use the powers of the office for his own legislation. Most likely this presidential loss of control of the national agenda will prove temporary—ended either by Clinton's hand or that of his successor.

In dealing with Congress the president often uses tactics like campaigning for a supporter's reelection or threatening to block a member of Congress's local public works project. (See "Presidential Arm Twisting.") President Clinton is noted for "killing Congress with kindness"—inviting members to dine at the White House, playing golf with them, and phoning their sick relatives. Such courtesies build loyalties.

Presidential Arm Twisting

West Virginia Senator Robert Byrd, who has had his arm twisted by presidents of both parties, offered an imaginary dialogue of what a White House phone call is like:

"Hello, Mr. President."

"Bob, I have been wanting to talk to you about something. . . . I know you have some moneys in the appropriations bill for the Gallipolis Locks and Dam."

"Yes, sir."

"The people of West Virginia, in my opinion, are to be complimented in having you as their Senator. I know you have worked hard for that funding. . . . By the way, Bob, we have this piece of legislation that is going to be coming up in the Senate in a few days to authorize moneys for the Contras in Central America. Gee, I wish you would support that, Bob. . . . It will be used only for food and medicines. . . . I respect you for your opposition to that funding, but I wish you would see your way to vote with us next time on that. Can you do it?"

"Well, I will certainly be glad to think about it, Mr. President. . . ."

"Well, Bob, I hope you will. And by the way, that money for the heart research center in Morgantown that you have worked for, I will bet your people love you for that."

"Yes, Mr. President. There is a lot of support for that in West Virginia."

"Bob, I have given a lot of thought to that. Be sure and take another look at that item we have, funds for the Contras."

Source: The New York Times, July 26, 1985, p. A10. Copyright © 1985 by The New York Times Company. Reprinted by permission.

The president's main constitutional power as chief legislator is the *veto*. If a president disapproves of a bill passed by Congress, he may refuse to sign it and return it to Congress with his objections. The president can also *pocket veto* a bill by refusing to sign it within ten days of Congress adjourning. Congress may override the veto by a two-thirds vote of each house, though this happens in only 3 percent of vetoes. The veto is most often used as a threat to influence a bill while it is still before Congress.

After a long effort by recent presidents Congress passed a limited *item veto* in 1996 allowing the president to veto sections of some money bills. The item veto has been challenged as unconstitutional because it violates Article I which requires the President to veto entire bills. (See "The Limited Line-Item Veto.")

Party Leader

A president is also head of his party. As party leader, the president has a number of major duties: to choose a vice president after his own nomination; to distribute a few thousand offices and numerous favors to the party faithful; and to demonstrate that he is at least trying to fulfill the *party platform*, the party's program adopted at his nominating convention. The president is also the chief campaigner and fundraiser for his party. He names the national chairperson and usually exerts a great deal of influence over the national party machinery.

The president's control over his party is limited, however, by the decentralized nature of American politics. Congressional members of the president's party can oppose his programs, and he has few sanctions to use against them. He has no power to refuse members of Congress the party's nomination, or to keep them from reaching positions of power in Congress through seniority. Presidents also vary in how much they wish to be involved in their party's affairs. President Carter was often criticized for not strengthening the party, whereas President Clinton has kept close control of the Democratic party organization. In fact, President Clinton was considerably weakened by his party's 1994 losses in congressional and state offices. Approaching reelection he made a visible effort to detach his own policies from those of his unpopular party's officeholders.

THE PRESIDENT AND THE PUBLIC

A major result of the president's many powers and roles is his influence over mass opinion. His visibility, his standing as a symbol of the nation, and his position as a single human being compared with a frequently impersonal government, give the chief executive a great deal of influence in the political game.

Yet all this visibility may also work against him. After all, a president is chosen by election and has to keep the voters happy to keep himself and his party in office. Usually this means accomplishing his administration's goals as well as maintaining his own personal popularity. But these two aims are not always compatible. Two modern presidents, Lyndon Johnson and Richard Nixon, left office widely unpopular, Johnson because of the Vietnam War and Nixon because of Watergate. In both cases the public attention focused on them by the mass media probably hastened their decline. Jimmy Carter, who had fairly good relations with the press, lost his bid for reelection under the widespread perception that his was a "failed presidency."

Some presidents have been luckier. President Reagan showed himself to be history's most skillful chief executive at using the media to directly reach out and touch people with his sincerity. While President Bush resisted being shaped by media managers, his informality and spontaneous chats with reporters clearly benefited him. His up-and-down approval rate from 90 percent in March 1991 to 37 percent in June 1992 reflected both his skills and his limits in public communications.

President Clinton's relaxed manner as well as his lawyer's command of policy details did not quite overcome his early rocky relations with the media. He preferred going around national reporters by holding few press conferences, favoring instead local speaking opportunities like town hall meetings. As his Administration gained experience in dealing with the media and as

The Limited Line-Item Veto

On April 9, 1996 President Clinton signed a limited line-item veto into law. This capped an effort begun by President Reagan 12 years before to give presidents more control over spending by allowing them to veto parts of bills. But like most times that Congress gives up power to the President there were a number of restrictions put on it.

The complex law gave the president the right to "cancel" some items in appropriations bills, new spending for certain programs, and narrow tax breaks for special interests. The bill allowed Congress to block these cancellations by a special "disapproval bill"—which in turn could be vetoed. The item veto would only go into effect on January 1, 1997 (unless a balanced budget was passed before then) when Republicans hoped Clinton would be ending his term in office.

Despite the claims of its supporters the line-item veto seemed unlikely to change relations between the president and congress, or the government's traditional spending habits.

public attention shifted to the Republican majority in Congress, the president's standing with the press improved, if only slightly. (See "Clinton and the Media" in Chapter 8.)

While keeping up his standing with other branches of the government and the public at large, the president must still try to carry out the tasks of his office and the goals of his administration. In doing so, his most critical relationship is with the bureaucracy, the huge organization that does things ranging from launching satellites into orbit to teaching adults to read. What makes up this bureaucracy and how the president handles it are the focus of the rest of this chapter.

THE FEDERAL BUREAUCRACY

The federal bureaucracy carries out most of the work of governing. Despite the bad implications of the word, a *bureaucrat* is simply an administrator, a member of the large administrative organization—the bureaucracy—that carries out the policies of the government. The great growth of the national government and the tasks it has confronted during this century have produced an administrative system unequaled in size and complexity. Whether this bureaucracy is the servant or master of government often varies from case to case.

Most of the bureaucracy is within, or close to, the executive branch. Its structure can be broken down into the executive office of the president, the cabinet departments, the executive agencies, and the regulatory commissions. (See Figure 3.1.)

Executive Office of the President

The *executive office* was established in 1939 to advise the president and to assist him in managing the bureaucracy. It has grown steadily in size and influence until today it includes eight agencies and some 1,400 people. (See Figure 3.2.) Three of the most important agencies of the executive office are the White House office, the National Security Council, and the Office of Management and Budget.

The *White House office* is a direct extension of the president. Its members are not subject to Senate approval. In recent years, centralization of executive power has increased the authority of the White House staff at the expense of the cabinet officers—and even the president. Leon Panetta, Bill Clinton's chief of staff, has often been criticized for the White House's failures, including their slowness in making presidential appointments. The president's administrative style has been criticized as *ad hocracy*, not only because of its unplanned, last-minute nature but also for its tendency to follow changing opinion polls. In an often disorganized White House led by a famously undisciplined president, a competent administrator like Panetta may still be blamed. But these criticisms also reflect an important function of a president's staff—to steer attacks away from the chief executive, and on to his appointees. As one staffer put it, we are the president's "javelin catchers." (See "First Lady, First Target.")

The *National Security Council (NSC)* was established early in the Cold War (1947) to help the president coordinate American military and foreign policies. These policies mainly involve the departments of State

Figure 3.1   The Government of the United States.

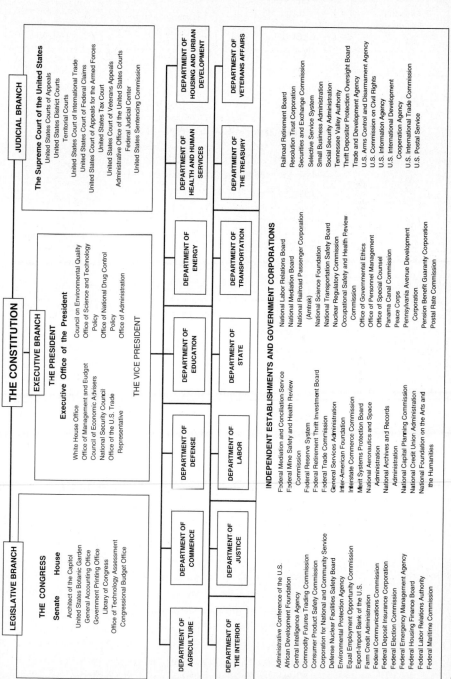

THE CONSTITUTION

LEGISLATIVE BRANCH

THE CONGRESS

Senate   House

Architect of the Capitol
United States Botanic Garden
General Accounting Office
Government Printing Office
Library of Congress
Office of Technology Assessment
Congressional Budget Office

EXECUTIVE BRANCH

THE PRESIDENT

Executive Office of the President

White House Office
Office of Management and Budget
Council of Economic Advisers
National Security Council
Office of the U.S. Trade
    Representative

Council on Environmental Quality
Office of Science and Technology
    Policy
Office of National Drug Control
    Policy
Office of Administration

THE VICE PRESIDENT

JUDICIAL BRANCH

The Supreme Court of the United States

United States Courts of Appeals
United States District Courts
Territorial Courts
United States Court of International Trade
United States Court of Federal Claims
United States Court of Appeals for the Armed Forces
United States Tax Court
United States Court of Veterans Appeals
Administrative Office of the United States Courts
Federal Judicial Center
United States Sentencing Commission

DEPARTMENT OF AGRICULTURE

DEPARTMENT OF COMMERCE

DEPARTMENT OF DEFENSE

DEPARTMENT OF EDUCATION

DEPARTMENT OF ENERGY

DEPARTMENT OF HEALTH AND HUMAN SERVICES

DEPARTMENT OF HOUSING AND URBAN DEVELOPMENT

DEPARTMENT OF THE INTERIOR

DEPARTMENT OF JUSTICE

DEPARTMENT OF LABOR

DEPARTMENT OF STATE

DEPARTMENT OF TRANSPORTATION

DEPARTMENT OF THE TREASURY

DEPARTMENT OF VETERANS AFFAIRS

INDEPENDENT ESTABLISHMENTS AND GOVERNMENT CORPORATIONS

Administrative Conference of the U.S.
African Development Foundation
Central Intelligence Agency
Commodity Futures Trading Commission
Consumer Product Safety Commission
Corporation for National and Community Service
Defense Nuclear Facilities Safety Board
Environmental Protection Agency
Equal Employment Opportunity Commission
Export-Import Bank of the U.S.
Farm Credit Administration
Federal Communications Commission
Federal Deposit Insurance Corporation
Federal Election Commission
Federal Emergency Management Agency
Federal Housing Finance Board
Federal Labor Relations Authority
Federal Maritime Commission

Federal Mediation and Conciliation Service
Federal Mine Safety and Health Review
    Commission
Federal Reserve System
Federal Retirement Thrift Investment Board
Federal Trade Commission
General Services Administration
Inter-American Foundation
Interstate Commerce Commission
Merit Systems Protection Board
National Aeronautics and Space
    Administration
National Archives and Records
    Administration
National Capital Planning Commission
National Credit Union Administration
National Foundation on the Arts and
    the Humanities

National Labor Relations Board
National Mediation Board
National Railroad Passenger Corporation
    (Amtrak)
National Science Foundation
National Transportation Safety Board
Nuclear Regulatory Commission
Occupational Safety and Health Review
    Commission
Office of Governmental Ethics
Office of Personnel Management
Office of Special Counsel
Panama Canal Commission
Peace Corps
Pennsylvania Avenue Development
    Corporation
Pension Benefit Guaranty Corporation
Postal Rate Commission

Railroad Retirement Board
Resolution Trust Corporation
Securities and Exchange Commission
Selective Service System
Small Business Administration
Social Security Administration
Tennessee Valley Authority
Thrift Depositor Protection Oversight Board
Trade and Development Agency
U.S. Arms Control and Disarmament Agency
U.S. Commission on Civil Rights
U.S. Information Agency
U.S. International Development
    Cooperation Agency
U.S. International Trade Commission
U.S. Postal Service

Source: U.S. Government Manual, 1995–1996.

Figure 3.2   Executive Office of the President.

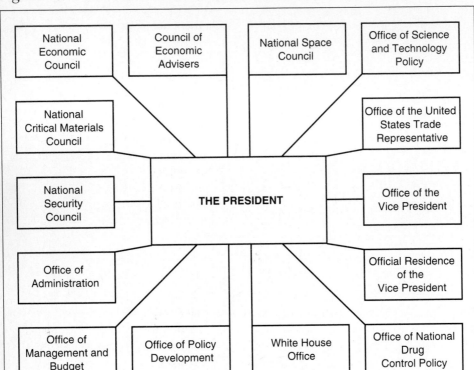

Source: U.S. Government Manual, 1995–1996.

and Defense, which are represented on the council. (The Central Intelligence Agency, though an executive agency, also falls under the authority of the NSC.) Presidents have varied in how much they wished to use the NSC. Under President Reagan, NSC staffers took on operational duties including antiterrorist actions and funding guerrillas abroad. When these activities, which had been performed by the NSC to keep them secret from Congress, were publicized in the Iran-Contra hearings in 1987, the NSC was forced back into a narrower advisory role. Under Clinton's national security adviser, Tony Lake, the NSC took on more of the character of a think tank that proposed policy options. Complaints soon followed that the NSC was providing too

First Lady, First Target

The first lady, the president's wife, is not mentioned in the Constitution, but seems to be mentioned everywhere else. She often acts as an unofficial representative of the president at openings, charity events, and other public occasions. Recent wives, notably Hillary Clinton and Nancy Reagan, have acted as close advisers to their husbands, despite frequent criticism. First Lady Nancy Reagan was described as Reagan's "most trusted adviser" and voiced strong opinions on decisions affecting her husband, including the removal of one of his chiefs of staff. For her efforts, critics called her an "Iron Butterfly." Barbara Bush generally enjoyed a more favorable press, keeping private any advice she gave her husband. Hillary Clinton was given a rough ride, at first as "the feminist wife from hell," and later for her role as a lawyer in the Whitewater scandal. But her influence over presidential appointments and in campaigning for healthcare reform established her as the most powerful first lady in history.

little central direction over administration policies concerning Bosnia and China, and that the president did not pay enough attention to foreign policy.

The *National Economic Council (NEC)* was established in 1993 because President Clinton decided that the United States needed an organization similar to the NSC to manage orderly economic policy making. Robert Rubin, formerly the head of the investment bank Goldman, Sachs & Co. was selected as the NEC's first chairman. The NEC included more than 20 cabinet members plus various top aides, and was expected to coordinate all the executive branch's trade-related activities. Rubin acted as an honest broker and policy coordinator among Clinton's cabinet officials and became Secretary of the Treasury in December 1994. He was replaced by Laura D'Andrea Tyson, the chair of the Council of Economic Advisors, the following February.

The *Office of Management and Budget (OMB)* was created by President Nixon in 1970 to replace the Bureau of the Budget. Departments of the executive branch submit competing claims for shares in the federal budget to OMB. Besides preparing the budget, OMB is an important general-management arm of the president. It helps the president control the executive branch by overseeing all the agencies and their success in accomplishing their programs. Preparing and administering the annual budget (which is then submitted to Congress for approval) gives OMB tremendous power within the government.

The *Council of Economic Advisers* is another important unit of the executive office. It is a three-member council of economic experts, appointed with Senate approval, which helps the president form a national economic policy and gives him advice on economic developments.

The Cabinet Departments

The *cabinet departments*, created by Congress, are the major agencies of the federal government. Originally there were only three (the departments of State, War, and the Treasury); today there are fourteen. The expansion of the cabinet has been due largely to the growth of problems that people wanted the federal government to deal with. Recently there have been competing efforts to both remove departments and create new ones. President Reagan entered office promising to abolish two cabinet departments—Education and Energy—and left office having created a new one—Veterans in 1988. Early in his term President Clinton proposed raising the Environmental Protection Agency (EPA) to cabinet status. But by the end of his term, the cabinet was again falling victim to the public distaste for government. Republicans in Congress proposed to eliminate three departments—Commerce, Education and Energy—as part of their effort to downsize the federal bureaucracy.

Each cabinet department is headed by a secretary, who is appointed by the president with the consent of the Senate (which is usually given). Cabinet secretaries hold office as long as the president wishes. Because cabinet secretaries have large bureaucracies to manage, however, they have less loyalty to the president than do members of the executive office. Pressures from their staff and constant involvement with the problems of their agencies may cause secretaries to act more like lobbyists for their departments than representatives of the president. Because of this detachment they often play a secondary role to the White House office. Cabinet secretaries in the Clinton administration frequently complained that they were not included in important decisions and that young, and arrogant, White House staffers were blocking their access to the president.

This does not mean that these cabinet secretaries are removed from partisan politics. The late Ron Brown, Commerce Secretary, was accused of putting businessmen who were financial contributors to President Clinton's campaign on the department's trade missions overseas. The Republican complaint was only half-heartedly denied.

How much the president uses the cabinet as a whole is strictly up to him. The cabinet has no power as a body. Although many presidents, including Reagan and Clinton, entered office promising to give the cabinet more power, things haven't worked out that way. President Clinton hardly ever used the cabinet as a

whole, except for ceremonial photo opportunities. He has on occasion called several secretaries in at a time for real decision-making meetings. But in this role they functioned only as advisors to the president. The lack of a policy-making role by the cabinet is illustrated in a story about President Lincoln being opposed by his entire cabinet on an issue. He remarked, "Seven nays, one aye; the ayes have it."

The amount of control each cabinet head has over his or her own department varies greatly. President Clinton generally allowed his cabinet secretaries wide scope over their own departments. However, often a department may be a loose structure containing strong, relatively independent groups. For example, the attorney general has authority over the FBI, which is in the Justice Department, but J. Edgar Hoover's lengthy rule as director of the FBI limited the cabinet secretary's influence. More recently, in April 1993 Attorney General Janet Reno acknowledged her responsibility for the disastrous raid on a religious compound in Waco, Texas. Others pointed out that the FBI planned the final attack, lobbied for it, and kept control on the ground.

The Executive Agencies

Executive agencies are simply important agencies of the executive branch that are not in the cabinet. Their heads are appointed by the president with approval of the Senate, but they are not considered major enough to be part of the cabinet. Examples of these are the Office of Personnel Management (OPM), the National Aeronautics and Space Administration (NASA), and the Central Intelligence Agency (CIA).

Under executive agencies we might include *government corporations,* which began as semi-independent but have come increasingly under presidential control. Government corporations, like private corporations, perform business activities such as operating a transportation system or developing and selling electricity. They are usually governed by a board of directors, have limited legislative control over them, and allow for flexible administration. The Tennessee Valley Authority (TVA) is a government corporation, set up in the 1930s to develop electricity for the Tennessee Valley. The United States Postal Service is another, established in 1970 when Congress abolished the Post Office as a cabinet department and set it up as a semi-independent, government-owned corporation.

The Regulatory Commissions

Regulatory commissions are charged with regulating and making rules for certain parts of the economy. Examples are the Interstate Commerce Commission (ICC), which regulates railroads, buses, and trucking, and the Federal Communications Commission (FCC), which oversees telephone, radio, and television operations. (The important Federal Reserve Board, under its chairman, Alan Greenspan, is a special type of regulatory agency that determines general monetary policies, like interest rates, for Federal Reserve Banks.) Although the president appoints the members of the commissions and chooses who chairs them, the commissions are relatively independent of all branches of the government. They are bipartisan (members come from both parties); the president has only a limited right to remove commissioners, who generally serve longer terms than the president; and there is no presidential veto over their actions. These commissions also have all three capacities of government: They can make rules that have the force of law (legislative), administer and enforce these regulations (executive), and conduct hearings and issue orders (judicial). Their decisions can be reviewed by federal courts, however, and their authority can be reduced by Congress.

The reasoning behind these commissions is that Congress and the president felt that parts of the economy required detailed oversight on complicated matters that Congress didn't have the technical ability to ensure. They were independent because their decisions were not supposed to be made on a partisan basis, but instead should rest on their expertise. The independence of these commissions from the rest of the government has meant, however, that the public has little control over their activities. The commissions often come under pressure from the groups they are regulating, and the lack of governmental controls has sometimes led them to negotiate with, rather than regulate, important economic interests. They have often been charged with being captives of the wealthy economic groups they oversee (see pp. 14–15). However, some commissions, like the Food and Drug Administration (FDA), have been accused of overregulating the economy. Under its current Commissioner, David A. Kessler, the FDA banned most uses of silicone-gel breast implants, restricted false labeling of "fresh" foods, and attempted to put restrictions on tobacco as a drug.

PROBLEMS OF BUREAUCRACY

The word *bureaucracy* is often used to imply incompetence and red tape; the faceless administrator unthinkingly following rules despite their impact on peoples' lives. The problems with bureaucracies seem to be related to their size rather than the nature of the public or private organizations they serve. As reflected by negative comments heard in Eastern Europe after the political upheavals in those countries, socialist and capitalist bureaucracies may have more in common than the political regimes they serve. The size and complexity of any large bureaucracy make it hard to tell who is responsible for a particular action, inhibiting public oversight. In the 1990s public outrage rose against a bureaucracy with too much power under too little control. These feelings helped antigovernment politicians gain positions of power where they then faced the dilemma of both guiding and depending on bureaucrats to carry out their policies. (See "Blame FDR for the Bureaucracy.")

The fact that bureaucrats are experts in their own areas is a major source of their influence in government, but the limits of their vision present problems. A member of Congress or a president wanting information and advice on tax policy, housing programs, or environmental costs would probably go to the bureaucrat in charge

Blame FDR For the Bureaucracy

For many critics of big government Franklin Delano Roosevelt, the creator of the modern bureaucracy, is to blame for the government we have. The only president to be elected to four terms, FDR brought the United States through the Great Depression of the 1930s and World War II. To fight the depression, Roosevelt started 30 new federal agencies, including well-known programs like the Social Security Administration. Later, to pay for the war, payroll deductions allowed the government to automatically collect income taxes, and therefore to double the number of federal employees. Taxes poured into Washington at six times the rate as before the war.

The growth in government has continued since FDR. Government employment has tripled. Federal taxes now take 20 percent of the nation's gross domestic product, four times more than in Roosevelt's first years. Social Security and other entitlement programs which were part of FDR's New Deal take half of the entire federal budget.

Nor have recent politicians stopped this growth. The federal budget stands at $1.5 trillion a year, nearly three times what it was when Jimmy Carter was president. Under Bill Clinton, the cost of government has increased and no major agency of government has yet been abolished. In fact, no president of either party has stopped the growth of the modern bureaucracy. Perhaps this means the blame lies less with FDR and his successors than with the demands placed on government—from caring for the elderly to arming the military—by all of us.

of the issue. The problem is how to get these experts in the bureaucracy to see beyond their own narrow fields of expertise to the broader public interest. During the recent debates over cutting the defense budget, bureaucrats often viewed the world through their own departments' interests—the navy thought the nation needed its bases, the air force knew security demanded its jets, and the army, of course, required adequate troop levels. More objective questions concerning the changed global threat often had to be posed by others.

Rise of the Civil Service

In the first century of the federal government, the usual method of choosing government bureaucrats was known as the *spoils system.* Taken from the phrase "to the victor belong the spoils," the spoils system meant that victorious politicians filled government positions with their supporters. This system of widespread patronage got its start during the administration of Andrew Jackson (1828–1836) and may have peaked under Abraham Lincoln (1860–1865). Those bureaucrats did not even need to be knowledgeable in their fields. But as the tasks expected of bureaucrats became more complex and corruption grew, pressure for reform also increased.

In 1881, President James Garfield was assassinated by a disappointed (and crazy) office seeker. The new president, Chester Arthur, backed by public outrage over the murder, supported the Civil Service Reform Act (also known as the Pendleton Act), which was passed by Congress in 1883. The act set up a bipartisan Civil Service Commission under which government employees were chosen by merit through examinations. At first only about 10 percent of federal employees were covered by civil service, but the system has grown and now covers practically the entire bureaucracy. This has considerably diminished the spoils system and has added stability to government activity. The president today fills only about 5,000 patronage jobs, of which fewer than one-third are at a policy-making level. While weakening the spoils system, it has also weakened presidential control of the bureaucracy; the bureaucrats know they will have their jobs long after the current administration passes into history.

Bureaucrats as Policymakers

The traditional idea of *public administration,* was that *policy* and *administration* were two different functions of government. The president and Congress, elected by the people, should make policy. The bureaucracy, which was not elected, should carry it out. The goal of bureaucracy was "efficiency." According to this ideal model, bureaucrats were supposed to administer policy and supply expert knowledge to elected policymakers. Today most political scientists consider this traditional view incomplete and a bit naive.

The political conflicts that influence policies do not stop when Congress passes a law. They continue when these policies are administered. In order to pass a bill, Congress must often reach a compromise that results in a vaguely worded law. That leaves it to the administrators to referee the debate—on, say, how clean is clean water—in applying the law. Before the bill is passed, bureaucrats may have influenced the process by their advice and information, even to the point of lobbying the bill through Congress. Afterward they often face applying the law to changed political and economic situations not foreseen by those who drafted it. And, of course, bureaucracies have interests of their own, such as increasing their budget or protecting their "turf." The result is that the model of a bureaucrat as a politically neutral administrator looks like a single musical note in a symphony of sounds. Bureaucrats carry other tunes as well.

Bureaucracies are involved in policy making because they exercise legislative, judicial, and executive power. For example, the Internal Revenue Service (IRS) holds hearings on tax cases and makes judicial findings. These legislative and judicial powers have been delegated by Congress. In exercising executive power, federal bureaucracies draw up long-range plans, and then make decisions about day-to-day operations, from aid to Bosnia to the space program. Other decisions, such as how to divide money among competing programs, involve the most serious policy questions in the government. Federal bureaucracies share in this decision making.

The President and the Bureaucracy

Curiously, the bureaucracy is both an important support for the president and a major limit on his actions. The federal bureaucracy gives the president access to more information than his opponents are likely to have, and allows him to initiate policies to which others must react. To carry out his policies, the president must rely on the information, advice, and actions of subordinates. Keeping control over the 3 million employees of the executive branch is a full-time job in itself. As political scientist Richard Neustadt commented, the president

The President and the Mouse

The problems presidents have with their bureaucracies are not always limited to major policy matters. An example from the Carter presidency:

When a couple of mice scampered across the President's study one evening last spring, an alarm went out to the General Services Administration, housekeeper of Federal buildings. Some weeks later, another mouse climbed up inside a wall of the Oval Office and died. The President's office was bathed in the odor of dead mouse as Carter prepared to greet visiting Latin American dignitaries. An emergency call went out to GSA. But it refused to touch the matter. Officials insisted that they had exterminated all the "inside" mice in the White House and this errant mouse must have come from outside, and therefore was the responsibility of the Interior Department. Interior demurred, saying that the dead mouse was now inside the White House. President Carter summoned officials from both agencies to his desk and exploded: 'I can't even get a damn mouse out of my office.' Ultimately, it took an interagency task force to get rid of the mouse.

Source: Hedrick Smith, "Problems of a Problem Solver," *The New York Times Magazine*, January 8, 1978. Copyright © 1978 by The New York Times Company. Reprinted by permission.

spends much of his time finding out what his subordinates are doing in his name.

Members of the bureaucracy acting as policymakers may work to protect their own interests or may respond to pressures from economic concerns threatened by presidential policies. In doing so, they may ignore the president's orders, and delay or even sabotage his programs. (Even on trivial matters, see "The President and the Mouse.") Often these departments have long-standing rivalries with each other: Labor versus Agriculture on food prices, State versus Defense over foreign policy. The president must act as a judge over these conflicts and yet maintain close ties with both sides. Cabinet officials appointed by the president may represent their own departments' interests against those of the president. Does the secretary of defense represent the president to the Defense Department, or the department to the president? Clearly both, but conflict often results.

Presidential power thus often boils down to the power to persuade. The president's ability to gain acceptance for his policies depends on his skill in controlling the executive branch bureaucracy and then in "selling" these policies to other political players, the most important of which is Congress. A successful blend of presidential management and maneuvering around Congress is seen in this foreign policy case study of George Bush and the war with Iraq.

Case Study

PRESIDENT BUSH, CONGRESS, AND THE WAR WITH IRAQ

On August 2, 1990, Iraq unexpectedly invaded and annexed its small, oil-rich neighbor, Kuwait. This set off a tense, five-month diplomatic and military confrontation with the United States that turned into war in January 1991. The war quickly ended in success for the American-led international coalition. President George Bush's relationship with Congress during this crisis illustrates both a president's power with Congress and the limits legislators can place on his dominant position in foreign policy.

The Crisis Begins, the President Acts, Congress Reacts

After the invasion, Bush quickly denounced it and issued an executive order banning economic relations with Iraq. Following discussions with his policy advisers and allies (notably British Prime Minister Margaret Thatcher), Bush stiffened the U.S. response. On August 5 he vowed that the invasion "will not stand" and ordered U.S. soldiers to Saudi Arabia to defend it against possible Iraqi attack. Bush gave a TV address from the Oval Office of the White House explaining the mission of Operation Desert Shield as "defensive" and praising the UN for passing sanctions against Iraq. Privately Bush had set the goal of liberating Kuwait and had concluded that this could not be accomplished without war. He concealed the military action he had in mind from both the public and Congress.

Congress swiftly backed the president, denouncing the invasion and passing an economic sanctions bill that put the executive order into law. Although the measures passed unanimously, congressional leaders quietly complained that the president had not informed them prior to deploying troops. Legislators made clear that any use of troops in hostile actions would require authorization by Congress.

While polls indicated some 77 percent of the public backed the president's actions, there was uncertainty whether sanctions alone would work. Members of Congress worried that the longer the crisis went on, the less popular support it would have. They pressed the president to explain American policy in grander terms than protecting the West's supply of oil, which most suspected as being the root cause. In future speeches Bush compared the Iraqi invasion to the expansion of Nazi Germany before World War II, and pledged to stop it. On August 22, Bush called up nearly 50,000 reservists to active duty, the first such mobilization since the Vietnam War.

The Administration Campaigns for Congress's Support

President Bush had to deal with two major concerns expressed in Congress. The first was that foreign allies were not going to contribute enough to the effort, causing the United States to bear the cost alone. Working the phone and his personal contacts with world leaders, Bush got allies, especially Germany and Japan, to increase their financial commitments. His friendships with Chinese and Russian leaders helped guarantee their support for the United Nations resolutions.

Of greater concern throughout the crisis was Congress's worry about the use of force by the president. Members recalled the Gulf of Tonkin Resolution in 1964, which President Johnson used to justify expanded involvement in Vietnam. While they asked the president to follow the War Powers Act to get Congress's approval to commit troops, they knew that no president had ever considered this 1973 law to be constitutional. They agonized that any support for Bush would be considered a "blank check" for future actions. By early October, Congress had passed nonbinding resolutions supporting actions "to deter Iraqi aggression," which its leaders declared was not an authorization for the use of force.

The president and his advisers wished to keep all their options open. Bush had concluded that the international coalition and public support he enjoyed wouldn't last long enough for sanctions to work. While he was moving toward

the military option, he didn't share this conclusion even with
his military commanders. He knew that the military could be
expected to leak information about the difficulty of battle
and their need for more resources in an effort to protect
themselves should things not turn out well.

Secretary of State James Baker, in testimony before the
House and Senate foreign affairs committees, declared that
the administration already had the authority to use military
force in the Persian Gulf. In mid-October he rejected requests for advance congressional authorization of military action. Such approval, he said, would rule out a fast response
or the element of surprise by U.S. forces. Baker declared, "I
cannot give you a blank-check commitment that we will, in
every case, do nothing until we consult with all 535 members
of Congress."

The President Raises the Stakes

Two days after the November congressional elections, President Bush jolted Congress and the nation by ordering a
massive new buildup of U.S. forces to develop "an adequate
offensive military option." His plans to double U.S. troops
to some 430,000 were revealed to congressional leaders
only hours before in order to prevent effective opposition.
Still there was a firestorm of criticism. Some wanted Congress called back for a special session. Bush reassured congressional leaders at a White House meeting that this increase did not mean war was inevitable. In a gesture toward
Congress, the president invited several leaders to join him
for Thanksgiving with the troops in Saudi Arabia. But, symbols aside, the president had escalated the conflict on
his own.

Many in Congress argued that Bush wasn't giving economic sanctions enough time to work. However, Congress's
major weapon would be to withhold funds for U.S. troops
already in a threatening battlefield overseas. This was too
politically risky and won little support. The president still
did not admit that he needed congressional approval for
military action.

He also outflanked Congress when he won UN approval on November 29 for the use of force unless Iraq
withdrew from Kuwait by January 15, 1991. This was an answer to domestic complaints that the United States was "going it alone." The same week of the UN vote, the Senate
Armed Services Committee held hearings marked by skep-
tical testimony by former military officials pointing to the

troop buildup as leading to a costly war. But the UN vote
put Congress in a difficult position. As Secretary Baker said,
it allowed him to say to members of congress, "You mean
you are not willing to support the president, but the prime
minister of Ethiopia will support the president." Of course,
Ethiopia was not risking half a million of its young men and
women.

The President Seeks a Resolution

While negotiations with Iraq on withdrawal went nowhere,
public support for the president increased. In a poll in early
December nearly two-thirds of those surveyed said the
United States should go to war with Iraq sometime after January 15. Sixty percent endorsed Bush's actions. The administration's skillful efforts to demonize Saddam Hussein worked,
aided by the harsh actions of Iraqi troops in Kuwait. A diverse
group of conservative hardliners, supporters of Israel, and liberals formed the Committee for Peace and Security in the
Gulf, which backed the president. On the other side, antiwar
marches were held in 20 cities across the country.

On January 8, after months of hesitation, the White
House sent Congress a letter formally asking for approval for a
potential war in the Gulf. Bush's letter avoided any suggestion
that he was required—either by the Constitution or the War
Powers Act—to obtain congressional approval. Instead, the
president stressed that the resolution would support the UN
resolution and would send a strong signal to Saddam of U.S.
determination. It was the first such request by a president
since the Gulf of Tonkin Resolution in 1964. The president's
change in position came both from his need for Congress's
support and his recognition that he would probably get it.

The president won the vote on January 12, three days
before the UN deadline. Most Democrats opposed the measure, which passed 52–47 in the Senate and 250–183 in the
House. While the divided vote showed the continuing doubts
over going to war, Congress had little choice. The president's
commitment of 400,000 troops, the 12 UN resolutions supporting these efforts, and the coalition of allies and Arab
states behind him, as well as American public opinion, made
Congress's support hard to withhold. Bush later maintained
that he would have gone to war with Iraq even if he had not
won approval from Congress.

On the evening of January 16, 1991, Operation Desert
Shield became Operation Desert Storm as waves of jets attacked Iraqi positions. After 38 days of bombing, Iraq re-

jected the allied demand to withdraw and the ground offensive began on February 23. In the next 100 hours the allies triumphed. Kuwait was freed. Iraqi casualties were estimated in the tens of thousands; 304 Americans died.

On March 6, Bush was invited to address a joint session of Congress. His popularity stood at 89 percent, a record high for modern presidents. As he spoke members of Congress stood and cheered, waving tiny American flags.

Conclusion

President Bush's actions to counter Iraq's invasion of Kuwait show how much power, at least in foreign affairs, lies with the chief executive. By seizing the initiative, committing American troops overseas, and putting together an international coalition supporting him, Bush put Congress in a difficult position if it chose to oppose him. With public opinion behind the president, members of Congress could question and complain, but couldn't easily stop him by the time the issue came to a vote in January. Presidential leadership was critical in mobilizing Congress and the public against a foreign threat.

Source: 1991 Congressional Quarterly Almanac.

WRAP-UP

This chapter has introduced the executive players in the political game—the president and the bureaucracy. We have seen how the presidency has irregularly but vastly grown in influence from a limited grant of constitutional powers, and we have looked at three different presidential styles as well as a psychological approach to a president's personality. The six major roles a president fills—chief of state, chief diplomat, commander-in-chief, chief executive, chief legislator, and party leader—show how broad his power has become. In the last 50 years, government power has been centralized, in the federal government relative to the states, and in the president relative to the Congress.

The bureaucracy within the executive branch generally reinforces the president's power. Yet its size, its roles in policy making, and its internal complexity—

from the executive office to the cabinet departments, executive agencies, and regulatory commissions—limit the president's control over the bureaucracy. In the Iraq case study we saw a president using his power over the military bureaucracy to commit the nation, and the Congress, to war.

The president as both an individual and an institution will continue to play a central role in the American political game. Often presidents have seemed weak and ineffective in managing the bureaucracy and getting their programs acted on by Congress. People have tended to focus their dissatisfaction with government on individual presidents. Most of us still look for a presidential Moses to lead us out of a wilderness of domestic and foreign troubles. Which is part of the problem.

Presidents are political leaders. They hold a powerful office restrained by all sorts of historical, political and legal limits. They may mislead us by promising to do more than they know the political game allows. But we also play a part. If we expect them to be heroes or symbols, priests or kings, we are bound to be disappointed. We may have to cool our expectations of what presidents can do to change our country and improve our lives. In that way we can, as citizens of a democracy, more realistically judge our chief executive when the time comes to vote.

Thought Questions

1. What are the major reasons for the growth in the power of the president? How are current antigovernment feelings likely to affect this growth?
2. How does the executive branch bureaucracy both limit and support the power of the president?
3. Do you think the president and bureaucracy are too powerful or not powerful enough? Give some current examples to back up your argument.
4. What shapes peoples' expectations of their president? Is it possible for any president to accomplish what people expect?
5. Is the current pattern of a strong congress and a weak president likely to continue? What factors led to this situa-

tion? How is it different from previous periods of a Democratic Congress and a Republican president?

Suggested Readings

Duffy, Michael, and Dan Goodgame. *Marching in Place.* New York: Simon & Schuster, 1992.

Two *Time Magazine* reporters critique the status quo presidency of George Bush.

Greenstein, Fred I. *The Hidden-Hand Presidency.* Baltimore: Johns Hopkins University Press, 1994. Pb

A good scholarly second look at how effective General Eisenhower was as president, much to the surprise of many of his critics.

Langston, Thomas S. *With Reverence and Contempt: How Americans Think About Their President.* Baltimore: Johns Hopkins University Press, 1995.

Spirited if pessimistic essays on the dilemmas facing a president, and the public who raise him to nearly religious heights.

Maltese, John Anthony. *Spin Control.* 2nd ed. Chapel Hill: The University of North Carolina Press, 1994. Pb.

A history of how the White House organizes and "spins" presidential news.

Pfiffner, James P. *The Modern Presidency.* New York: St. Martin's Press, 1994.

Traces the development of the "presidential branch" standing apart from the rest of the executive branch. Stops before Clinton.

Reedy, George. *The Twilight of the Presidency.* New York: NAL Books, 1987.

An aide of President Johnson gives an insider's classic, and depressing, look at the presidency.

Woodward, Bob. *The Agenda: Inside The Clinton White House.* New York: Pocket Books, 1995. Pb.

A revealing look at the first-year seat-of-the-pants economic policy making by the president and his staff.

CHAPTER FOUR

The Legislative Branch: Congress

According to the Constitution, Congress was to be at the center of the American political game. The framers' experience with King George III of England and his often autocratic governors had left the colonists with a deep suspicion of strong executive authority. As a result, the Constitution gave many detailed powers and responsibilities to the Congress but far fewer to the president.

Through its major function, lawmaking, Congress creates the rules that govern all the political players. Article I of the Constitution gives Congress the power to levy taxes, borrow money, raise armies, declare war, determine the nature of the federal judiciary, regulate commerce, coin money, and "make all Laws which shall be necessary and proper for carrying into Execution the foregoing powers, and all other Powers vested by this Constitution in the Government of the United States, or in any Department or Officer thereof."

The powers of Congress limit many of the powers given to the president. The president was named the commander-in-chief of the armed services, but he could not declare war or raise armies without Congress's approval. The president was to be the chief administrative officer of the government, but there would be no government to administer if the Congress did not create it. He could appoint executive officials and negotiate foreign treaties only if the Senate agreed. Both the raising of money through taxes and the spending of it by the government required approval by Congress. Finally, Congress was given the power to impeach and remove the president.

Through most of the nineteenth century, Congress was the major player in shaping the nation's policies. By the end of the nineteenth century, Woodrow Wilson could proclaim, "Congress is the dominant, nay, the irresistible power of the federal system." Wilson was later to change his mind, and since the Great Depression and

World War II the executive branch generally increased in influence compared with Congress. (Of course, even during this long cycle of executive ascendancy there were periods of weak presidents and assertive congresses.)

Now with the rise of Republican majorities in both houses committed to major reforms, Congress often seems dominant. Under strong leaders like Speaker Newt Gingrich, Congress has asserted its right to determine the national agenda—which issues will be considered, what solutions will be offered. To this agenda the president and the public react. And along with this increased presence comes much of the blame for Washington's failures.

The Legislative branch remains vital to the political game. In this chapter we will examine the structure of Congress, how it was designed to operate, and how it actually carries out its functions today.

MAKEUP OF THE SENATE AND HOUSE

The Congress of the United States is *bicameral*, made up of two branches: the Senate and the House of Representatives. The Senate consists of two senators from each state regardless of the size of the state. House members are distributed according to population so that the larger the state's population, the more representatives it gets. The Constitution requires that each state, no matter how small it may be, have at least one representative. These provisions are the result of a political compromise between the small states and the large states during the writing of the Constitution.

As the country has grown, so too has the size of Congress. The first Congress consisted of 26 senators and 65 representatives. With each new state added to the Union, the Senate has grown by two, so that it now has 100 members. As the nation's population grew, the size of the House of Representatives grew also. In 1922 the Congress passed a law setting the maximum size of the House at 435 members, where it remains today. In the first House each member represented around

50,000 citizens. The average representative now serves 572,500 constituents.

Role of the Legislator

There are many questions about what the role of a legislator should be, questions as old as the idea of representative assemblies. Should a representative follow his or her own judgment about what is best or do only what his or her constituents wish ("re-present" them)? What should a representative do if the interests of his or her district seem to conflict with the needs of the nation as a whole? Should a legislator recognize a "greater good" beyond the boundaries of the district?

One reason for all these questions is that members of Congress are both *national* and *local* representatives. They are national representatives who make up one branch of the national government, are paid by that federal government, and are required to support and defend the interests of the entire nation. Yet they are elected by local districts or states. In running for election, legislators must satisfy local constituents that they are looking out not only for the national interest but for local interests as well. In controversial areas such as cutting the defense budget by closing military bases, the national interest may be very different from local popular opinion. Congressional representatives must both represent a small interest and compromise it to form a coalition large enough to pass bills. And they can't forget a warning heard often in Congress: "To be a good representative, you first have to be a representative"—a reminder that usually gives constituents' opinions the upper hand.

Who Are the Legislators?

A member of the House of Representatives must be at least 25 years old, a citizen of the United States for seven years, and a resident of the state in which he or she is elected. A senator must be 30 years old, nine years a citizen, and a resident of the state that elects him or her. State residency is a fairly loose requirement, however. Robert Kennedy rented a New York City apartment and declared it his prime residence just before entering the New York Senate race in 1964.

Senators serve six-year terms and are elected by the entire state's population. Every two years, during the national elections, one-third of the Senate seeks reelection. The other senators do not run because they are only one-third or two-thirds of the way through their terms.

The Constitution originally provided that members of the Senate would be elected by their state legislatures. The purpose was to remove the choice from the masses of citizens and try to ensure that more conservative elements would pick the senators. This procedure was changed by the Seventeenth Amendment, ratified in 1913. Senators are now elected by the voters of each state.

Members of the House of Representatives (called "Congressmen") serve two years. They are elected from congressional districts within the states. No congressional district ever crosses state borders.

Congress is composed overwhelmingly of white males, and it tends to reflect the values of upper-middle-class America. Almost half the members of Congress are lawyers. Other common professions are business, banking, education, farming, and journalism. Women and blacks are underrepresented in Congress for many reasons, including the selection of candidates by party organizations, lack of voter organization, and voter apathy. The 1992 elections, however, brought more women and minority group members into Congress than any previous election in American history. The 1994 congressional elections, sometimes referred to as "the year of the angry white male," leveled off this trend. (See "The 104th Congress.")

Until the 1840s the average length of service in the House was less than two years, and in the Senate less than four, meaning that many members were resigning for better opportunities. There remains a fair amount of turnover. In the 104th Congress, one-fourth of the Senate and nearly half of the House has less than three years' experience.

The 104th Congress

The November 1994 elections for the 104th Congress placed the Republican party in charge of both houses. The Republicans regained control of the Senate for the first time since 1986, and their first majority in the House since 1954. All 167 Republican incumbents returned to office, and 85 of the 98 new members were Republicans. Although the 98 freshman House members elected in 1994 was not as great as the 124 newcomers in 1992, the trend toward high levels of turnover in Congress continued.

While the number of representatives who are women or minorities significantly increased in the 103rd Congress, there were no such increases in the 104th. Blacks in the House remained the same at 39, including three freshman members. Senator Carol Moseley-Braun of Illinois is still the only black in the Senate. The number of Asians and Pacific Islanders was unchanged—6 in the House and 2 in the Senate. Hispanics lost a representative, going from 19 to 18. Colorado Senator Ben Nighthorse Campbell, who switched from Democrat to Republican, continues as the sole Native American in Congress. Although 1992 was the "Year of the Woman," when the Senate added 5 new women members and the House gained 19, in 1994 women accounted for only 2 new members, one in the House and one in the Senate. Women make up 13 percent of the 104th Congress.

Roman Catholics are still the largest religion at 27 percent, while 6 percent of the 104th Congress is Jewish. Four major Protestant groups (Baptists, Episcopalians, Methodists, and Presbyterians) account for 43 percent of Congress. Although lawyers continued to be the best-represented occupation, their numbers dropped from 58 percent to 42 percent. Most of the remaining members came from business, banking, government and education.

The youngest member of the newly elected House was Rhode Island's Patrick J. Kennedy, 27 (Senator Kennedy's son). Professional athletes added to their numbers with Steve Largent, congressman from Oklahoma and star football receiver for the Seattle Seahawks. And fans of 1970s pop music were undoubtedly cheered that Sonny Bono would no longer be singing. Cher's former mate was elected to a House seat in California.

Careerism—the tendency for legislators to see service in Congress as a lifetime career—still exists. Tradition holds that the leadership in both houses consist of the most senior members. Although Speaker of the House Newt Gingrich drew attention by occasionally breaking with the seniority tradition in the appointment of committee chairs, the present House chairmen average more than 18 years of service. However, Republicans have placed limits on the number of consecutive terms members can serve as committee chair and in leadership positions. The current unpopularity of *incumbents* has led many of the new members of Congress—calling themselves "citizen legislators"—to vow to stay in office for only a few terms.

It does seem ironic that although high-level executive branch administrators and members of the judiciary may be appointed from outside fields, it's a lifetime career to become a leader in a representative assembly. The problem with careerism is that, although it may guarantee loyalty to their institution, it may also separate members from a changing society.

As popular disgust for entrenched government grew, proposals for *term limits* on members of Congress gained support. Twenty-three states adopted measures to limit the number of times their congressmen and senators could run for reelection. Congress, led by Republicans who had embraced term limits in their Contract with America, tried to join in by voting on several different constitutional amendments that would restrict members to 6 or 12 years in office. They all failed.

Even more damaging for supporters of term limits was a May 1995 Supreme Court ruling (*U.S. Term Limits* v. *Thornton*) that threw out term limits imposed by the states. The Court held that states could not restrict who could run for federal offices without an amendment to the Constitution. That seemed to put an end to term limits. As one supporter, Republican Senator Dan Coats of Indiana, said about the chances of Congress voting for such an amendment, "I don't think there's any way to get two-thirds of the people in this place who are willing to say goodbye to their jobs."

Malapportionment and Reapportionment

The drawing of House districts is up to the state governors and legislatures, who have often used these powers to boost their own party and penalize the party that is out of power. In the past, *malapportionment* (large differences in the populations of congressional districts)

Advantages of Incumbency

During elections to Congress, the advantages of incumbency (being currently in office) are considerable. The incumbent is well known, and by issuing "official" statements or making "official" trips to his district, he can get a lot of free publicity that his opponents would have to pay for. Members of the House have office and staff budgets of approximately $350,000 a year; senators are given at least that and often considerably more if their states are large. Both receive 32 government-paid round trips to their districts each year. Facilities for making television or radio tapes are available in Washington at a low cost. And there is the *frank*, the privilege of free official mailing enjoyed by Congress. Two hundred million pieces of mail, much of it quite partisan, are sent free under the frank every year.

Despite the low public opinion of the effectiveness of Congress, incumbent representatives often do well running for Congress by running against Congress. Coupled with the usually low voter turnout in congressional races and the frequent one-party dominance of districts, it is no wonder that incumbents usually win. The election of 1994 was no exception. Despite strong anti-incumbency sentiment, 90 percent of House incumbents and 92 percent of Senate incumbents who sought reelection won.

was common in many areas of the country. Districts would be drawn up so that minority-party districts included more voters than majority-party districts. In this way, each minority-party voter would count for less. In 1960, Michigan's 16th district had 802,994 people, whereas the 12th had only 177,431.

In addition, the art of *gerrymandering* was practiced. The name comes from Massachusetts Governor Elbridge Gerry, who in 1812 helped to draw a long, misshapen district composed of a string of towns north of Boston. When painter Gilbert Stuart saw a drawing of the oddly shaped district, he penciled in claws, wings, and a head and said, "that will do for a salamander!" His editor replied, "Better say a gerrymander." The two most common forms of gerrymandering are "packing" and "cracking." *Packing* involves drawing up a district so that it has a large majority of supporters, to ensure a "safe" seat. *Cracking* means splitting up an opponents' supporters into minorities in a number of districts to weaken their influence.

Such practices have long been attacked by reformers. In 1964 a Supreme Court decision held that legislative districts at both the state and national levels must be as close to equal in population as possible. Many of the worst abuses of malapportionment were ended by the Court's decision. But politics remains vital to the drawing of districts, as can be seen in the conflicts over the shifts caused by the 1990 Census.

At the beginning of each decade the Census Bureau counts the nation's population, and the House of Representatives is reapportioned to reflect the change in each state's population. The population has not only grown since the last census in 1980 but has continued to shift toward the South and West of the country. After the 1990 Census, because the number of seats in the House is limited by law to 435, seventeen seats switched to the so-called Sunbelt. New York was the big loser, with three of its seats being lost, and California the big winner, gaining seven seats. The state legislatures shaped the new districts, combining them in states losing population (or not gaining as much as other states) and splitting up districts in states gaining voters. (See Figure 4.1.)

There has been much controversy surrounding the creation of new congressional districts following the 1990 Census. Based on 1982 amendments to the Voting Rights Act, state legislatures created or gerrymandered districts that were racially representative of a state's population. They designed minority districts in which the minorities became the majority of the voting population. An example of this type of racial gerrymandering occurred in the creation of North Carolina's 12th Congressional District. This district, in an attempt to include as many black voters as possible, snakes across thirteen counties in half the state. (See Figure 4.2.)

Attempting to benefit from the creation of these minority-voting districts was the Republican party, which hoped to become more competitive in a greater number of districts. The minority districts did weaken Democratic support in surrounding districts by lowering the number of Democratic-voting minorities. The redistricting clearly played a role in Republican gains in the South in 1994. However, these 17 new black or his-

Figure 4.1 Redrawing the Lines. Nineteen House seats shifted states as a result of data from the 1990 Census; eight states gained seats and thirteen lost seats.

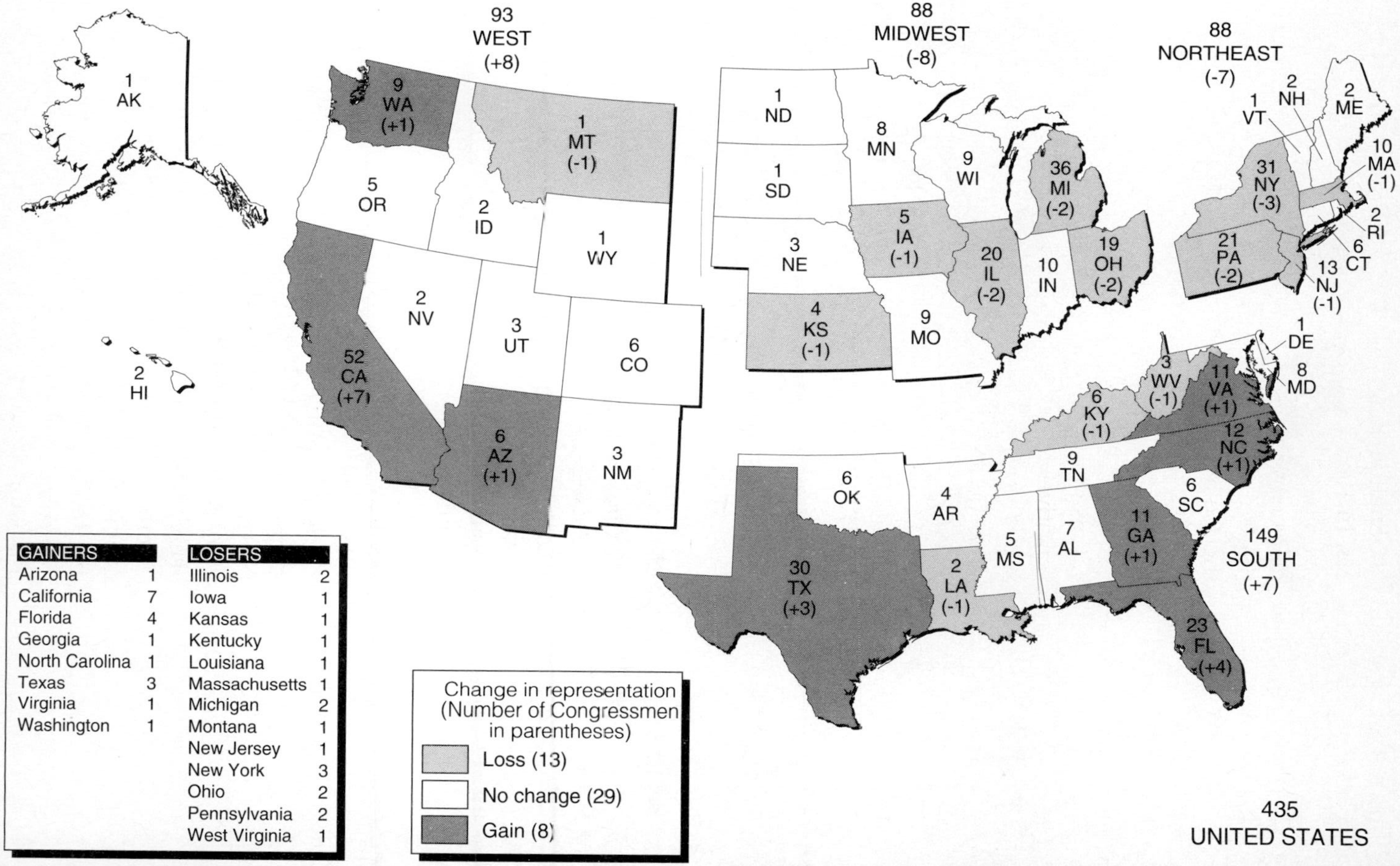

GAINERS	
Arizona	1
California	7
Florida	4
Georgia	1
North Carolina	1
Texas	3
Virginia	1
Washington	1

LOSERS	
Illinois	2
Iowa	1
Kansas	1
Kentucky	1
Louisiana	1
Massachusetts	1
Michigan	2
Montana	1
New Jersey	1
New York	3
Ohio	2
Pennsylvania	2
West Virginia	1

Figure 4.2   Racial Gerrymandering.

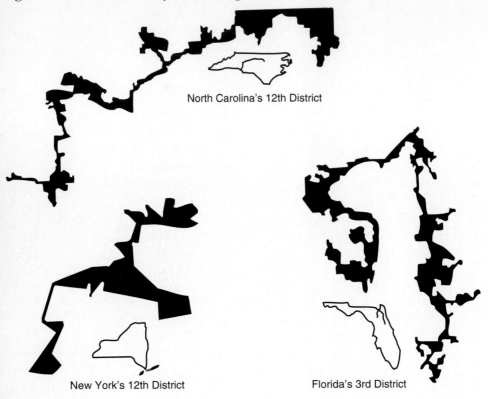

North Carolina's 12th District

New York's 12th District

Florida's 3rd District

panic districts also resulted in large gains in minorities elected to Congress. In 1992 African Americans in the House rose from 26 to 39, and Hispanics went from 12 to 19.

The Supreme Court looked at this gerrymandering and didn't like what it saw. In a 1993 ruling (*Shaw* v. *Reno*), the Court questioned whether North Carolina's "bizarrely shaped" 12th district was an effort to segregate the races for purposes of voting. In another 5–4 ruling in 1995 the Court struck down a Georgia congressional district because it violated the Constitution's guarantees of equal protection. In this case, *Miller* v. *Johnson,* the Court doubted whether it would approve any district lines for which race was the "predominant factor." While allowing race to be a consideration in drawing districts, the Court seemed to question the premise that minorities benefit when they are placed in minority-dominant voting districts. It seemed likely that most of these districts would eventually have to be redrawn to meet the Court's approval.

Organization of the House of Representatives

The organization of both branches of Congress is based on political party lines. The *majority party* in each house is the one with the greatest number of members. Being the majority party is quite important because that party chooses the major officers of the branch of Congress, controls debate on the floor, selects all committee chairs, and has a majority on all committees. Until 1994 the Democrats had controlled both houses of Congress for 40 years, except for the years 1980–1986 when the Republicans ran the Senate. In 1994 the Republicans became the majority in both houses.

In the House of Representatives, the majority party chooses from among its members the *Speaker of the House.* He does not have to be the oldest or longest-serving member, but he will certainly be well respected and is likely to have served a long apprenticeship in other party posts. During some periods, such as 1890 to 1910, the Speaker exercised almost dictatorial powers. The Speaker still retains considerable power, especially recently, through his control over the majority party. He also greatly influences how the committee system operates, which we will look at later in this chapter. The selection of the Speaker takes place every two years, at the beginning of Congress, in the majority party caucus.

In 1994 Newt Gingrich of Georgia became the first Republican Speaker of the House since 1954. He led the Republican majority toward achieving a national "mandate for change" to both shrink the federal government and make it operate more efficiently. Believing that the best place to start this process was within Congress itself, he ushered in many rule changes, cutting staffs and eliminating entire committees. He tightened the coordination of activities among House leaders, limited the number of subcommittees within each committee, and reorganized the jurisdictions of many committees. Through the force of his own personality and by relying on the loyalty of the large class of freshman Republicans, he greatly increased the power of the Speaker. (See "Prime Minister Gingrich.")

The *caucus* of each political party in the House or Senate is simply a gathering of all the members of that party serving there. The Republican majority caucus in the House is referred to as the Republican *Conference.* The conference chooses a *majority leader* who is second in command to the Speaker. The majority leader works closely with the Speaker and schedules legislation for debate on the House floor. Republican Dick Armey of Texas is majority leader, which makes him number two to the Speaker.

Prime Minister Gingrich

The cohesion shown by the new House Republican majority resulted in their campaign platform, Contract with America, passing the House in the first 100 days of the session with an average of only five Republicans dissenting on 33 roll call votes. (Of course it was then altered, delayed, or eliminated by the Senate.) Much of this unity reflected the leadership of House Speaker Newt Gingrich.

The Republican from Georgia gained power in several ways. His help in their campaigns—through fundraising, speaking appearances, and even recruiting them to run—gave Gingrich great standing among freshman Republicans. With his party's backing he handpicked committee and subcommittee chairs, not always on the basis of seniority, thus assuring their loyalty to him. He freed himself up from the day-to-day business of the House by turning over many of these tasks to the House Majority Leader aided by multiple weekly meetings of party leaders. This division of labor left Gingrich so comfortable that he recalled that Senator Majority Leader Robert Dole "was shocked when I couldn't even tell him what was on the House floor that day."

Gingrich was left to determine the agenda of his party and, some would claim, the nation. He saw himself as a kind of Prime Minister of a counter government chosen by the House, the U.S. equivalent of the British House of Commons. Despite being pictured as radical and unpredictable, he used his frequent media appearances to turn the speakership into a powerful pulpit presenting an alternative conservative direction for the country to rival that of the president's.

Source: Congressional Quarterly, February 4, 1995, 331; *The Washington Post,* July 17, 1995, A-12.

The Speaker and majority leader are assisted by *majority whips.* (The word *whip* comes from English fox hunting, where the "whipper-in" keeps the dogs from running away.) The whips help coordinate party positions on legislation, pass information and directions between the leadership and other party members, make sure party members know when a particular vote is coming, try to persuade wavering representatives to vote with the leadership, and conduct informal surveys to check the likely outcome of votes. Being at the center of the congressional process, these party leaders possess more information than other legislators, which adds to their power.

The minority party in the House, currently the Democrats, select in their caucus a *minority leader* and *minority whips.* Like the majority party's leader and whips, their duties are to coordinate party positions. The minority leader is usually his or her party's candidate for Speaker should it become the majority party. Richard Gephardt of Missouri is the Democrats' minority leader.

The Democratic and Republican caucuses in the House run their affairs in slightly different ways. The Republican party chooses a *Steering Committee* to function as an executive committee of the caucus. The Steering Committee helps chart party policy in the House, and assigns Republican members to committees. It also nominates committee chairs, who must be approved by the Republican Conference. The Republicans restructured the Steering Committee after winning their House majority, and it now has a weighted voting system which gives the Speaker 5 of the 30 votes in the committee, reflecting his increased power.

The Democrats also have a Steering Committee, which was divided into two after the 1994 elections. The *Steering Panel* nominates committee members and ranking minority members, and the *Policy Committee* studies issues, writes bills, and publicizes them. The Steering Panel had to adjust to the Democrats no longer controlling committees and was forced to remove members from many committees. It relied almost exclusively on seniority in making these decisions.

Organization of the Senate

The Senate has no Speaker. The *president of the Senate* is the vice president of the United States. He has the right to preside over the Senate chamber and to vote in case of a tie. Presiding is a rarely exercised function, one filled only when an important vote is scheduled.

The honorary post of president *pro tem* (from *pro tempore,* meaning "for the time being") of the Senate is given to the senator from the majority party who has served longest in the Senate—currently Strom Thurmond (R-S.Car.), a Senator since 1954. His only power is to preside in the absence of the vice president, but he hardly ever does so. Because the vast majority of Senate work takes place in committees, the job of presiding over a Senate chamber that may be dull and nearly vacant usually falls to a junior senator, who is asked to do so by the Senate majority leader.

The *majority leader of the Senate* is the nearest equivalent to the Speaker of the House. He schedules debate on the Senate floor, assigns bills to committees, coordinates party policy, and appoints members of special committees. Republican Trent Lott of Mississippi replaced Robert Dole of Kansas after Dole resigned from the Senate to run for president. The Senate majority leader is assisted by a whip and assistant whips. The minority party in the Senate selects a *minority leader* and a *minority whip,* who likewise coordinate party positions and manage floor strategy. The minority leader is now Democrat Tom Daschle of South Dakota.

In the Senate the Republicans have a *Committee on Committees,* which assigns members to committees, and a *Policy Committee,* which charts legislative tactics. The party caucus, called the *Republican Conference,* consists of all Republicans in the Senate. Each of these groups is chaired by a leading Republican Senator. Senate Democrats are organized in much the same way. A *Steering Committee* assigns members to committees and a *Policy Committee* coordinates strategy. Unlike the Republican organizations, the Senate Democratic leader chairs the Democratic caucus (called the *Demo-*

cratic Conference), the Steering Committee, and the Policy Committee.

HOW DOES CONGRESS OPERATE?

Legislation may be introduced in either the House or the Senate, or in both houses at the same time. The only exceptions to this rule are money-raising bills, which the Constitution states must originate in the House, and appropriations (spending) bills, which by custom also begin there. Approximately 20,000 bills are introduced in Congress each year. (See Figure 4.3.) They may be part of the president's program, they may be drafted by individual members or by committees, or they may be the result of alliances between Congress and the executive bureaucracy or lobbyists. Only 5 percent of these bills become law.

With cohesive Republican majorities in both houses of Congress, it is likely the Republican party will introduce most of the legislation passed by Congress. However, the Senate and House act separately and may amend or revise bills as they see fit. For any bill to become law it must ultimately be passed by both houses of Congress in identical language and approved by the president or passed over his veto.

The Congress operates by division of labor. Most of the work of Congress goes on not on the House or Senate floor, but in committees. House committees may have anywhere from 20 to 50 representatives; Senate committees usually have 10 to 20 senators. If they did not break down into committees, the Senate and House would move much more slowly and could deal with far fewer issues because they could consider only one subject at a time. It is almost impossible to imagine Congress operating without the committee system.

When a piece of legislation is introduced in either the Senate or the House, it is assigned to a committee. The committee (or, often, one of its subcommittees) reviews the bill and decides whether to recommend it to the whole House or Senate. Between 80 and 90 percent of the bills introduced in Congress die in committee. Because the committee system is central to the opera-

Figure 4.3 How a Bill Becomes a Law.

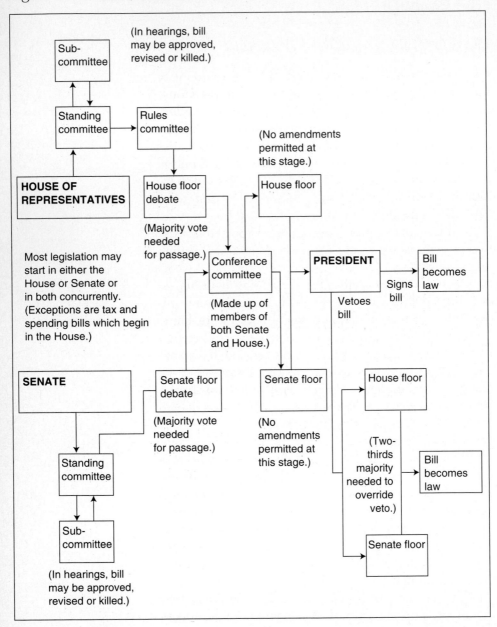

tion of Congress, it will be discussed more fully later in this chapter.

Floor Debate in the House and Senate

Once a bill has been approved by committee (and in the House by the Rules Committee), it is sent to the House or Senate floor for debate. There it is placed on a calendar. *Calendars* are the business agendas or schedules in Congress. Certain calendars are for routine or minor legislation, others for more important bills, and one in the House, the "discharge calendar," can be used to try to force a bill out of committee against the committee's wishes. (It is rarely successful.)

In the House, floor debate is controlled by the Speaker. He schedules bills for consideration and then makes sure the committees deliver their bills in the correct form and at the right time. He has the right to preside over debate. House members are commonly restricted to a few minutes of talk each. The Senate, being smaller, is able to operate more informally. In general, power is more widely distributed in the Senate than in the House. Even junior (new) senators, for example, often chair subcommittees. The Senate majority leader schedules bills for debate, but his control during debate is much less than the House Speaker's.

When debate on a bill has ended, it is put to a vote. A simple majority of the legislators present is needed for passage. Whether a bill begins in the Senate or the House, it must sooner or later be submitted to the other branch, where the whole procedure of committee review and floor action will be repeated. Then, any differences between the House and Senate versions of a bill must be eliminated before it can be sent to the president for his signature or veto.

Both in committees and on the floor of Congress, members of the same political party do not always vote together. In the fights over the North American Free Trade Agreement (NAFTA), which President Clinton strongly supported, most Republicans were behind the measure, and the Democrats were divided, with most opposing it. Regional coalitions of Republicans and

Democrats have united to prevent the closing of local military bases.

More often, President Clinton found himself facing a unified Republican opposition; even to the extent that every Republican in both houses of Congress opposed his budget package in 1993. When they became the minority Democrats generally returned the favor by voting against Republican budget proposals in 1995. The most frequent division in Congress remains that between Republicans and Democrats. (See Table 4.1.)

Filibuster

In the Senate, except under very unusual circumstances, debate is unlimited. Senators may talk on a subject for as long as they wish and they will not be cut off. Never-ending talk by one or a number of senators designed to delay or block action in the Senate is called a *filibuster.* The original filibuster was a type of pirate ship. Its current meaning probably comes from the image of a lone individual defying the rules. Senators engaged in a filibuster usually talk for several hours at a time (sometimes reading the Bible or the Washington phone directory) before giving up the floor to an ally.

Table 4.1   Major Differences Between the House and the Senate

HOUSE	SENATE
Larger (435)	Smaller (100)
Shorter term of office (2 years)	Longer term of office (6 years)
More procedural restraints on members	Fewer procedural restraints on members
Narrower constituency	Broader, more varied constituency
Policy specialists	Policy generalists
Less press and media coverage	More press and media coverage
More powerful leadership	Less powerful leaders
Less prestigious	More prestigious
Briefer floor debates	Longer floor debates
Less reliant on staff	More reliant on staff
More partisan	Less partisan

Source: Walter J. Oleszck, *Congressional Procedures and the Policy Process,* 3rd ed. (Washington, D.C.: Congressional Quarterly Press, 1989), p. 24.

Senator Strom Thurmond of South Carolina set the individual filibuster record in 1957 by speaking against a civil rights act for 24 hours and 18 minutes nonstop. (See "A National Town Meeting?")

Rule 22 (of the Senate Rules—a set of regulations governing Senate behavior) protects the filibuster unless three-fifths of the Senate votes for an end to debate. This is the only vote in Congress based on the total number of legislators. All other votes in both the Senate and House are based on the number of members who are present and voting. Voting to end debate is called *cloture*. Because many senators, especially those of the minority party, see advantages in having the option of a filibuster available, cloture is rarely successful. Senator Robert Byrd (D-W. Va.), a former majority leader, has used his mastery of parliamentary rules to slow the Senate to a crawl when he believed it was heading in the wrong direction. Relying on the Democrats to use their numbers to prevent a three-fifths vote to close off debate, his "Byrdlock" slowed debate on measures like the balanced budget amendment.

Filibusters are most effective late in a session of the Senate when legislation has piled up. Senators are eager to adjourn, and they feel the pressures of any delaying tactic. If 60 senators cannot be found to invoke cloture, a compromise is likely. Democrats as the minority party,

A National Town Meeting?

C-SPAN (Cable Special Public Affairs Network), which started on the air in 1979, expanded as the public's apparent appetite for raw, unedited views of government in action grew. Beginning with the House, C-SPAN later added coverage of the Senate in 1986. The federally supported C-SPAN televises uninterrupted coverage of the proceedings of both bodies on the floor and in committee. It also broadcasts other public interest events and viewer call-in interviews with public figures. Starting with less than a million dollars, C-SPAN grew to a $20 million operation that is carried by cable systems serving 60 million households. The initial fear that members would grandstand in front of the camera gave way to an appreciation among members of Congress of the value of free TV exposure for incumbents' reelection hopes.

like the Republicans when they were the minority, frequently use the filibuster to prevent majority actions. The House, being larger and harder to manage, has decided it cannot afford the luxury of unlimited debate. Hence, filibusters are not allowed in the House.

Presidential Veto

Even after it has been approved by both the House and Senate, a bill may still be killed by a presidential veto. The president may veto any legislation he wishes. The threat of a veto is especially important for a president who has to bargain with hostile congressional majorities, as shown in Clinton's budget fights with a Republican Congress.

In most instances a president may not veto only part of a bill. He must veto it all or accept it all. However, the 104th Congress approval of a limited *item veto* for certain financial bills has theoretically given the president more power in influencing legislation. But of course, Congress has the last word: If Congress *overrides* a veto, the bill becomes law. To override a veto requires two-thirds approval of each house of Congress. Vetoes are rarely overridden.

The president must act on a bill within ten working days. If he does not sign it within that period while Congress remains in session, the bill becomes law without his signature. If Congress adjourns before the ten days are up, and the president does not sign the bill, it does not become law; this is called a "pocket veto."

Because the limited item veto does not cover most bills Congress has an advantage in any confrontation with the president by using *riders.* A rider is a piece of legislation attached as an amendment to another bill, which may deal with a totally different issue. Commonly, the rider contains provisions that the president does not like, whereas the "parent" bill to which the rider is attached is favored by the president. Either he vetoes the rider he does not like and thus also the main bill that he desires, or he accepts the unwanted rider in order to get the rest of the bill. Before the limited item veto these riders helped increase government spending and the

---

The White House Looks for Votes

A veto is not the only tool a president has to bargain with Congress. To get a 1986 tax reform passed in the House, the Reagan White House had to make deals, even with members of their own party to gain needed votes:

Members who were still sitting on the fence saw this as an opportunity to swap their votes for favors from the White House, and they began horse trading. Eager to get fifty supporters, the administration team was more than willing to deal. Representative George Gekas of Pennsylvania said he would change his vote if the administration would take a look at his proposal to have staggered filing dates for tax returns; [Secretary of the Treasury James] Baker agreed. Representative Nancy Johnson of Connecticut promised to switch if the cabinet would consider placing import quotas on machine tools; Baker promised to look into that as well. One congressman asked Baker to come to his state and help in his reelection campaign; Baker said he would. "Boy, they weren't bashful," Baker recalls.

Source: Jeffrey H. Birnbaum and Alan S. Murray, *Showdown at Gucci Gulch* (New York: Random House, 1988), p. 172.

---

deficit. For this reason many Republicans supported the item veto, even for a Democratic president. (See "The White House Looks for Votes.")

Finally, passing legislation does not automatically make anything happen. If money is needed for the government's wishes (as expressed in a bill) to be carried out, the entire legislative process must be gone through *twice*—once to pass the bill authorizing the activity, and a second time to pass a bill appropriating the money to do it. The goals of the authorizing bill will not come into being if the appropriations process does not provide the funds.

THE COMMITTEE SYSTEM

As we have mentioned, much of the work of Congress takes place within committees rather than on the "floor" of the House or Senate. Often, although not always, floor debate is little more than a formality designed to make a public record. On an average day, a visitor to the Senate or House chamber might find a dozen or fewer members talking with each other while a colleague de-

scribes the superiority of Idaho potatoes or the reason
Pennsylvania named the firefly its official state insect.
At the same moment, many of the committee rooms
would be filled with activity.

How Committees Work

The four types of committees in Congress are standing,
conference, select, and joint.

Standing committees are the basic working units of
Congress. They were started early in the nation's history
because Congress found it could do more work faster if
it broke down into smaller, specialized groups. There
are 19 standing committees in the House and 17 in the
Senate, most focusing on one or two general subjects.
Representatives serve on one or two standing committees, senators on three or four. Usually these committees break down into subcommittees for a further division of labor. The House has 86 subcommittees and the
Senate has 69. This is a dramatic reduction from the
number of subcommittees in the 103rd Congress, when
there were 147 in the House and 87 in the Senate.

Before any bill can be sent to the floor for consideration by the entire Senate or House, it must be approved by a majority vote in the standing committee to
which it is assigned. A committee's examination of a
proposed bill may include holding public hearings in
which interested parties, including the executive bureaucracies and lobbyists, are invited to testify. Often
the actual work on a bill assigned to a standing committee goes on in one of its subcommittees. If the full committee then approves the bill, it will be sent to the floor
of the Senate or House with a report describing the
committee's findings and the reasons the committee
thinks the bill should be passed. If the bill is considered
unnecessary or undesirable by the committee, it will be
killed. The bill's sponsors may resubmit it in a later
Congress, but if the committee involved continues to
reject it, it will fail again.

A *conference committee* is a temporary body including both senators and representatives, created solely to
iron out the differences between House and Senate versions of one bill. These differences come about because

of amendments attached to the bill by one chamber but not the other or because the two houses have passed different bills dealing with the same subject. Before a bill can be sent to the president for his action, it must be passed in identical language by both houses.

The Speaker of the House and the Senate majority leader have the authority to appoint the members of conference committees. However, in practice they allow the chairs of the relevant standing committees to do this and typically appoint the senior members of these committees. The conference committee engages in bargaining and trade-offs to reach a compromise; once this job is finished, it is disbanded.

When (and if) the conference committee reaches agreement, the new substitute bill is then sent back to the House and Senate floors for approval or disapproval. This bill cannot be amended; it must be accepted or rejected as is. If this rule were not in force, of course, the bill might be amended again in different ways in the House and Senate, thereby requiring another conference committee, and so on.

Select committees are set up to do specific, usually temporary, jobs, often to conduct an investigation. A recent example, the Senate Special Committee on Whitewater, was set up by the 104th Congress to uncover any illegal activity in President Clinton's involvement with a failed Arkansas real estate project in the 1980s.

Joint committees are permanent bodies including both senators and representatives. Usually these committees coordinate policy on routine matters, such as printing or the congressional library. The Joint Economic Committee, however, has important tasks of studying and reporting to Congress its recommendations on the president's annual economic report. Reformers often favor greater use of joint committees in Congress to save time, money, and confusion. The two branches are jealous of their separate powers, however, and joint committees remain the exception.

Committee Chairmen and the Seniority System

By the unwritten rule of *seniority*, the chair of any committee is typically the majority-party member who has served longest (consecutively) on the committee. While the current congressional leadership has usually followed seniority they have made it clear that acceptance of the party's legislative agenda would be part of the job requirements for any committee chairman.

Some of the chairmen's power comes about naturally through the work of their committees, their understanding of congressional procedures, and their wide contacts within the government, which are results of long legislative service. They influence the hiring and firing of majority-party staff, schedule committee meetings and agenda, and have something to say about the appointment of new members to their committees. The seniority system has been a long tradition in Congress, though it is not written down anywhere in the rules of the House or Senate. Still, for more than 50 years, the custom was almost never broken.

Starting in the mid-1970s, a combination of scandals and the desire of the growing number of junior Democratic representatives and senators for a "piece of the action," led to several committee chairs being ousted and an increase in the power of subcommittees and the party caucus. Seniority was not considered crucial in appointing subcommittee chairmen, especially in the Senate, where first-term senators usually chaired a subcommittee. These changes also represented a revolt within the Democratic party against the power of committee chairs, many of whom were long-serving conservative Southern Democrats.

With the Republican takeover of both houses of Congress in 1994, party leadership was strengthened at the expense of the committees. Interestingly, this was done differently in the House and the Senate: The power of committee chairs in the House was strengthened, while their authority in the Senate was weakened. The House Republican Conference gave committee chairmen the authority to select subcommittee chairs and to hire all committee staff. Subcommittees were barred from having their own staff. The purpose of these changes was to both shrink the size of committees and to centralize power in the party leadership. In the House, the committee heads were seen as furthering this goal.

Meanwhile, the Senate Republican Conference gave committee members the power to nominate their chairs, prevented heads of most standing committees from chairing subcommittees, and imposed term limits on their committee chairmen (as did the House). These limits on the seniority system in the Senate were sparked by Republican freshman members. Many of them had recently served in the House and were used to greater party control over members.

Nonetheless, the seniority system (often called the "senility system") lives on in the House and the Senate. Attacked as out-of-date and undemocratic, it has allowed members who are popular in their districts and states to accumulate substantial national power. It has also allowed minorities in the Democratic party and moderate Republicans to gain positions of power. Seniority ensures that an experienced person will become chairman and, more importantly, has provided a predictable system of succession without constant fights over control of the chair. But the new leaders and majority caucuses of Congress no longer feel the need to automatically follow a custom that limits their own influence. Current party leaders committed to their own legislative program have loosened the hold of seniority and with it some of the independence of the committee system.

Specialization, Reciprocity, and Party Loyalty

Two other informal rules, though weakened, support the power of committees in Congress. The first, *specialization,* is closely related to the second, *reciprocity.* Specialization means that once assigned to a committee or subcommittee, a member of Congress is expected to specialize in its work and become expert in that area. Particularly in the House, members are not expected to follow all legislation in Congress equally, or to speak out on widely varying issues. The result of this system is that committees and their individual members become experts in their own work but may not know much about other areas.

This potential problem is resolved through the informal rule of *reciprocity.* Here members look for guidance in voting on legislation outside their committee's field to members of committees that do specialize in it. Legislators tend to vote the way their party's representatives on the most closely concerned committee tell them to vote, because that committee knows most about the legislation and because the members want the same support and respect when their committee's business is involved. Specialization and reciprocity, then, are two sides of the same coin. You develop expertise in an area and other members follow your lead in that area. You, in turn, follow the lead of others more knowledgeable than you in areas outside your expertise.

This process has been diluted in the Senate, and more recently in the House. Greater party control of the legislative agenda has reduced the ability of the committees to take the lead in their particular field. Because senators commonly serve on three or four committees, their areas of specialization are more varied and less intense. Still, the general pattern operates both in the Senate and the House. Indeed, were it not for specialization and reciprocity, the work of Congress would proceed more slowly, with more confusion.

In recent years party loyalty has increased in Congress in both parties. The votes in which the majority of the two parties oppose each other have increased. Members now vote with their party about 80 percent of the time whereas 20 years ago loyalty was only seen in 70 percent of the votes. The parties are more united and more different. As the Democratic party continues to lose its more conservative members from the South, and as the number of conservative Republicans has increased, the parties have become more polarized—there are now fewer liberal Republicans, fewer conservative Democrats and fewer moderates in both parties. As a result, recent congresses have become more partisan, often with a nasty tone to the place. (See "Congress: Personal, Mean, and Nasty?")

There are certainly fewer mavericks. *Mavericks* are those members of Congress who show less loyalty to their party and do not abide by the informal rules. Usually mavericks represent constituencies that are not like the typical voters of their party: For example, conservative Democrats from Republican-leaning districts or liberal Republicans from Democratic-leaning districts. Mavericks may be popular in their home districts, but they are unlikely to be popular in Congress. They may receive unattractive committee assignments or be shunned by their colleagues. As Speaker Sam Rayburn was fond of saying to new members of Congress, "To get along you've got to go along."

Assignment to a committee or subcommittee are vital to a legislator's power. These patterns of influence tend to keep committees stable and discourage "hopping" from one to another. Once members of Congress have been assigned to a committee, they will not be removed against their wishes unless the ratio between the parties should shift, including a change in the majority party as happened when the Republicans won control of Congress in 1994. The Republicans then became the majority in every committee in both houses of Congress. Democrats, in turn, found themselves losing seats in these committees to make room for Republican members.

Congress: Personal, Mean, and Nasty?

The rules of both houses of Congress forbid personal insults. But recently the rhetoric has gotten down and dirty, perhaps reaching a new depth with the partial government shutdown in 1995 and early 1996. Each side blamed the other for the budget impasse leading to some of the following:

- When Speaker Gingrich complained he had been snubbed by the president, Democrats held up a newspaper headline referring to him as a "crybaby."
- The Speaker called Clinton "deliberately dishonest."

- One GOP congressman accused Democrats of "down-in-the-dirt gutter politics."
- Republicans turned off the microphones on Democratic speakers.
- A Democrat shoved a Republican starting a general melee.

Whether the causes were negative campaign advertising, the Speaker's history of personal attacks, the intensity of the budget debate, or the late-night sessions and frayed nerves, the consequences for Congress were that, in the words of one congressman, "The civility's gone out of the well."

The Budget Process

The "power of the purse" is one of Congress's basic constitutional powers. Historically, the power to control government spending and taxes has not meant that Congress had the ability to control them coherently. The large number of committees and decentralized power bases in Congress has meant that overall spending (expenditures) was seldom related to taxes (revenues), and neither fit into a national economic policy. The responsibility for putting together a comprehensive government budget and national economic policy thus fell to the president. For the last 20 years Congress has struggled to change this.

In 1974 Congress passed the Budget Act (the Congressional Budget and Impoundment Control Act). The Budget Act enabled Congress to propose an alternative to the president's budget based on an examination of all spending and tax measures and the overall needs of the economy. Rather than merely debating the merits of individual government programs, Congress could now examine formerly isolated parts of the budget and evaluate them for their influence on the economy. The Budget Act did this in several ways.

The act set up House and Senate Budget committees. The House Budget Committee members are drawn mainly from the Ways and Means and Appropriations committees, with one member from each of the other standing committees. Members and the chair are rotated periodically without regard to seniority. Members of the Senate Budget Committee are selected in the same way as members of other committees in the Senate. The committees guide the Congress in setting total spending, tax, and debt levels. Aiding the two Budget committees is a *Congressional Budget Office* (CBO) established by the act. The nonpartisan CBO provides experts to analyze the president's budget proposals and to match Congress's numerous spending decisions with the established budget targets.

The budget works its way through Congress on a series of deadlines. The goal is to have a completed budget by the beginning of the government's fiscal year, October 1. The process starts when the president submits his budget to Congress in January. All the committees in Congress then submit their estimates and views of the budget to the Budget committees, which gather them in a first resolution. Congress must vote on this resolution, which sets overall spending and tax levels, by April 15. The various parts of this first resolution then go back to the standing committees concerned with the particular subject or program. By mid-June the standing committees' recommendations have gone back to the Budget committees, which draw up a reconciliation bill that is then voted on by Congress. This part of the process is called *reconciliation* because it attempts to balance the separate standing committees' decisions with the targets set by the first resolution.

By 1985 it was as clear as the then-record $220 billion deficit that the budget process was not working. In a radical attempt to lower the deficit, Congress passed an antideficit measure called Gramm-Rudman. The law required five years of federal deficit reductions of $36 billion a year resulting in a balanced budget (zero deficits) by fiscal 1991. These reductions, by less spending or more taxes, would take place in the normal budget process but—and this was the radical part—if Congress failed to meet the deficit target, automatic cuts would be made in defense and nondefense programs. In 1986 the Supreme Court ruled that imposing automatic cuts was unconstitutional.

Without the automatic cuts Congress was unable to keep to the Gramm-Rudman deficit-reduction schedule. Congress did cut defense, reduced farm aid, and slowed down government spending to less than 1 percent annual growth. But Congress also "cooked the books" by some questionable practices like selling government holdings, which resulted in one-time gains, and pushing federal paydays into the next fiscal year. The political consensus was not yet in place to reduce the deficit.

In 1993 President Clinton introduced an ambitious deficit-reduction package that promised to reduce the deficit by $500 billion over the next five years. The White House claimed that half of the reduction would come from tax increases (mostly on the wealthy) and half from cutting government spending. Republican opponents charged the bill's numbers were suspect and that it was too "tax heavy." After considerable debate and changes by Congress, a version of the bill was passed in August 1993.

With the rise of Republican majorities in both houses, balancing the budget became a major political goal. The defeat of the balanced budget amendment (see Case Study: The Balanced Budget Amendment) moved Republican leaders to the practical task of actually balancing the budget. In June 1995 they agreed on a complex plan that aimed to balance the budget in seven years while giving taxpayers a $245 billion tax cut. The Republicans did what the Democrats charged they could never do—actually spell out their cuts in government spending. The GOP also preserved tax breaks for the wealthy and programs that helped business—welfare for the rich, critics charged. President Clinton, attempting not to be irrelevant to the process, came up with a balanced budget with far fewer tax cuts and less painful reductions in popular programs like Medicare. Disagreements over the budget between the president and Congress led to a government shutdown in late 1995 and early 1996. Both finally agreed on balancing the budget in seven years but disagreed on everything else. Both sides played fast and loose with their numbers and put off the most difficult spending cuts for several years in the future.

Major Committees in the House

With the coming of the budget process and the political focus on the deficit, power centered even more than it had on those committees shaping the taxing and spending policies of the government. In the old days, power came through seniority to all committee chairmen. While this still has some truth, power is now concentrated in the House leaders of the majority party and in the senior majority party members of a few elite committees. Members of less fortunate committees spend a good deal of time trying to get help from members of the key committees. These House committees, besides Budget, are Rules, Ways and Means, and Appropriations.

Almost all legislation approved by committees in the House must pass through the Rules Committee before reaching the House floor. The Rules Committee's name comes from its function: If the committee approves a bill for transmission to the House floor, it assigns a "rule" to that bill setting the terms of a debate. The Rules Committee can, for example, assign a "closed rule," which forbids any amendments and forces the House into a "take it or leave it" position. Thus the Rules Committee acts as a traffic cop. It has the power to delay or even stop legislation; it can amend bills or send them back to committee for revision; and it can decide in cases where two committees have bills on the same subject which one gets sent to the floor. At the start of the 104th Congress, Gerald Solomon (R-N.Y.) unsuccessfully challenged Newt Gingrich (R-Ga.) to be Speaker of the House. Despite the challenge, Gingrich did not oppose Solomon becoming chairman of the Rules Committee and this powerful committee largely followed the wishes of the speaker.

The Ways and Means Committee deals with tax legislation, or the raising of revenue for the government. Because all money-raising bills begin in the House, any tax legislation goes first to Ways and Means, making this committee a central power in Congress. Chairman Bill Archer (R-Tx.) was in a key position for moving much of the Republican "Contract with America" legislation through the House. Ways and Means has been the key committee on issues such as welfare reform, tax reform, and proposed changes in the Social Security system. In "reconciliation," it and the Senate Finance Committee are important in deciding where the Budget Committee's spending cuts will fall.

The Ways and Means Committee raises money; the Appropriations Committee deals with how government spends that money. When the federal budget is presented to Congress by the president each year, it is sent to the House Appropriations Committee and its 11 subcommittees as the first stage in congressional review. Because the power to tax and spend is the power to make or break programs, industries, and interest groups, and because specialization and reciprocity nudge Congress to follow the lead of its committees, the importance of Ways and Means and Appropriations is clear. While Appropriations is limited by the budget process on its overall spending, it can still decide where it will spend money or make cuts. It has become a key place for doing favors for other members, such as passing their *pork-barrel* bills—legislation designed to produce visible benefits, such as local highways and post offices, for constituents.

Major Committees in the Senate

The most important committees in the Senate (besides Budget) are Appropriations, Finance, and Foreign Relations. The Senate Appropriations Committee receives appropriations bills after they have been passed by the House. Its procedures are very much like those of its House counterpart, with the important distinction that the Senate committee tends to act as a "court of appeals," adding money to or subtracting it from the amounts granted by the House. If passed by the House, tax legislation then goes to the Senate Finance Committee, the Senate's equivalent to Ways and Means in the House.

The Senate Foreign Relations Committee is a watchdog over the president's dominant position in foreign policy. Its importance comes from the Senate's role in confirming appointments of ambassadors and approving or disapproving treaties. Under its chairman, conservative Senator Jesse Helms, Republican of North Carolina, it has pushed for cutting foreign aid (which is less than 1 percent of the federal budget) and for reorganizing the foreign affairs bureaucracy. To pressure the administration to adopt his reforms, Senator Helms used his powers as chairman to hold up nominations of ambassadors and other high-level foreign policy appointments needing Senate approval.

The Senate also has a Rules Committee, but it is much less important than its House counterpart. The Senate has fewer than one-fourth as many members as

Congressional Staff

Despite recent efforts to shrink staff, the U.S. Congress remains the most heavily staffed legislature in the world, with over 35,000 total employees in the legislative branch. Gingrich's Republican House reduced its committee staff from 2,100 to 1,407. The Senate followed, lowering its number of committee staff from 1,185 to 950. However, personal staffers for members of Congress have gone untouched. Even junior representatives can have 18 full-time staffers and 4 part-time employees. By comparison, the 650 members of the British House of Commons get by with about 1,000 employees.

Congress found it difficult to cut staff further than this because, other than voting, a member's staff is likely to do everything he or she does. Staffers will organize hearings, negotiate agreements with other members' staffs, research proposals, speak with voters, and promote legislation. Staffers will often initiate policies and then "sell" them to their bosses. Lobbyists understand the importance of the staff and spend much of their time cultivating relationships with them. Because staff influence is best exercised quietly, it may be difficult to see, yet it is always present.

the House. Thus the problem of coordination is not as great and the Senate simply decided that it did not need to set up a strong "traffic cop" to screen legislation. (See "Congressional Staff.")

OTHER POWERS OF CONGRESS

So far we have discussed the legislative powers of Congress. Congress also has several nonlegislative powers, which of course can affect legislation. Among these are *oversight* of the executive branch and *investigation*. Congress created the various executive agencies and departments and specified their duties and powers. It can change them at any time. In addition, Congress appropriates the funds those agencies need to perform their jobs. These powers give Congress both an interest in what the executive branch is doing and the means to find out. For example, Congress can decide who will and who will not receive food stamps and at what price, and judge whether environmentalists or loggers will influence the uses of federal lands. In short, the annual appropriations process gives Congress the chance to ask what the bureaucracies are doing; tell them what they ought to be doing; and, finally, give money for what Congress wants and withhold money for what it doesn't want.

The General Accounting Office (GAO) is an agency created by Congress to help with its oversight function. Congress uses the GAO to examine certain government programs or departments. Many of the stories about scandals in government that appear on shows like "60 Minutes" start as GAO reports.

In addition, Congress has the power to investigate. If Congress, or a committee (or a committee chair), decides that something is not being done properly, an investigation may be launched. The subject might be foreign policy decision making in the executive branch, a price rise in heating oil, or campaign contributions by the savings and loan industry. In other words, Congress can investigate whatever it wishes.

Congressional investigations are not welcomed by executive departments. The Senate Special Committee on Whitewater investigated the actions of White House officials for removing sensitive papers from the office of Deputy White House Counsel Vincent Foster, following his suicide. The Committee wanted to know if staffers or even the first lady hid or destroyed documents relevant to their investigation of Whitewater. Shortly before this, two House subcommittees investigated executive branch actions during the 1993 siege of the Branch Davidian compound near Waco, Texas.

Congressional investigations have sometimes proven dangerous to civil liberties. In the 1950s, Senator Joseph McCarthy's Permanent Investigations Subcommittee and the House Un-American Activities Committee ruined the reputations of many innocent people, forced able persons out of government service, and whipped up fear throughout the country with charges of disloyalty and communist sympathies.

The Senate also has the power to approve or reject most presidential appointments, including ambassadors, cabinet members, and military officers. Many presidential appointments within the executive branch are routine, and there is a tendency in the Senate to agree that the president has a right to have the persons he wishes working with him. Still, Dr. Henry Foster, President Clinton's nominee for Surgeon General, was rejected by the Senate after he admitted that he had performed a number of abortions. The "behind-the-scenes" pressure of Senate dissatisfaction undoubtedly causes presidents not to make certain nominations in the first place. The Senate often takes a more active role in presidential appointments to the independent regulatory commissions and the Supreme Court, as shown by the close Senate vote in October 1991, following televised committee hearings on Clarence Thomas's nomination to the Supreme Court.

Congress also has certain judicial functions. The House of Representatives can *impeach* (bring charges against) a federal official by a simple majority vote. Then, the Senate holds a trial on these charges. If two-thirds of the Senate votes to uphold the charges and to convict the official, that official is removed from office.

Impeachment is difficult, slow, and cumbersome. Several federal judges have been impeached and convicted in the past. Only one president was ever impeached, Andrew Johnson in 1868, and he was not convicted by the Senate. Richard Nixon resigned the presidency in 1974 (the only president ever to do so) in the face of almost certain impeachment by the House and conviction by the Senate. Despite the difficulty of impeachment, the process does remain an ultimate power over the executive in the hands of the legislative branch.

Case Study

THE BALANCED BUDGET AMENDMENT

The new Republican House majority came into office in January 1995 with an ambitious agenda: They planned to vote on each of the ten planks of their Contract with America within 100 days. To underline their belief in restraining government, the first item considered was the balanced budget

amendment. It required federal spending to not exceed the government's revenue each year, except in times of war or other emergencies. A similar proposed amendment had failed by only 12 votes the previous year. With more than 50 new Republicans in the House, GOP leaders believed the amendment could now pass.

History suggested that problems awaited them. In every year since 1970, the United States government had spent more money than it had taken in. The year 1995 saw a budget deficit of $176 billion while the accumulated deficit stood at almost $5 trillion. Just the annual interest payments on this deficit totaled $235 billion, 15 percent of the federal budget. Although economists disagree on how the government's debt affects the U.S. economy, these deficits have been pointed to, notably by Ross Perot in his 1992 presidential campaign, as evidence of Washington's lack of political will to control spending and "balance the books."

The Players: Their Positions and their Arguments

Supporters of the amendment argued that without it, Congress would never have the backbone to balance the budget. However, Democrats, including the Clinton administration, argued that political courage cannot be written into the Constitution. The Republicans had not explained what programs they would cut to balance the budget. Opponents were concerned that the amendment would restrict the government's ability to increase spending during economic downturns, allowing recessions to become more severe. Democrats were also looking out for their voters, such as the poor and the elderly, who depended on government programs.

Groups outside the federal government sought a role. Most state legislatures and governors supported the amendment. Over the past 20 years, 32 states had passed resolutions (2 short of the 34 necessary) calling for a constitutional convention on a balanced budget amendment. Much of the support from the states was based on Congress first passing legislation ending the federal government's "unfunded mandates." (See "Unfunded Mandates.")

Conservative interest groups, such as the Christian Coalition, the National Taxpayers' Union, and the U.S. Chamber of Commerce, mobilized grassroots support for the amendment. They used fax networks and computer databases to generate thousands of calls to Congress. Other interest groups worked to block the amendment. One of the largest and most influential was the American Association of

Retired Persons, which worried about the cuts it would require in federal programs for the elderly.

Media coverage of the debate was mostly negative. It focused on the spending cuts that would follow passage of the
amendment. For example, ABC ran 14 stories which focused
on the harm cuts in government spending could cause. Only
one story emphasized Republican arguments. Meanwhile,
polls indicated that 80 percent of Americans favored the
amendment. However, when told that a balanced budget
would require significant cuts in spending for Social Security,
Medicaid, and education, popular support dropped to under
30 percent.

Balancing Supporters: The House

The amendment quickly got caught up in the legislative
process. The House Judiciary Committee swiftly approved
the version of the amendment outlined in the Contract with
America It was sent to the House floor on a party-line vote.
However, a different version of the amendment, called the
Stenholm-Schaefer plan, which budget-cutters in the House
had rallied around for years, was offered on the House floor.
(Under House rules, rival proposals from the floor are allowed when there is a vote on a Constitutional amendment).

Unfunded Mandates

Congressional Republicans knew that
support by the governors for the balanced budget amendment would be essential to passing it in the 50 state legislatures. Obtaining this backing
required the federal government to
limit its unfunded mandates. These are
federal laws that mandate actions by
the states, but do not provide the states
with the funding necessary to meet the
laws' requirements. They have been
bitterly opposed by many governors.
For example, in the case of the "motor
voter" bill, which allowed citizens to
register to vote when they got their drivers license, several governors, includ-

ing Pete Wilson of California, refused
to pay any added costs to implement it.

The governors' concerns with the
amendment was that congress would
balance the budget on their backs—
by simply rewriting laws so that the
states would have to pay for more
federal programs. Thus in the middle
of the debate over the balanced
budget amendment the House and
Senate took time out to pass a bill
which restricted the government's
ability to impose unfunded mandates
on the states. Former governor Bill
Clinton signed the bill into law in
March 1995.

The amendment in the Contract had a clause requiring a three-fifths majority in the House to pass any tax increases. The Stenholm-Schaefer plan did not have this requirement.

The problem for the Republican leadership was that to get the two-thirds majority necessary to pass a constitutional amendment they needed support from at least 60 Democrats. But the Democrats believed that the Contract with America version would make it impossible to raise taxes and would severely restrict government policies. On the other side, the leadership faced a revolt within their own party from a dozen freshman who refused to support the Stenholm-Schaefer plan, because they had promised in their campaigns to support the Contract. Without the votes of these Republicans, and without the support of many Democrats, neither version of the amendment would pass.

Speaker Newt Gingrich dealt with this dilemma in two ways. First, he decided to vote on both versions of the amendment on the same day using an unusual voting rule. Normally, in situations where the Congress votes on multiple bills dealing with the same issue, the "King of the Hill" rule is used, which requires that the bill which is passed last becomes the one voted on for final passage. In this case, the House leadership used the "Queen of the Hill" rule, which requires instead that the version of the bill which receives the most votes becomes the final version. Second, the GOP leader promised the rebellious freshman Republicans to propose a separate tax limitation constitutional amendment in 1996.

The party leadership was successful: The promise of a tax limitation amendment persuaded the GOP freshman to vote for the Stenholm-Schaefer plan. Having a vote on both versions of the amendment allowed the freshman to meet their promise of supporting the Contract with America version, and it let the Democrats vote for their version of the amendment. In the end, the Contract version of the amendment received a 253–173 preliminary vote, short of the 290 votes needed. The Stenholm-Schaefer plan received a 293–139 vote. Because of the "Queen of the Hill" rule, this was the version voted on for final passage. It passed 300–132.

Obstacles in the Senate

The vote on the amendment in the Senate promised to be slower and more uncertain. Democratic opposition to the amendment was stronger than in the House. The rules and procedures of the Senate provided them with more opportunities to block its passage. For these reasons the Clinton administration focused its efforts to stop the amendment in the Senate.

The Senate version of the amendment followed the Stenholm-Schaefer plan, and was approved by the Senate Judiciary Committee on January 18 on a 15–3 vote. Sixty-seven votes were required on the Senate floor for the amendment to be sent to the states for approval. By early February, all but one Republican supported it. About half of the Democrats were opposed, and the remaining Democrats were split between supporters of the amendment and those who were undecided. The Senate spent the month of February in debate.

The Democrats used various tactics to prevent passage. Behind the scenes, Senator Robert Byrd (D-W.Va.) used his mastery of Senate rules to slow down the process. This strategy of delay allowed Democrats to gain time to erode public support for the measure. As Senator Byrd put it, "Let the fresh air in and let's inspect this piece of garbage." Minority Leader Tom Daschle (D-S.D.) offered a "right to know" clause that would require Congress to specify how it would balance the budget before the amendment was passed. Democrats believed that the measure would loose support if people knew what government programs would disappear.

President Clinton took a low-profile approach. He privately leaned hard on Democratic Senators to oppose the bill. But when Senator Tom Harkin (D-Iowa) told him, ". . . if he felt so strongly, he ought to go on national television and tell the American people," the president, "just laughed." Clinton was unwilling to invest political capital in a public campaign to defeat the popular balanced budget amendment.

Many of the undecided Senators supported the idea of the amendment, but had specific concerns. Democrats proposed making money for Social Security "off-budget." They were concerned that this trust fund for retirees might be used to pay for shortfalls in government revenue. The Republicans, feeling that they had strong public support, killed almost all proposed changes. The GOP feared that changes would mean a House/Senate conference committee, and that a modified amendment would fail in the House.

On February 28, Majority Leader Robert Dole delayed the final vote on the amendment, because the Republicans were one vote short. Veteran Senator Mark Hatfield (R-Ore.) was the lone Republican opposing the amendment. He was intensely lobbied by fellow Republicans. Senator Dole implored him, "I've never asked you for anything in all these years, . . . what's wrong with sending it out to the states, including Oregon?" But Senator Hatfield refused, saying that his conscience prevented him from changing his vote. Unlike the House, where the leadership has considerable control over its members, Republicans had little leverage.

On March 2, the balanced budget amendment failed by one vote. Senate Minority Leader Daschle said it would have easily passed if the Republicans had allowed the Social Security exemption. After the vote, angry freshman Republicans, not accustomed to the folkways of the Senate led an unsuccessful attempt to strip Senator Hatfield of his Appropriations Committee chairmanship.

As for the balanced budget amendment, Senate Majority Leader Dole resolved to bring it up again and again. In June 1996 shortly before resigning from the Senate to run for president, Dole brought the amendment to the floor for a vote. It was defeated. Senator Hatfield was the only Republican voting no.

WRAP-UP

The United States Congress consists of two houses, the Senate and the House of Representatives. Two senators are selected from each state, and they serve for six years. Representatives are allocated to states according to population; they serve for two years. The Senate, with 100 members, is smaller, more informal, and more prestigious than the House, with its 435 members. The House is more tightly controlled by the majority party leadership, especially under its new speaker Republican Newt Gingrich.

The House and Senate operate separately, but before any legislation can be sent to the president for signing, it must be passed in identical language by both branches. In the House, floor debate, the agenda for legislation, and even committee priorities, are controlled by the Speaker of the House, who is elected by the majority party. The Speaker works closely with the House majority leader and whips. The Senate has no speaker; floor debate is managed by the Senate majority leader. Each branch also has minority leaders and minority whips.

Since 1994 the Republicans have been the majority party in both houses. While much of the work of the House and Senate goes on in committees and subcommittees, party leadership has asserted itself under the Republicans. Acting on behalf of the party leaders, the committee chairmen (who are always from the majority party) exercise considerable power, especially in the House. Despite some recent exceptions, chairmen are almost always chosen on the basis of seniority—longest consecutive service on the committee. The recent attention to the budget, and the willingness of members to follow specialization and reciprocity, has increased the importance of the taxing and spending committees.

All legislation other than revenue-raising and appropriations bills (which must start in the House) can be introduced in either the House or the Senate. It is then assigned to the relevant committee for examination and change. If approved by committee, the bill is sent to the floor of the House or Senate (going through the Rules Committee in the House). When approved there, the bill goes to the other chamber for a similar process. If the House and Senate pass different versions, they will be ironed out by a conference committee. When both branches of Congress have approved the same bill, it is sent to the president. He may sign it, veto it, pocket veto it, or allow it to become law without his signature. If he vetoes it Congress may try to override by a two-thirds vote in each house. Of course the president has no veto over a constitutional amendment, but the two-thirds vote required in each house (not to mention the three-quarters of the state legislatures) make passing an amendment very difficult, as seen by the unsuccessful efforts to pass the balanced budget amendment in 1995.

Congressional procedures seem complex and confusing because they are complex and confusing. Congress has often been criticized for being slow, unresponsive, and even unrepresentative. Certainly the procedures discussed in this chapter often involve much time-consuming duplication. The seniority system, the filibuster in the Senate, and the overall fragmentation of power into committees may sometimes frustrate majority wishes. But they have not stopped Congress from quickly acting on legislation with broad popular support. The recent 104th Congress has clearly demonstrated the ability of Congress to respond to the demands of the people who elected them in 1994 and vote on the legislation which they promised.

If Congress is sometimes slow to solve national problems, it may be because the country itself does not agree on the nature of the problem or the way to fix it. If Congress sometimes bogs down in party disputes or struggles to reach a watered-down compromise, it may be because a country as large as the United States includes strongly opposing opinions that the Congress reflects. If special interests seem to receive special treatment from Congress, this preference may simply be an accurate reflection of the political power of these players.

Congress was not set up to make government run more efficiently. It was established to reflect the wishes of the people governed, to be the democratic centerpiece. Congress acts best not when it acts least, but when it represents to the rest of the government the public support and public monies on which the government ultimately rests.

Thought Questions

1. In recent years, many commentators have argued that Congress has interfered too much in the operations of the executive branch. In what ways does Congress influence the executive? What changes would you recommend in this role?
2. Think about the "unwritten rules" of seniority, specialization, and reciprocity. How do these rules help Congress to operate? What are their drawbacks?
3. To what extent does the majority party control what goes on in Congress? How does this differ in the House and the Senate? Does this control make Congress more effective? More representative?
4. Congress has been described as an arena of widely dispersed power centers faced with the constant threat of stalemate. Is this description accurate? Are there any advantages to such a system?

Suggested Readings

Cohen, Richard E. *Washington At Work: Back Rooms and Clean Air.* New York: Macmillan , 1992.
> A how-a-bill-becomes-law account by an experienced Washington reporter. Goes behind closed doors to look at how and why Congress passed the 1990 Clean Air Act Amendments.

Harris, Fred R. *In Defense of Congress.* New York: St. Martin's Press, 1995.
> This former Oklamoma senator does what the title claims, defends "the greatest and most powerful national legislature in the world."

Kelly, Brian. *Adventures in Porkland—How Washington Wastes Your Money and Why They Won't Stop.* New York: Villard Books, 1992.
> A scandalous account of the inner workings of the powerful House and Senate Appropriations committees and the scramble to spend the American people's tax money.

Kennedy, John F. *Profiles in Courage.* New York: Harper & Row, 1956. Pb.
> The future president wrote these prize-winning profiles of members of Congress who stood up to the popular pressures of their time and sacrificed their careers to do what they thought was right.

Light, Paul C. *Forging Legislation.* New York: W.W.Norton, 1992.
> A detailed case study of the fight over creating a new cabinet department, Veterans Affairs, and how Congress involves itself in public administration.

Price, David E. *The Congressional Experience.* Boulder, Colo.: Westview Press, 1992.
> A political science professor and then congressman from North Carolina, discusses what it takes to get to Congress and then stay there. Alas, he lost his reelection.

Thomas, Sue. *How Women Legislate.* New York: Oxford University Press, 1994.
> How the rise in the numbers of women serving in legislatures change the representative bodies as well as the women elected to them.

Waldman, Steven. *The Bill.* Revised and updated. New York: Penguin Books, 1995. Pb.
> The case of a Clinton campaign promise to create national service for college students colliding with Washington interests in the halls of Congress.

CHAPTER FIVE

The Judicial Branch: The Supreme Court and the Federal Court System

The Constitution is brief and to the point in providing for the judicial player: "The judicial Power of the United States shall be vested in one supreme Court, and in such inferior Courts as the Congress may from time to time ordain and establish" (Article III, Section 1). Congress did set up two major levels of federal courts below the Supreme Court—federal district courts and courts of appeals. It has also established several special federal courts as the need for them has arisen. The federal court system is responsible for judging cases involving the United States Constitution and federal laws.

Parallel to this judicial structure is the state court system. Each state has its own judicial system to try cases that come under state law (though it may also deal with cases under the United States Constitution and laws). Issues involving the Constitution may be appealed to the United States Supreme Court. In this chapter we will focus on the federal court system and particularly the Supreme Court; state courts are set up in much the same way.

FEDERAL COURT SYSTEM

United States District Courts

At the base of the federal court system are the *United States district courts*. These are the courts of *original jurisdiction*. Except in a few special instances, all cases involving federal law are tried first in the district courts. There are 94 district courts in the United States and its possessions, with at least one federal district court in each state. The larger, more populous states have more district courts. New York, for example, has four. Each district has between 1 and 28 judges, for a total of 649 district judges in the country. These judges preside over most federal cases, including civil rights cases, controversies involving more than $10,000, antitrust suits, and counterfeiting cases. The large volume of cases they handle (almost 280,000) has led to long delays in administering justice. At one time it took an average of almost four years to complete a civil case in the Southern District of New York.

Courts of Appeals

Above the district courts are the *courts of appeals* (sometimes called by their old name, *circuit courts of appeals*). These courts have only *appellate jurisdiction;* that is, they hear *appeals* from the district courts and from important regulatory commissions, like the Interstate Commerce Commission. If you took a civil rights case to your district court and lost, you could appeal the decision and have the case brought before a court of appeals. The United States is divided into thirteen courts of appeals. There are twelve geographic *circuits* (eleven plus one in Washington, D.C.), and one U.S. Court of Appeal for the Federal Circuit dealing with appeals from special federal courts like the U.S. Claims Court. Each of the thirteen courts has between 6 and 28 judges, depending on the volume of work. Usually three judges hear each case. One hundred seventy-nine circuit court judges handle 46,000 cases annually. These are the final courts of appeal for most cases, but a hundred or so cases each year are appealed further to the Supreme Court. (See Figure 5.1.)

Special Federal Courts

Special federal courts have been created by Congress to handle certain cases. The *United States Claims Court* deals with people's claims against government seizure of property. The *United States Court of Military Appeals* (often called "the GI Supreme Court"), composed of three civilians, is the final judge of court-martial convictions. The United States Supreme Court can review only certain types of military cases.

Figure 5.1 Federal Court Structure and the Flow of Cases to the Supreme Court.

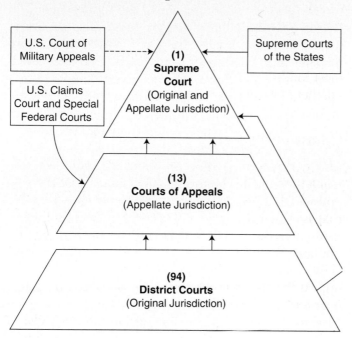

The Judges

All federal judges, including Supreme Court justices, are nominated to the bench by the president and must be approved by the Senate. Although it is usually given, confirmation by the Senate is not merely an empty ritual. In 1987 Robert H. Bork's nomination was defeated after bitter attacks from liberal groups fearful of conservative dominance on the bench. And Anita Hill's 1991 televised accusations of sexual harassment by Clarence Thomas followed by the close vote (52–48) to confirm him to the Supreme Court showed how intense the politics surrounding appointment to the Supreme Court have become.

Under the Constitution, all federal judges hold office for life "during good behavior" and can be removed only by impeachment. This has rarely happened. However, in October 1989 the Senate removed a Florida judge (who is now a congressman), Alcee Hastings, in a controversial case involving bribery. To further protect them from political pressures, judges' salaries cannot be reduced during their time in office.

Despite these protections, the appointment of judges is a very political matter. Judges are almost always selected on a party basis and usually as a reward for their political services to the party. One commentator called the judiciary "the place to put political workhorses out to pasture." In this partisan spirit, 93 percent of Lyndon Johnson's appointments to federal judgeships were Democrats, whereas 93 percent of Richard Nixon's were Republicans.

This power of the president to influence the makeup of one of the three major branches of the government is extremely important. Some observers feel that President Reagan's most lasting political influence may be his appointment of enough justices to create a conservative majority on the Supreme Court. (See "Presidents and the Court.") President Carter, on the other hand, was the first full-term president in history not to put even one justice on the Supreme Court. After Congress passed a law expanding the judiciary, Carter appointed an unprecedented number of lower federal court judges, including more women and blacks than all the presidents before him combined.

Presidents and the Court

Supreme Court justices have a way of disappointing the president appointing them. Theodore Roosevelt said of famed justice Oliver Wendell Holmes: "He has the backbone of a banana." President Eisenhower was so angered at Chief Justice Earl Warren's rulings that he called Warren's appointment "the biggest damn-fool mistake I ever made." The controversy set off by the Warren Court's activism led President Nixon to appoint Warren Burger as chief justice to replace Earl Warren

when he retired in 1969. Nixon hoped Burger would inspire greater political restraint in the Court. But the Burger Court, in *U.S.* v. *Nixon* (1974), ruled that President Nixon had to surrender to the special Watergate prosecutor the White House tapes of his conversations about often-illegal activities. The president, who resigned shortly afterward, was not pleased by this clear example of the strength and independence of the Court.

Twelve years of Ronald Reagan's and George Bush's judicial appointments created a conservative impact on the courts. By 1993 Reagan/Bush judges represented about two-thirds of all appellate court judges with majorities in nine of thirteen appellate courts. More than half of the nation's 828 federal appeals and district court judges were appointed by Reagan or Bush. By the end of President Clinton's term, about half the federal judges will likely be Democrats.

A majority of the Supreme Court has been appointed by Reagan and Bush. In 1981 President Reagan appointed the first woman to the Supreme Court, Sandra Day O'Connor. When Chief Justice Warren Burger resigned in 1986, the president elevated Justice Rehnquist to be chief justice and nominated an equally conservative Antonin Scalia to be the first justice of Italian descent. Reagan's 1988 selection of Anthony Kennedy after the Senate had rejected Robert Bork was aimed at pointing the Court in a conservative direction. President Bush's 1990 appointment of a moderate New Hampshire judge David Souter reflected a more low-key approach. But in 1991 his appointment of Clarence Thomas was considered a more hard-line conservative selection.

Only the two most recent appointees were chosen by a Democrat, President Clinton. When he selected Ruth Bader Ginsburg in 1993 she was labeled a middle-of-the-road judge. Similarly Stephen G. Breyer was also considered a moderate when he was appointed in 1994. They have voted together 87 percent of the time and have consistently been part of the Court's liberal wing.

To ensure local party influence, the Senate follows a custom called *senatorial courtesy* in confirming federal judges below the Supreme Court. This is the practice by which senators will not vote for nominees who are unacceptable to the senator from the state concerned. This gives the Senate the whip hand in appointing federal district judges. How the senators of the various states divide up these nominees is left up to them. In some instances the senator of the party *not* in the White House is given one of every four nominations for federal judges in his state. So, for example, with Bill Clin-

ton in the Oval Office, New York Republican Senator Al D'Amato gets one nomination for every three that Democratic Senator Daniel Moynihan controls. When a Republican is president, the ratio is reversed.

Jurisdiction

Jurisdiction refers to the matters over which a court may exercise its authority. The jurisdiction of the federal courts falls into two broad categories: In the first group, it depends on the *subject of the case;* in the second, on the *parties to the case,* no matter what the subject. The federal courts have jurisdiction over all subjects related to the Constitution and over treaties of the United States. (Admiralty and maritime cases involving international law are also included.) Jurisdiction determined by parties includes cases involving ambassadors and other foreign representatives; controversies in which the United States is a party; and controversies between two or more states or between a state or citizen of the United States and a foreign citizen or state. The federal court system's last and largest source of cases is suits between citizens of different states.

This definition does not mean that the federal courts have the *only* jurisdiction over such cases. Federal courts have *exclusive jurisdiction* in some cases, such as cases involving crimes against the laws of the United States. But in other cases they have *concurrent jurisdiction,* shared with state courts. For example, some suits between citizens of different states may be heard by both federal and state courts.

UNITED STATES SUPREME COURT

At the head of the federal court system stands the *Supreme Court of the United States,* composed of a chief justice and eight associate justices. (See Table 5.1.) Congress can set by law the number of justices on the Supreme Court. Although the number has varied from time to time, it has remained at nine since 1869. Though the Supreme Court has some *original jurisdiction* (some cases can be presented first to that court), most of the cases it hears are appeals of lower court de-

Table 5.1   The Supreme Court, 1997

Justice	Date of Birth	Appointed by	Date Appointed
William H. Rehnquist, Jr. (chief justice)	1924	Nixon	1971
John Paul Stevens	1920	Ford	1975
Sandra Day O'Connor	1930	Reagan	1981
Antonin Scalia	1936	Reagan	1986
Anthony Kennedy	1936	Reagan	1988
David Souter	1939	Bush	1990
Clarence Thomas	1946	Bush	1991
Ruth Bader Ginsburg	1933	Clinton	1993
Stephen G. Breyer	1938	Clinton	1994

cisions, which involve its *appellate jurisdiction.* If your civil rights case lost in both the district court and the court of appeals, you might be able to get it heard by the Supreme Court.

Actually, very few cases ever reach the Supreme Court. Of more than 10 million cases tried every year in American courts (federal and state), only some 8,000 petitions for review make it to the Supreme Court. Of these, the Court heard oral arguments and wrote opinions in 75 cases in the 1995–96 term. The other petitions were affirmed or reversed by written *memorandum orders.* Many cases that reach the Supreme Court involve constitutional issues. The majority of these 5,000 cases come to the Court in the form of petitions (written requests) for a *writ of certiorari* (*certiorari* means to be informed of something). A writ of certiorari is an order to the lower court to send the entire record of the case to the higher court for review. Someone who has lost a case in a lower court may petition for this writ. It is granted when four justices of the Supreme Court feel that the issues raised are important enough to merit a review. The Court denies between 85 and 90 percent of all such applications. This procedure keeps control over the appeal process in the hands of the Supreme Court, allowing it to keep a maximum of decisions in the lower courts. It also enables the Court to influence the actions of lower court judges by establishing guiding decisions on certain crucial cases.

The Final Authority?

The Supreme Court has been prominent in American political history because it has been thought to have "final" authority over what the Constitution means. Historically, however, a ruling of the Court has not always been the final word. The Court itself has reversed its decisions. (See Case Study: Separate but Equal?) If the Court interprets a law in a way Congress doesn't like, Congress will often overrule the Court simply by rewriting the statute. Amendments to the Constitution also have reversed decisions by the Court. An 1895 Court decision striking down the federal income tax was overcome by the Sixteenth Amendment in 1913, which allowed such taxes. In 1990 Congress passed a Civil Rights Restoration Act which extended civil rights protection to all programs of colleges accepting federal aid. The Act overturned a court ruling that limited this protection.

The strength of the Court's "final" authority is also affected by the other branches of government. Congress and the president, as well as the Supreme Court, have taken their turn in interpreting vague parts of the Constitution to meet the demands of the time and the needs of those in power. The president's right to involve the country in the Korean and Vietnam wars without a declaration of war would seem to fly in the face of the war-making powers given to Congress by the Constitution. Yet without a challenge by the courts and Congress, the president's interpretation of the Constitution stood.

Despite this shared role in changing the Constitution, the Supreme Court, by its constant interpretation and reinterpretation of the Constitution through its rulings, breathes life into 200-year-old words. A brief history of the Court will show how this has been done.

Early Years of the Court

The Supreme Court did not begin life as the powerful institution we know today. In its early years interest in the Court was slight. No cases at all were brought to the Supreme Court in its first three years. Many leaders, such as Patrick Henry and Alexander Hamilton, refused appointments to serve as judges; and court sessions were held in such places as basement apartments. When the federal city was first planned, the Court was completely overlooked with no building or chamber provided for it.

Under the leadership of John Marshall the Court's influence greatly increased. (See "Chief Justice John Marshall.") Two landmark decisions marked its growth in power. The first established *judicial review,* the power not only to declare acts and laws of any state and local government unconstitutional, but also to strike down acts of any branch of the federal government. The second major decision established the principle of *na-*

Chief Justice John Marshall

"Marshall found the Constitution paper and he made it power."

—James A. Garfield

John Marshall served as the fourth, and arguably greatest, chief justice from 1801 to 1835. He applied his genius to a single mission: building the government of a united nation. Raising the prestige and power of the Supreme Court from the low level he found it was necessary so that it could serve that mission. Similarly, he shaped constitutional law so that it too could preserve a strong central government into an unlimited future.

Marshall acted more like a statesman than a judge. In his major decisions on judicial review and national supremacy he was not strictly interpreting and applying the law. He was establishing principles for a growing nation. Interestingly, his lack of legal training—less than three months of law classes, and poorly attended at that—may have helped him. Rather than deciding cases legalistically, he acted like a legislator breaking with the past. His experience in General Washington's army at Valley Forge may have provided his most important education by reminding him of the price of disunity. For Marshall the Constitution must serve always its goal of creating a lasting union. This underlines his most famous phrase, "We must never forget that it is a *constitution* that we are expounding."

Source: See Bernard Schwartz, *A History of the Supreme Court* (New York: Oxford University Press, 1993), Chapter 2.

tional supremacy, that the United States laws and Constitution are the supreme law of the land and that state laws that are in conflict with federal laws cannot stand.

Judicial Review and National Supremacy

The principle of judicial review was established in the case of *Marbury* v. *Madison* (1803) in which the Supreme Court for the first time struck down an act of Congress. The case illustrates how shrewd Chief Justice John Marshall was as a politician. Shortly before leaving office, President John Adams (who had nominated Marshall to the court) appointed a number of minor judicial officials in order to maintain the influence of his party in the coming administration of his opponent, Thomas Jefferson. When Jefferson took office, he discovered that one of the commissions, that of William Marbury, had not actually been delivered. Jefferson ordered his secretary of state, James Madison, to hold it up. Under a section of the Judiciary Act of 1789, Marbury sued in the Supreme Court to compel delivery of the commission. Marshall was then confronted with deciding a case between his political allies and his enemy, Jefferson, who was not only president but also intent on weakening the power of the conservative Supreme Court. What Marshall did was to dismiss Marbury's case, ruling that the section of the Judiciary Act under which he had sued was unconstitutional (the Act allowed the Supreme Court original jurisdiction in a case not mentioned by the Constitution). By doing so he clearly asserted that the Supreme Court, on the basis of its interpretation of the Constitution, could set limits on the actions of Congress. The Court supported Jefferson's argument that he did not have to deliver the commission. How could the president object?

Another early decision established that states could not interfere with the functioning of the federal government. In this case, *McCulloch* v. *Maryland* (1819), the state of Maryland attempted to tax the Baltimore branch of the unpopular Bank of the United States, established by the federal government. Chief Justice Marshall, speaking for a unanimous court, ruled that the federal government "though limited in its powers, is supreme within its sphere of action." He also found that although the Constitution did not specifically allow Congress to create a bank, Article I, Section 8 gave Congress the power to make all laws "necessary and proper" for carrying out its authority. *Implied powers* based on this clause was to be used later in broadly expanding the duties that Congress could undertake.

Then in 1857 came the famous *Dred Scott* case (*Dred Scott* v. *Sandford*). Here, the Court ruled that a slave (Dred Scott) was not automatically free merely because his owner had taken him to a state not allowing slavery. Congress, the Court said, had no right to interfere with property rights guaranteed by the Constitution. The Court went on to say that the *Missouri Compromise* (1820), which had attempted to resolve the slavery issue by dividing the new western territories into slave and free parts, was invalid. In terms of constitutional development, this unpopular decision was the first time an act of Congress of any great importance was struck down by the courts. As such, the Dred Scott case marked a critical expansion of judicial powers.

The Court After the Civil War

The end of the Civil War signalled the end of the major political conflict that had dominated the first 75 years of the Republic—*states' rights* versus *federal powers*. With unity achieved, rapid national growth began. The resulting economic expansion and the unrestrained growth of giant monopolies created a new demand for government regulation of the economy. The Supreme Court became more active, and judicial power was greatly enlarged. In just nine years (1864–1873), ten acts of Congress were struck down, compared with only two acts in the previous 74 years.

Not only was the Court more active, it was also more conservative. In the view of many, the Court became an instrument for protecting the property rights of the rich and ignoring popular demands for government regulation.

In the twentieth century, the Court found itself up against the growing power of the executive branch. The presidency was widely felt to be the most effective place in the government to regulate the social and economic changes brought about by the post–Civil War industrialization. But the Supreme Court continued to resist the expansion of state and federal regulatory power, even though much of the legislation it struck down (such as minimum wage and child labor laws) was widely popular. Between 1890 and 1936, the Court declared 46 laws unconstitutional in full or in part.

It was President Franklin D. Roosevelt who caused the Court's policy to change. He countered the Court's opposition to his New Deal measures with a threat to pack the Court with new judges of his own choosing, the so-called *court-packing* bill. Although Roosevelt's plan was unsuccessful and aroused a storm of public and congressional opposition, in 1937 the Court nevertheless backed down—the famous "switch in time that saved nine"—and turned away from economic policy making.

The Modern Courts

Since 1937, Supreme Court decisions have shown three major trends. First, the Court has invalidated much less federal legislation than it had in the previous 50 years. Generally only a few federal laws have been held unconstitutional, and in most of these cases the legislation struck down was not very significant. In a second area, the Court has avoided protecting private property rights. The Court in the modern era has not been greatly concerned with guarding economic interests from government policy making.

A third area in which the Court has shown more positive interest is increased judicial protection for civil liberties. While reducing property rights in importance, the Court has sought to preserve and protect the rights of individuals against the increased powers of the government. First Amendment freedoms of speech, press, religion, and assembly have been developed and expanded by modern Supreme Courts. With Earl Warren as chief justice (1953–1969), the Supreme Court moved in the areas of reapportionment, racial discrimination, and the rights of defendants in criminal cases.

In decisions dealing with *reapportionment,* beginning with *Baker* v. *Carr* (1962), the Warren Court established the principle of "one man, one vote" for election districts. The Court ruled that districts should be drawn based on equality of population so that each citizen's vote would count as much as another's. In moving to eliminate *racial discrimination,* the Court has been a leading force in cutting away racism in schooling, voting, housing, and the use of public facilities.

Another major interest of the Warren Court's decisions, the rights of criminal defendants, has seen the Court throw the protection of the Bill of Rights around people accused of crimes by state and federal authorities. The Court has insisted on an impoverished defendant's basic right to a lawyer; declared that illegally seized evidence cannot be used in state criminal trials; and held that suspects must be advised of their constitutional right to silence, and to have a lawyer, before questioning. This last area, summed up as the *Miranda* decision (*Miranda* v. *Arizona,* 1966), is familiar to all fans of TV detective series.

The Supreme Court under Warren Burger (1969–1986) was less activist than the Warren Court, but not as conservative as some had expected. On the liberal side, the Burger Court legalized abortions except in the last ten weeks of pregnancy, declined to stop publication of the Pentagon Papers (official papers on the government's planning for the Vietnam War unofficially leaked to the press), and severely limited capital punishment. The Burger Court also declined to interfere with massive busing to integrate schools in cities like Boston and Los Angeles.

This is not the whole story of the Burger Court. In more conservative directions, the Court allowed local communities, within limits, to define obscenity and ban those works considered pornographic. (See "The Burger Court's Porno Movies.") Perhaps the most important changes the Burger Court made were in the rights of the accused. Here the Court allowed the police broader powers in searching without a warrant— deciding, for example, that persons detained on minor

charges (like traffic violations) may be searched for evidence of more serious crimes (like possession of drugs)—a decision strengthened in 1996 by the Rehnquist Court. The Court also permitted illegally obtained information to be used at a trial and the police to continue their questioning after a suspect has claimed the right of silence. However, the Burger Court left the Miranda decision in place.

The Rehnquist Court (1986–)

The present-day *Rehnquist Court* may mark another departure in the direction of Supreme Court decisions. The 1986 appointment of William Rehnquist as chief justice came from the Reagan administration's hope for a more conservative, more restrained court. In its first years, the Rehnquist Court, lacking a conservative majority, did not dramatically break with past Court rulings. In some areas, like civil liberties, including the decisions allowing flag burning (see Case Study in Chapter 6) the Court zigged and zagged with little of the clear

---

The Burger Court's Porno Movies

The Justices take their obligation to research opinions so seriously that in one area of law—obscenity—the result has led to a lot of snickering both on and off the bench. Since 1957, the Court has tried repeatedly to define obscenity. The subject has become so familiar at the Supreme Court building that a screening room has been set up in the basement for the Justices and their clerks to watch the dirty movies submitted as exhibits in obscenity cases. Justice Douglas never goes to the dirty movies because he thinks all expression—obscene or not—is protected by the First Amendment. And Chief Justice Burger rarely, if ever, goes because he is offended by the stuff. But every-

one else shows up from time to time.

Justice Blackmun watches in what clerks describe as "a near-catatonic state." Justice Marshall usually laughs his way through it all. . . . The late Justice Harlan used dutifully to attend the Court's porno flicks even though he was virtually blind; Justice Stewart would sit next to Harlan and narrate for him, explaining what was going on in each scene. Once every few minutes, Harlan would exclaim in his proper way, "By George, extraordinary!"

Source: From Nina Totenberg, "Behind the Marble, Beneath the Robes," *The New York Times Magazine,* March 16, 1975. Copyright © 1975 by The New York Times Company. Reprinted by permission.

direction Rehnquist's Republican backers had hoped for. In other areas, like abortion, the Court sounded conservative but placed few limits on the practice while affirming the basic right to an abortion.

Then in an unusually active 1994–1995 term the Rehnquist Court demonstrated a clear conservative direction in major decisions affecting race, religion, and federalism. In three 5–4 decisions the Court narrowed the use of race in hiring minority contractors for government programs, in attracting suburban students into city schools, and in drawing boundaries for congressional districts. In another 5–4 decision the Court ruled that a state university could not refuse funds for a student-run Christian magazine (*Rosenberger* v. *Rector and Visitors of University of Virginia*). This marked the first time the Court had approved government funding for a religious activity.

The Court also delivered significant rulings concerning government power. As discussed in the last chapter, *U.S. Term Limits Inc.* v. *Thornton* forbid the states to set term limits for members of Congress because it added to the qualifications for office already listed in the Constitution—age, citizenship, and residency. Perhaps most important for the debate on federalism was the case of *United States* v. *Lopez*. Here the Court ruled that Congress had exceeded its authority to regulate interstate commerce when it passed a law intended to keep guns out of schools. This marked the first time in 60 years that the Court had limited Congress's power to regulate interstate commerce. Because previous Courts had allowed the Commerce Clause to be used since the New Deal to expand federal authority, the Court's ruling marked its forceful emergence into the current debate over power in the federal system.

These decisions hint that we may have begun another phase in the history of the modern court. A new majority—caused by two moderate justices, O'Connor and Kennedy joining a conservative core of Rehnquist, Scalia, and Thomas—seems willing to restrain central government power in order to preserve property rights and the authority of the states. Decisions in the 1996 term reinforced the conclusion that the Court wants the federal government to leave the states alone. The Court's emphasis on the grant of *limited power* given the federal government is consistent with current trends seen in the other branches of government and in public opinion.

All of these decisions rested on a thin 5–4 conservative majority, with O'Connor and Kennedy remaining the swing votes. This newly energized Court represents the delayed results of the Reagan/Bush appointments of conservative justices. It remains to be seen whether the Chief Justice can keep his conservative majority in future decisions. If Rehnquist can, then the 1995 term may mark a decisive change in the Supreme Court.

STRENGTHS AND WEAKNESSES OF THE SUPREME COURT

The United States Supreme Court has been called "the least dangerous branch of government." Despite its great power of judicial review, the Court is the weakest of the three branches. It must depend on the other parts of the government to enforce its decisions. Its authority to cancel actions of the other branches of the federal government is in fact seldom used and strictly limited. These limits are found both within the Court and in the political system as a whole.

Internal Limits on the Court

Most of the limits on the power of the Court are found within the judicial system, in the traditional practices of the Court. For one thing, a long-held interpretation of the Constitution requires that an *actual case* be presented to the Court for it to exercise judicial review. The Court cannot take the lead in declaring laws unconstitutional. It cannot give advisory opinions. It must wait for a real controversy brought by someone actually injured by the law to make its way through the lower courts. This means that years may pass after a law is put on the books before the Court can rule on it. (The Supreme Court's *Dred Scott* decision struck down the Missouri Compromise passed 37 years before.)

Another important limit on the Court's actions is the practice that the Court will not attempt to resolve *political questions*. A political question is an issue on which the Constitution or laws give final say to another branch of government, or one the Court feels it lacks the capability to solve. Political questions often crop up in foreign relations. The justices of the Court lack important secret information; they are not experts in diplomacy; and they recognize the dominance of the presidency over the conduct of foreign affairs. Consequently, a federal court in December 1990 used the doctrine of political questions to avoid deciding whether President Bush could use force against Iraq without congressional approval, saying it was "premature" to decide before Congress passed a resolution requiring congressional authorization.

The Court has narrowed or expanded its definition of a political question at various times. For many years, the Court used this doctrine of political questions as grounds for refusing to consider reapportionment of state legislatures and congressional districts. In 1962, however, the Court reversed its position and forced state legislatures to draw boundaries to create districts with more nearly equal populations. A political question, then, can be whatever issue the Supreme Court wants to avoid.

Just as the Court attempts to avoid political questions, so too it often avoids *constitutional issues*. The Court will not decide a case on the basis of a constitutional question unless there is no other way to dispose of the case. The Court usually will not declare a law unconstitutional unless it clearly violates the Constitution. In general, the Court will assume that a law is valid unless proved otherwise. Although we have stressed the role of the Court in applying the Constitution, the vast majority of cases it decides deal with interpretations of less important federal and state laws.

A final internal limit on the Court is that of *precedent or stare decisis* ("to study by the decision"). Justices generally follow previous Court decisions in cases involving the same issue. Recent abortion cases have illustrated the reluctance of the Court to reverse precedents, in this instance *Roe* v. *Wade*. Yet as the conservative majority on the Rehnquist Court has shown, at times the Court will not follow precedent if they feel the prior cases did not follow the intent of the Constitution or the justices' own principles. Often the Court tries to be consistent with precedent even when changing the law.

What these and the other limits on the Court's power mean is that the Court usually avoids most of the constitutional questions pressed upon it. For both political and legal reasons the Court will often duck an issue that is too controversial, on which the law is uncertain or no political consensus has formed. It may simply not hear the case, or it may decide it for reasons other than the major issue involved. Knowing the difficulty of enforcing a ruling against strong public opinion, the Court generally seeks to avoid such a confrontation. This self-imposed restraint may make the use of judicial review scattered and often long delayed. But one can argue that the Court has maintained its great authority by refusing in most instances to use its power of judicial review.

External Limits on the Court

Other limits on the Court come from the duties the Constitution gives to other parts of the government, especially to Congress. Congress has the right to set when and how often the Court will meet, to establish the number of justices, and to limit the Court's jurisdiction. This last power sometimes has been used to keep the Court out of areas in which Congress wished to avoid judicial involvement. For example, the bill establishing the Alaska pipeline excluded the Court from exercising jurisdiction (on possible damage to the environment) under the Environmental Protection Act. Also, Congress may pass legislation so detailed that it limits the Court's scope in interpreting the law. Finally, the Senate has the duty of approving the president's nominations to the bench, and Congress has the seldom-used power to impeach Supreme Court justices.

These limits on the Court reflect the very real weaknesses of that body. With no army or bureaucracy to enforce its decisions, the Court must depend on other parts of the government and all the political players to accept and carry out its decisions. (President Andrew Jackson, violently disagreeing with a Supreme Court decision, once remarked: "John Marshall has rendered his decision; now let him enforce it!") Yet with few exceptions, the Court's decisions have been enforced and accepted. And when opposed, this weak and semi-isolated branch of government has been able to overcome resistance. Why?

Strengths of the Court

Three major strengths of the Court rest on (1) its enormous prestige; (2) the fragmented nature of the American constitutional structure; and (3) the American legal profession, which acts like the Court's constituency.

The Court's *prestige* is unquestionable. Despite public dissent to many of its decisions in areas like school busing and abortion, the Court retains its high public standing. Opinion polls have shown that the position of a judge is one of the most respected in our society. This respect is due not only to the generally high quality of the people who become judges, but also to the judicial process itself. Anyone who watched the marathon O.J. Simpson murder trial can recall the aspects of theater in the legal process: the judge sitting on a raised platform dressed in robes; the formal speeches addressed to "your honor"; the use of Latin phrases; the oath on the Bible. All create a heavy impression of dignity and solemnity, which often masks the fact that a judge is simply a public administrator judging controversies. The Supreme Court, which presides over this judicial system, has added prestige because it is seen as the guardian of the Constitution and often is equated with that document in people's eyes.

Another strength of the Court lies in the *fragmented nature of the American system of government.* With separation of powers dividing up power among the branches of the federal government, and federalism dividing power between the states and federal government, conflict is inevitable. This division of power creates a need for an umpire, and the Court largely fills this role.

In acting as an umpire, however, the Court is hardly neutral. Its decisions are political (they determine who gets what, when, and how), and to enforce them it needs political support. The other political players might not give this support to decisions they strongly disagree with. Consequently, the Court's rulings generally reflect the practices and values of the country's dominant political forces. As an umpire, the Court enforces the constitutional rules of the game as practiced by the political game's most powerful players, of which it is also one.

A final source of support for the Court is the *legal profession*. There are some 780,000 lawyers in the United States. Yet lawyers occupy all the major judicial positions, and more lawyers than any other occupational group hold offices in national, state, and city governments. Other countries manage with far fewer lawyers and far fewer issues winding up in court. Some scholars argue that lawyers use their domination of elected offices to pass laws and regulations that create new demands for their skills. (See "Too Many Lawyers?") The American Bar Association (ABA), with about half the lawyers in the country as members, represents the legal profession. The ABA reviews nominees to the bench, and its comments on a candidate's fitness have a great deal of influence on whether he or she is appointed. Because of their own commitment to law, as well as some similarity in educational and social backgrounds, lawyers generally back the Court.

Too Many Lawyers?

COUNTRY	TOTAL	PER 100,000 PEOPLE
United States	780,000	312
Canada	42,170	169
England	68,000	134
Japan	124,000	102
France	27,700	49

Source: The Economist, July 18, 1992.

THE COURT AS A POLITICAL PLAYER

Clearly the Supreme Court is a *political institution* that sets national policy by interpreting the law. In applying the Constitution and laws to the cases before it, the Court clearly makes political choices. In arriving at decisions on controversial questions of national policy, the Court is acting in the political game. The procedures may be legal; the decisions may be phrased in lawyers' language; but to view the court solely as a legal institution is to ignore its important political role. "We are under the Constitution, but the Constitution is what the judges say it is," declared former Chief Justice Charles Evans Hughes. In interpreting the meaning of the Constitution, each Supreme Court must operate within the political climate of its time. Clearly the judges not only read the Constitution, they read the newspaper as well. The Court must rely on others, especially the executive branch, to enforce its rulings. The Court cannot ignore the reactions to its decisions in Congress or in the nation, because as a political player, its influence ultimately rests on the acceptance of these decisions by the other political players and the public. Nor, generally, are the Court's opinions long out of line with the dominant views in the legislative and executive branches. (See "The Court Waits for an Election.")

Judicial Activism Versus Judicial Restraint

The question of how the political and legal power of the Court should be applied has centered on the use of judicial review. Should judicial authority be active or restrained? How far should the Court go in shaping policy when it may conflict with other branches of the government? The two sides of this debate are reflected in the competing practices of *judicial restraint* and *judicial activism.*

Judicial restraint is the idea that the Court should not impose its views on other branches of the government or on the states unless there is a clear violation of the Constitution. Judicial restraint (often called self-restraint) calls for a passive role in which the Court lets the other branches of the government lead the way in

The Court Waits for an Election

Civil rights decisions have never been far removed from politics. Here is an example of the Court keeping an eye on the political arena in a landmark case:

"Why doesn't the Supreme Court pass the school desegregation case?" asked one of Chief Justice Vinson's law clerks in 1952. *Brown* v. *Board of Education of Topeka, Kansas,* had arrived on the Court's docket in 1951, but it was carried over for oral argument the next term and then consolidated with four other cases and reargued in December 1953. The landmark ruling did not come down until May 17, 1954.

"Well," Justice Frankfurter explained, "we're holding it for the election"— 1952 was a presidential election year. "You're holding it for the election?" the clerk persisted in disbelief. "I thought the Supreme Court was supposed to decide cases without regard to elections." "When you have a major social political issue of this magnitude, timing and public reactions are important considerations, and," Frankfurter continued, "we do not think this is the time to decide it."

Source: David M. O'Brien, *Storm Center: The Supreme Court in American Politics* (New York: W. W. Norton, 1986).

setting policy on controversial political issues. The Court intervenes in these issues only with great reluctance. Felix Frankfurter and Oliver Wendell Holmes Jr. are two of the more famous justices of the Supreme Court identified with judicial restraint. Frankfurter often argued that social improvement should be left to more appropriate parts of the federal and state government. The Court, he declared, should avoid conflicts with other branches of the federal government whenever possible.

Judicial activism is the view that the Supreme Court should be an active, creative partner with the legislative and executive branches in shaping government policy. Judicial activists seek to apply the Court's authority to solving economic and political problems ignored by other parts of the government. In this view the Court is more than an umpire of the American political game: It is an active participant as well. The Supreme Court under Earl Warren for the most part practiced judicial activism. In its rulings on reapportionment, school desegregation, and the right to counsel, the Warren Court broadly and boldly changed national policy.

It is important not to confuse judicial activism versus restraint with liberal versus conservative. Although many modern activist justices, such as Earl Warren and Thurgood Marshall, have taken liberal positions on issues like school integration and toleration of dissent, this wasn't always so. John Marshall's court was both activist (in establishing judicial review) and conservative (in protecting private property rights). The conservative Supreme Court during the 1930s attempted to strike down most of Franklin D. Roosevelt's New Deal program as unconstitutional. And the recent Rehnquist Court decisions limiting affirmative action programs and federal authority over the states were seen as activist conservative reversals of liberal policies. On the restraint side, justices Frankfurter and Holmes were political liberals. Yet both believed it was not wise for the Court to dive into the midst of political battles to support policies they may have personally backed.

Case Study

SEPARATE BUT EQUAL?

The Supreme Court's role as a political player can be seen in the evolution of the "separate but equal" doctrine. By first approving this doctrine of racial segregation late in the nineteenth century and later abolishing it in the mid-twentieth century, the Court played a central role in establishing the national policy that governed relations between the races. The changing but always powerful position of the judiciary in the history of racial segregation shows how influential the Court's political role can be.

Political Background of Segregation

The end of the Civil War and the emancipation of the slaves did not give blacks the full rights of citizenship, nor did the passing of the Thirteenth Amendment in 1865 (which outlawed slavery), or the Fourteenth Amendment in 1868 (which extended "equal protection of the laws" to all citizens), or the Fifteenth Amendment in 1870 (which guaranteed the right to vote to all male citizens regardless of "race, color, or previous condition of servitude").

Between 1866 and 1877 the "radical Republicans" controlled Congress. Although the sometimes corrupt period of *Reconstruction* partly deserves the bad name it has gotten in the South, it was a time when blacks won a number of political rights. In 1875 Congress passed a civil rights act designed to prevent any public form of discrimination—in theaters, restaurants, transportation, and the like—against blacks. Congress's right to forbid a *state* to act contrary to the Constitution was unquestioned. But this law, based on the Fourteenth Amendment, assumed that Congress could also prevent racial discrimination by private individuals.

The Supreme Court disagreed. In 1883 it declared the Civil Rights Act of 1875 unconstitutional. The majority of the Court ruled that Congress could pass legislation only to correct *states'* violations of the Fourteenth Amendment. Congress had no power to enact "primary and direct" legislation on individuals; that was left to the states. This decision meant the federal government could not lawfully protect blacks against most forms of discrimination. In other words, white supremacy was beyond federal control.

With this blessing from the Supreme Court, the southern states passed a series of laws legitimizing segregation. These laws included all-white primary elections, elaborate tests to qualify for voting, and other racial restrictions. (See "American Apartheid.")

American Apartheid

Throughout the South during the late nineteenth and early twentieth centuries, Jim Crow laws (taking their name from a black-face minstrel song), were passed to prohibit blacks from using the same public facilities as whites. These state laws required segregated schools, hospitals, prisons, restaurants, toilets, railways, and waiting rooms. Some communities passed "Sundown Ordinances" that prohibited blacks from staying in town overnight. Blacks and whites could not even be buried in the same cemeteries.

There seemed to be no limit to the absurdity of segregation. New Orleans required separate districts for black and white prostitutes. In Oklahoma, blacks and whites could not use the same telephone booths. In North Carolina and Florida, school textbooks used by black children had to be stored separately from those used by white children. In Birmingham, the races were specifically prohibited from playing checkers together.

Separate but Equal

Segregation was given judicial approval in the landmark case of *Plessy* v. *Ferguson* (1896). Here, the Court upheld a Louisiana law requiring railroads to provide separate cars for the two races. The Court declared that segregation had nothing to do with the superiority of the white race, and that segregation was not contrary to the Fourteenth Amendment as long as the facilities were equal. The doctrine of "separate but equal" in *Plessy* v. *Ferguson* was allowed to become the law of the land in those states maintaining segregation.

In approving segregation and establishing the "separate but equal" doctrine, the Court was undoubtedly reflecting the temper of the time. To restore the South to the Union, the new congresses were willing to undo the radicals' efforts to protect blacks. It was the southern black who paid the price—exile halfway between slavery and freedom. And just as the Court was unwilling to prevent these violations of civil rights, so too were the executive and legislative branches.

Plessy v. *Ferguson* helped racial segregation continue as a southern tradition. For some 40 years the "separate but equal" doctrine was not seriously challenged. "Separate" was strictly enforced; "equal" was not. Schools, government services, and other public facilities for blacks were clearly separate from tax-supported white facilities, but just as clearly inferior to them. One can argue that the Court did not even support its own doctrine during this period.

By the late 1930s, the Court began to look more closely at so-called equal facilities. In *Missouri ex. rel. Gaines* v. *Canada* (1938), the court held that because the state did not have a law school for blacks it must admit them to the white law school. In *Sweatt* v. *Painter* (1950), a black (Sweatt) was denied admission to the University of Texas Law School on the grounds that Texas was building a law school for blacks. The Court found the new school would in no way be equal to the white one and ordered Sweatt admitted to the existing school.

Thus the Plessy doctrine of "separate but equal" was increasingly weakened by judicial decisions. By stressing the "equal" part of the doctrine, the Court was in fact making the doctrine impractical. (Texas was not likely to build a law school for blacks equal to its white one.) These decisions also reflected the Court's change in emphasis after 1937 from making economic policy to protecting individual rights more fully.

Still, the Court did not overrule *Plessy* in this period. The Court was following precedent. Paralleling the rulings of the Court were the actions of the executive branch and some northern states that were increasingly critical of racial segregation. In 1941 Roosevelt issued an executive order forbidding discrimination in government employment, and in 1948 Truman abolished segregation in the army. Congress, however, dominated by a conservative-oriented seniority system and blocked by southern filibusters, was unable to pass civil rights measures. Nonetheless, public attitudes toward segregation were changing, and the Supreme Court's rulings were reflecting that change.

The End of Separate but Equal

In 1954 the Supreme Court finally reversed *Plessy* v. *Ferguson* in *Brown* v. *Board of Education.* Here the Court held that segregated public schools violated the "equal protection of the laws" guaranteed in the Fourteenth Amendment. "Separate but equal" had no place in public education, the Court declared. Drawing on sociological and psychological studies of the harm done to black children by segregation, the Warren Court's unanimous decision stated that in fact separate was "inherently unequal." This finding was the beginning of the end of *legal segregation.*

The Court backed up its new equal protection stand in areas other than education. In the years following the *Brown* decision, it outlawed segregation in interstate transportation, upheld legislation guaranteeing voting rights for blacks, reversed convictions of civil rights leaders, and often protected civil rights demonstrations by court order. These decisions, though they stirred up opposition to the Court (including demands to impeach Earl Warren), helped a political movement apply pressures to wipe out racial discrimination. Civil rights groups were active in these cases, which shows how results sometimes can be gotten from one part of government (the courts) if another part (the Congress) is unwilling to act.

Congress finally joined in by passing civil rights acts in 1957, 1960, and 1964. The 1964 act, coming after continuing pressure and agitation by civil rights activists, was the first comprehensive legislation of its kind since 1875. The act prohibited discrimination in those public accommodations (hotels, restaurants, gas stations) involved in interstate commerce, and in most businesses, and enforced equal voting rights for blacks.

The Court acted to encourage and to force all levels of the government—federal, state, and local—as well as the private sector, to move toward full equality. The Court's support of busing to end segregation of schools caused by housing patterns aroused opposition in northern cities like Boston. By the 1980s President Reagan was calling *affirmative action* "reverse discrimination" against white males. Yet affirmative action expanded beyond remedies for discrimination against African Americans to include ill-defined goals of cultural diversity, which often seemed to mean counting by race to ensure "balance." At the same time it was applied to other groups from Asia and Latin America, with little historical claim to its benefits. As the programs spread, judicial and public support for affirmative action diminished. In recent decisions the Supreme Court has narrowed and struck down as many affirmative action plans as it has upheld. (See Civil Rights: Protecting People from People, pp. 184–191.)

Still, racism remains. And for this the Supreme Court as well as the rest of the political system must share responsibility. For it was the Supreme Court that struck down civil rights acts of the Reconstruction Era and failed to protect the rights of African Americans between 1883 and 1937 when they were most trampled on. And it was the Court that made "separate but equal" the legal justification for white supremacy. The Court's effort to put equal rights before the eyes of the nation was in many ways merely an undoing of its past mistakes.

Throughout this history of the "separate but equal" doctrine, the Court has acted politically as well as morally. At times the Court held back efforts at social and political reform; at other times it confused the efforts; and at still others it forced political and social changes more rapidly than some would have preferred. Yet as the history of "separate but equal" makes clear, whether we agree or disagree with the Court's stand, it is never removed too far or for too long from the positions dominating the political game as a whole.

WRAP-UP

The federal court system consists of United States district courts, courts of appeals, special federal courts, and the United States Supreme Court. Although very few of the cases tried in the United States ever reach the Supreme Court, it retains its position as the "final authority" over what the Constitution means. Yet the Court's decisions often are changed over the years, usually by the Court itself, in part reflecting the changing political climate. Our brief history of the Court showed this, as did the case study of "separate but equal," where the Court first allowed racial segregation and then gradually reversed its position.

The practices of judicial activism and judicial restraint are two sides of the debate over how far the political involvement of the Court should go. The Court is limited by a number of its own practices and, most important, by its dependence on other parts of the government to enforce its decisions. The Court's respect for these limits, as well as its own great prestige, has given it the strength to overcome most resistance. In recent years there has been frequent criticism of its decisions on abortion, term limits, and civil rights and liberties. This criticism has run up against solid support for the Court.

Secure within its limits and resting on its wide public respect, the Supreme Court of the United States remains a unique political player. No other government can boast of a long-held tradition that gives "nine old men" (and women, now), nonelected and serving for life, the duty of overturning the acts of popularly elected officials. Through this power of judicial review, the Court is deeply involved in making national policy, setting limits on how the political game is played, and bringing pressing social issues to the attention of the people and their leaders. Whether the Court continues to protect the rights of groups threatened by the most powerful players will depend on who the justices are and which forces prevail in the national political game.

Thought Questions

1. How did the Supreme Court become so important to our system of government? Would John Marshall be pleased?
2. Is the Supreme Court influenced too much or not enough by the executive and legislative branches of government and by public opinion?

3. Do the courts, rather than popularly elected officials of the government, generally appear to be more interested in defending constitutional rights? If so, why?
4. Why are justices more respected than other government officials? Do they deserve it?

Suggested Readings

Jacob, Herbert. *Law and Politics in the United States,* 2nd ed. New York: HarperCollins College Publishers, 1995. Pb
Expertly describes the legal system—from courts to cops—and its links and gatekeeping role to the broad political game.

Lewis, Anthony. *Gideon's Trumpet.* New York: Vintage Books, 1966. Pb.
A short story that traces the development of a case from a Florida jail to the United States Supreme Court.

Phelps, Timothy M., and Helen Winternitz. *Capital Games: Clarence Thomas, Anita Hill and the Story of a Supreme Court Justice.* New York: Hyperion, 1992.
Eyewitness account of the controversial confirmation hearings of Supreme Court Justice Clarence Thomas by the reporters who first leaked Anita Hill's story.

Schwartz, Bernard. *A History of the Supreme Court.* New York: Oxford University Press, 1993. Pb.
A readable, insightful chronicle of how the Supreme Court grew from small apartments to its position as guardian (and adapter) of the Constitution.

Simon, James F. *The Center Holds: The Power Struggle Inside the Rehnquist Court.* New York: Simon & Schuster, 1995.
Behind-the-scenes stories of how the Court reaches decisions. Its view that moderates have won seems overtaken by events in the 1995 session.

Woodward, Bob, and Scott Armstrong. *The Brethren: Inside the Supreme Court.* New York: Simon & Schuster, 1979. Pb.
Gossipy stories of the Burger Court and the bargaining that went on among the justices in reaching decisions.

CHAPTER SIX

Civil Rights and Liberties: Protecting the Players

Civil rights and liberties provide rules and limits for the political game. They describe the methods by which government is to be conducted, as well as some of the goals of politics. They tell us how to play—with due process of law—as well as why we ought to play, for example, to protect freedom of speech and religion, and equality under the law. American government was limited by the Constitution and Bill of Rights so that certain rules govern the relationships between people and their government, and other rules govern the relationships between groups of citizens. The two principles upon which these rules rest are straightforward: The government must not violate the civil rights and liberties of the people; the government must protect people from the actions of those who would violate their rights.

In this chapter we focus on how the courts and other players protect civil rights and liberties. We will see what these rights and liberties are, and how the protections provided by the Bill of Rights have expanded down through American history. Many different actors are involved in applying these protections, and a case study on flag burning will show some of them in action.

WHAT ARE CIVIL LIBERTIES AND RIGHTS?

Civil liberties are a set of protections against government restrictions on freedom of expression, such as freedom of speech and religion. Civil liberties are those First Amendment rights of freedom of speech, petition, assembly, and press which protect people against governmental actions that would interfere with their participation in a democratic political system. This definition also includes Fifth Amendment and Fourteenth Amendment guarantees of due process of law in courtroom proceedings and government agencies. The underlying principle here is that ours is a government of laws, rather than of arbitrary, unfair action. *Civil rights* are a set of protections for some groups, defined in terms of race, religion, ethnicity, or gender, against discrimination by others. Civil rights involve the protections granted in the Fourteenth Amendment to the Constitution recognizing that all citizens are entitled to be treated equally under the law. No members of a single racial, religious, or economically privileged group may claim or receive privileged treatment by virtue of group membership. Nor may the members of any group be discriminated against by other groups or by government officials.

Examples of civil rights and liberties issues are present in our everyday lives. Civil liberties involve your rights as a college student: Can school authorities censor the student newspaper? Suspend a student for making nasty remarks about another's sexual orientation? Establish a "civility" code barring "hate speech"? Other issues involve your rights as a member of the public to be informed: Can the government prevent a newspaper from publishing a story on "national security" grounds? Can it require reporters to reveal their sources to a grand jury investigating a crime? Can the government restrict information on making bombs sent over the Internet? How about sexual or racial harassment? (See "Codes, Colleges, and Free Speech.")

Everyone is affected by civil rights issues: Will you as a woman receive equal pay for equal work? As a Mexican American will you be discriminated against in hiring and promotion? Will affirmative action programs designed to make up for past discrimination against minorities and women lead to "reverse discrimination" against you as a white male?

These issues have emerged in American politics. In recent presidential elections issues such as a woman's right to an abortion and a teacher's right to refuse to say the Pledge of Allegiance became important. Members of rightwing militias along with the National Rifle Association claim that the Second Amendment forbids the gun control laws passed in recent years. Congress regularly grapples with civil rights issues: votes on proposals to bar discrimination against the disabled, bills to

Codes, Colleges, and Free Speech

A wave of speech codes has rolled over college campuses in the last few years. The University of Michigan was typical. In response to racial jokes on the radio station and anti-Semitic comments in the student newspaper, a new policy prohibited harassment of people based on their race, ethnicity, religion, sex, sexual orientation, creed, age, marital status, handicap, or Vietnam War veteran status. Activity that would create an "intimidating, hostile, or demeaning environment" was banned. Later a federal judge responding to an ACLU suit struck down these rules as unconstitutional. Similar speech codes exist at other colleges.

Critics argue that in applying these vague restrictions on speech universities undermined freedom of expression, a core value for a place of learning. There is some evidence of this. A San Francisco newspaper reported "widespread apprehension on several Bay Area campuses that certain topics—mainly centering on race relations, feminist issues, and gay rights—are off-limits for open discussion in social situations and even in the classroom."

Do these restrictions lead to a society that is less racist or sexist? Do certain groups need protection? In a debate at Harvard Law School on whether the school should punish racist speech, a white student said that such codes are necessary because without them black students would be driven away from colleges and thereby deprived of an equal opportunity for an education. A black student rose and said that the white student had a hell of a nerve to assume that in the face of a racist speech he would pack up his books and go home. He'd handled racism before and it was condescending to say that blacks had to be "protected" from racist speech. "It is more racist and insulting to say that to me than to call me a nigger."*

Source: Nat Hentoff, *Free Speech for Me—But Not for Thee* (New York: HarperPerennial, 1993), Chapter V, "The Pall of Orthodoxy on the Nation's Campuses."

Author's Note: Was use of this racist term appropriate here? Should the publisher/author have removed it?

limit federal funding for abortions in public hospitals, and measures making it easier to prove discrimination against women in employment. To get a grip on some of these current issues, we might first look at the past.

EXPANDING THE BILL OF RIGHTS

When the Bill of Rights was added to the Constitution in 1791, it applied only to the activities of the national government. The Congress that passed the Bill of

Rights in 1789 had no intention of restricting the activities of state governments. Since the early twentieth century, however, the protections of the Bill of Rights have gradually been extended to cover actions of state and local officials and private individuals. The federal courts have relied on the *Fourteenth Amendment* to do so. That amendment, ratified in 1868, says in part, "nor shall any State deprive any person of life, liberty or property, without due process of law, nor deny to any person within its jurisdiction the equal protection of the laws." The two key, if vague, phrases are "due process" and "equal protection."

The *equal protection* clause has been used to prevent state officials from engaging in racial or sex discrimination. It has also prevented discrimination by private individuals when that action (1) is aided by state action, such as a law; (2) furthers a state activity such as an election, or the activities of a political party; or (3) involves a fundamental state interest such as education or public safety. Therefore, the equal protection clause has been used to strike down state laws segregating students by race in public schools. It has been used to put an end to the "whites only" primaries that the Democratic parties of southern states used to hold prior to the general elections. Though individuals may practice racial or religious or gender discrimination when they decide whom they will invite to their homes or associate with in private clubs, they cannot discriminate in associations like private schools, because education involves a fundamental state interest. And private clubs that serve the public, or permit nonmembers to use their facilities, are now considered places of public accommodation, and if they discriminate in selecting members on the basis of race or gender, they may lose certain tax advantages.

The *due process* clause of the Fourteenth Amendment applies to state and local governments. But to say that states must act according to "due process of law" raises a basic question: What does "due process" mean? The debate over the meaning and application of due process illustrates the difficulty of expanding the coverage of the Bill of Rights to the states.

The issue involves the extent that Bill of Rights protections should be "incorporated" into the language of the Fourteenth Amendment so as to apply to the states. On one side of the debate over due process are the *partial incorporationists*. They believe that only some of the Bill of Rights should be included in the meaning of "due process" in the Fourteenth Amendment, mainly those procedures guaranteeing fair criminal trials and First Amendment freedoms of religion, speech, and press. Which rights are to be incorporated? Those that are considered *preferred freedoms*, that is, the liberties necessary for a democracy to function, which, in the words of Justice Brandeis, form the essence of "a scheme of ordered liberty." But not everything in the Bill of Rights need be considered fundamental. Partial incorporationists must decide first whether a right contained in the Bill of Rights should apply to the states, before they decide on the facts of a case involving an alleged violation of these rights.

On the other side of the debate are the *complete incorporationists*. They believe that the entire Bill of Rights was incorporated into the Fourteenth Amendment. Thus there is no need to consider which rights to apply and which to leave unincorporated. When a case comes before them, they incorporate the entire Bill of Rights and use it as a limitation against state action.

Consider the case of a prisoner held in a state penitentiary who sues the warden in federal court. The prisoner argues that two months of solitary confinement for a mess hall riot is a violation of the Eighth Amendment prohibition against "cruel and unusual punishment." Partial incorporationists first must decide whether or not the Eighth Amendment should be incorporated into the Fourteenth Amendment as a limitation on state prison officials. They might argue that it applies only to criminal trials in state courts and that prison discipline does not involve any "fundamental rights." Full incorporationists would automatically incorporate the Eighth Amendment into the Fourteenth Amendment: There would be no question that the amendment applied to state prison officials. The judge would decide only the question whether two months of solitary confinement did indeed equal "cruel and unusual punishment."

Full incorporation has never been embraced by the Supreme Court. Yet in the past 90 years, the cumulative effect of federal court decisions has been to incorporate almost all of the Bill of Rights into the Fourteenth Amendment. Those that have not been incorporated are trivial.

CIVIL LIBERTIES: PROTECTING PEOPLE FROM GOVERNMENT

For the framers of the Constitution the greatest danger to citizens lay in the abuse of government power. For this reason, the most important civil liberties are those that provide protection for players in the political game. Most of these "preferred freedoms" are derived from the *First Amendment,* which states:

"Congress shall make no law respecting an establishment of religion, or prohibiting the free exercise thereof; or abridging the freedom of speech, or of the press, or the right of the people peaceably to assemble, and to petition the Government for a redress of grievances."

The First Amendment's "rules of the game" are essential to allow democracy to work. They enable people to keep informed, to communicate with each other and with the government without fear. Remove these protections and it would be difficult for political players to function. The press, interest groups, and even members of Congress would find their ability to "go public" and organize to change government policies very restricted. The political party that lost an election might be prevented from getting out its message, making it difficult to contest the next election. The Bill of Rights, along with separation of powers and checks and balances, is a mechanism designed to protect a people with a historically healthy fear of unchecked governmental power.

Supreme Court Justice Oliver Wendell Holmes once wrote that a democratic society needs competition among ideas as much as an economic marketplace needs competition among producers. "When men have realized that time has upset many fighting faiths," he wrote, "they come to believe . . . that the ultimate good desired is better reached by free trade in ideas—that the best truth is the power of the thought to get itself accepted in the competition of the marketplace." Put another way, how can you be sure your opinion is correct unless you are willing to test it against the opinions of others who may differ with you? And how can wrong opinions ever be changed, even when held by a majority, unless there is freedom for other opinions to be expressed?

Fundamental to Holmes's thinking, however, is the belief that good ideas would drive bad ideas out of the market, and that the public can be expected to reject the false in favor of the true. Given the awesome power of modern communications, and the lack of knowledge about politics shown by many Americans, these calculations may not always be true. Propaganda sometimes overwhelms reason; the demagogue may defeat the statesman. But it is hard to see how restricting speech can provide better safeguards for democracy.

A look at recent thinking about four of the most important civil liberties—freedom of speech and religion, the right to privacy, and due process of law—will help us to understand how the Bill of Rights works to protect citizens.

Freedom of Speech

The First Amendment guarantee of freedom of speech has been widened to state governments under the Fourteenth Amendment. Its meaning has also been deepened by various court decisions. "Speech" now includes not only speaking, but also gesturing and mimicking, wearing buttons and armbands, raising signs, and leafleting passersby. The Supreme Court has upheld congressional laws that make it a crime to conspire to overthrow the government by force. But it has struck down convictions of communists based on their membership in the Communist party, because the government was infringing on their freedom of association. Just believing in the violent overthrow of the government, even a speech about revolution, is not a crime. Nor is mere membership in an organization that believes in violent overthrow of the government. The courts insist that if the government wishes to put communists in prison, it prove that they conspired (that is, took concrete action) to overthrow the government.

The First Amendment not only protects your right to say what you believe, it also protects you by prohibiting the government from forcing you to say anything you don't believe. In 1943, for example, schoolchildren who were Jehovah's Witnesses refused to say the Pledge of Allegiance, on the grounds that they would be worshipping "graven images" (the flag) against the tenets of their religion. The Supreme Court overturned their suspension from school by state officials, and Justice Robert Jackson wrote, "No official, high or petty, can prescribe what shall be orthodox in politics, nationalism, religion, or other matters of opinion, or force citizens to confess by word or act their faith therein." As Americans we have the freedom to refuse to say things that we do not believe.

The Supreme Court has given protection to what is called "speech plus." This involves symbolic actions, such as wearing buttons or burning flags. (See Case Study: Flag Burning and Flag Waving.) In one case, an antiwar student who entered a courthouse with the words "Fuck the Draft" written on the back of his jacket was held in contempt by a local judge. The decision was reversed by the Supreme Court. As one justice pointed out, "While the particular four-letter word being litigated here is perhaps more distasteful than most others of its genre, it nevertheless is often true that one man's vulgarity is another's lyric." (See "High School Civil Liberties.")

The First Amendment provides no protection to speech that directly leads to illegal conduct or that might be considered illegal conduct by itself. Shouting "fire" in a crowded theater (when there is no fire) is not considered speech, but rather a reckless action which the state may punish. Writing or speaking falsehoods

High School Civil Liberties

The yearbook of Brunswick High School in Brunswick, Maine, was the unlikely focus of a fight over free speech. Graduating seniors get to choose a brief quotation to run along with their yearbook picture. One senior had been thinking long and hard about capital punishment. Rather than write "a standard butterfly quote," she chose the following from a *Time* magazine story on capital punishment: "The executioner will pull this lever four times. Each time 2,000 volts will course through your body, making your eyeballs first bulge, then burst, and then boiling your brains. . . ."

While not exactly a joyful farewell to her high school years, she intended to "provoke some of my classmates to think a little more deeply. . . ." The reaction the 17-year-old got was more than she could have expected. The students running the yearbook vetoed it as "bad taste," the school principal called it "disruptive," and the school board turned thumbs down on printing it. With the help of the Maine Civil Liberties Union, however, the stubborn student took the school board and the principal to court. The federal judge referred to the First Amendment as preventing the government (in this case, the school board) from interfering with people's ability to voice their ideas, no matter how unpopular. Then the judge issued an injunction prohibiting the yearbook from being printed until the case was resolved.

Faced with not being able to print the yearbook at all, the school system eventually reached a settlement with the student that allowed the quote to remain. A lone voice had stood up to the majority (her classmates, principal, and school system) and, with a little help from the Constitution, had won.

about a person which is damaging (libel and slander) is not protected, and you can be sued. Making or selling child pornography is not protected speech and does not involve freedom of expression, and you go to jail for doing so. When an individual addresses abuse and "fighting words" at someone, particularly a police officer, convictions for disorderly conduct are usually upheld by the courts.

Questions of free speech have recently come to cyberspace. At the urging of groups like the Christian Coalition, several Senators downloaded hardcore pornography from the Internet. The result was the Communications Decency Act which passed Congress as part of the vast telecommunications bill of 1996. The Act punished making "indecent" material available to children over the Internet. In June 1996 a special federal three-judge panel unanimously rejected the law as a violation of free speech. One judge wrote, "As the most participatory form of mass speech yet developed, the Internet deserves the highest protection from government intrusion." (See "Freedom in Cyberspace.")

Freedom of Religion

Even before the adoption of the Constitution, the state of Virginia in 1786, set forth the fundamental principle in its Statute of Religious Freedom that "our civil rights have no dependence on our religious opinions." The Constitution provided that there would be no religious test for office, and the First Amendment provided for "free exercise of religion" and prohibited the establish-

---

Freedom in Cyberspace

In the early days of the Internet, users were able to create a unique "cyberspace" environment. It was a culture where they "left behind politicians, bureaucrats, police, army, and not only crime but the very concept of crime." However, as users have grown to over 30 million by 1996, concern has risen over issues such as electronic harassment, theft of sensitive information by "hackers," and pornography. Laws which deal with individual rights, safety, and the limits of free speech are confounded by three characteristics of the Internet:

- *It's global:* On the Internet, a computer across the world can be reached as easily as one across the room. How do you enforce national laws in this environment? One example of a problem lies in the "virtual" gambling casinos that have been set up on the Internet using computers located outside the United States. Parents in the United States have caught their kids gambling on the Internet with their parents' credit cards.

- *It's anonymous:* Disguising your name on the Internet is easy. An occasional contributor to a pornography newsgroup identifies himself as "George W. Bush, the governor of Texas," although everyone assumes it's not really the governor.

- *It's huge:* Terabytes, or trillions of bytes, of data are circulating on the Internet at any given moment. As one commentator put it, "trying to locate illegal or offensive data on the net would be harder than trying to isolate two paired words in all the world's telephone conversations and TV transmissions at once."

Sources: Gary Chapman, "The Unassailable Liberty of Cyberspace," *The New Republic,* July 1995. Tracy LaQuey, *The Internet Companion* (Reading: Addison-Wesley, 1993).

ment of an official religion by Congress. Yet there has never been a complete "wall of separation" between church and state in America. The armed forces have chaplains paid for by Congress; the Supreme Court chambers have a mural of Moses giving the Ten Commandments; the dollar bill proclaims "In God We Trust." Recently the rise in political importance of Christian fundamentalists has led them (along with some Catholics and Orthodox Jews) to try to redefine the nature of church-state relations.

The question of freedom of religion inevitably gets mixed up in the constitutional prohibition against the establishment of religion. To allow students to pray in school, a position favored by a large majority of Americans, may seem to be simply an issue of free exercise of religion. But if most children in the class are Protestant, should the prayer be from a Protestant denomination? And if so, which one? Will other children feel like outcasts, even if they are excused from saying the prayer and permitted to leave the room? The Clinton administration tried to clarify the legal limits of religion in public schools and to distinguish between what teachers cannot do, and what students can do. (See "Dos and Don'ts on Religion in Public Schools.")

Dos and Don'ts on Religion in Public Schools

Department of Education 1995 guidelines on religious activity in schools:

Permitted:

- Student prayer by individuals or groups
- Student-initiated discussions on religions
- Reading the Bible
- Saying grace before meals
- Wearing religious clothing or symbols
- Religious activities before or after school

Forbidden:

- Prayer endorsed or organized by teachers or administrators
- "Harassing" invitations to participate in prayer
- Teaching or encouraging a particular religion, rather than teaching about religion
- Denying school rooms to religious groups

Source: The New York Times, August 26, 1995.

While Americans strongly support freedom of religion, most also believe that the government must not favor one religion over another. Balancing these competing values is very difficult, as when a court is faced with a law passed by Congress or state legislature providing federal or state funds for parochial schools. The courts have upheld government funding of such schools, but only for their secular activities. Yet in 1995 the Supreme Court ruled against the University of Virginia for refusing to fund a student publication because it had a Christian orientation. How to recognize and accommodate some of the religious sentiments of the people, yet ensure that government does not infringe on religious freedom or favor one group over another, is a delicate matter. As the Supreme Court once confessed, "We can only dimly perceive the lines of demarcation in this extraordinarily sensitive area of constitutional law."

Rights of Privacy

To what extent do citizens have privacy rights against snooping by government officials or attempts to regulate their intimate social, sexual, and cultural behavior? Though nowhere mentioned in the Constitution, the First Amendment along with the Ninth Amendment, is sometimes read by the courts as creating a "zone of privacy" that shields individuals from government intrusion into their homes, phones, computers and bedrooms.

Some recent privacy issues have centered on sexual conduct. The state, according to the Supreme Court, cannot prevent couples from using contraceptive devices. Nor can states forbid abortions in the first trimester of pregnancy, though state regulations making it difficult for women to use abortion services without informing their spouses or waiting 24 hours after "family counseling" have been upheld. States may not forbid sexual relations between individuals of different races, as some states did to preserve the "purity" of the white race. In a notable 1996 decision, *Romer* v. *Evans*, the Court ruled that Colorado could not single out gays and prohibit local laws designed to end discrimination

against them. However the Supreme Court has not required states to recognize homosexual marriages on the
same footing as heterosexual marriages (though states
and cities are free to do so). Nor have courts ruled that
states must fund abortions for those who cannot pay for
them.

Due Process Rights

The Fifth Amendment and the Fourteenth Amendment prevent the national and state governments from
depriving persons of their lives, liberty, or property
without due process of law. Due process guarantees involve fundamental procedural fairness and impartial
rulings by government officials, especially in (but not
limited to) criminal courtrooms. In criminal trials the
right to due process includes the right to free counsel if
you cannot afford a lawyer and the right to have your
lawyer present at any police questioning; the right to
reasonable bail after being charged; the right to a
speedy trial; the right to confront and cross-examine
your accuser and witnesses testifying against you; the
right to remain silent (Remember O.J. Simpson refusing to testify?); the right to an impartial judge and a jury
of your peers, selected without racial bias; and the right
to appeal the decision to a higher court if you believe legal errors were committed by the judge.

These rights were granted in federal criminal trials
under the Fifth Amendment and the Sixth Amendment. As a result of Supreme Court decisions over the
years, these rights have also been established for state
criminal trials as well. In the 1970s the federal courts
also began to require some of these procedures in non-
criminal settings. Students could not be transferred,
suspended, or expelled from high schools or public universities without certain kinds of hearings. People on
welfare could not be purged from the rolls for fraud or
ineligibility without receiving "fair hearings."

Consider the case of a student who has participated
in a campus demonstration and is told by university
officials that she has violated rules and will be suspended for a semester. Surely she would want all the
due process guarantees she could obtain in order to

prove to these officials that she should not be suspended. Obtaining one due process right often leads to obtaining others. Once the college decides that students are entitled to a hearing, students may demand the right to bring their attorneys. The attorneys will insist on written transcripts and an appeals process. Often the very existence of a fair hearing procedure and the presence of lawyers will encourage informal settlements without a hearing—a money-saving step usually welcomed by all parties.

These due process issues are directly related to First Amendment political freedoms. It does little good to give people the right to protest to the government if officials can retaliate by cutting off essential services to protesters. Students or workers who are politically involved need legal protection from unfair action by school administrators or employers. Due process protects them. It also protects officials, because it requires them to meet high standards of fairness and procedure, and that is likely to ensure that their actions are viewed as legitimate.

CIVIL RIGHTS: PROTECTING PEOPLE FROM PEOPLE

Protecting people against state action is only half the game. Civil rights involve the national government in the protection of minorities (or women, who are a majority) against actions by state and local governments or private individuals and organizations.

Civil rights issues involve discrimination based on classifications of race, religion, gender, or national origin. A group that believes it is being discriminated against may try to obtain satisfaction from elected officials, or it may turn to the judiciary. African Americans may find it difficult to rent apartments because landlords discriminate against them. To combat discriminatory practices many states and the national government have passed fair housing laws, which make such discrimination illegal. Presidents have signed executive orders banning racial discrimination in public housing and in private housing that is financed through federal mortgage programs. In

1948 the Supreme Court ruled that racial covenants attached to deeds that restricted the sale of property to "Caucasians Only" were unconstitutional.

Civil rights issues are not always clearcut. Affirmative action programs have sometimes placed groups in opposition to one another. The woman who supports affirmative action in order to get a job may be in conflict with the African American who believes that these programs were designed primarily to redress wrongs committed against blacks. As the noted civil rights leader, Dr. Kenneth Clark, remarked, if women, blacks, Latinos, and Asians are all given affirmative action preferences almost three-quarters of the population would be protected.

Preferential admissions policies at universities have increasingly brought blacks and Latinos into conflict with whites who believe that these programs may result in "quotas" that decrease their chances of admission. These arguments and publicized incidents of unfairness in these programs have led to their increasing unpopularity. By 1995 the Regents of the University of California voted to end their affirmative action programs. The regents, with a push from Republican Governor Pete Wilson, declared that race and gender would no longer be considered in school admissions, hiring, and contracting. Opinion varied on how this would affect the numbers of minorities admitted.

Other arguments against affirmative action programs have come from within the African American community. Black conservatives charged that these programs were hurting blacks rather than helping them. They argued that preferential treatment allowed blacks with lower qualifications to gain entry into work or education. Not only did it reinforce a sense of victimization on their part, but it also publically stamped black professionals as less qualified than their white peers. Finally, these programs fueled white resentment against "reverse discrimination."

However valid these critics may be, they have not spelled out alternative policies that would speak to the burdens overwhelming many people in minority as well as white communities. Without programs that address poverty, crime, and unemployment, wherever they exist, criticisms of affirmative action can only be half correct—they leave an unfilled space for future efforts that can remedy these ills without the public disfavor of affirmative action. In this evolution the courts, too, will play a role.

Which People Need Protection? Suspect Classifications

The Fourteenth Amendment sets forth the right to "equal protection of the laws." However, the government may pass laws applying to some citizens and not to others, or applying different criteria to different classes of people. For example, working people with low incomes receive money from the government (in the form of the earned-income tax credit) while people who earn higher amounts of money pay taxes at several different rates, depending on how much income they receive.

What limits are placed on government classifications of people? Hardly any if the classifications involve wealth and income. In any economic issues the laws passed by Congress or state legislatures are routinely approved by the judiciary, under the doctrine of "presumptive legislative rationality." Courts assume that the lawmakers know what they are doing when they make such classifications. On the other hand, if lawmakers apply racial or religious or national origin classifications, the courts subject these to "close scrutiny," because these are *"suspect" classifications.* Here the burden of proof is on the government to demonstrate that the classification is not, on its face, unconstitutional.

Governments must, when the law or action touches a "suspect class," prove a compelling state interest for their action. The courts begin their scrutiny with the assumption that the action violates the equal protection guarantee, and it is up to the lawmakers to prove otherwise. Racial classifications are always considered suspect, and are almost always struck down. Gender classifications are not suspect. The court applies a "middle test," which is stricter than standards for wealth and income but looser than standards for race. While courts have struck down many gender classifications, they have upheld some: Women, for example, are not registered for the military and women who volunteer for the armed forces do not serve in combat positions. Women, because they give birth, may be given different medical benefits than men.

Race as a Suspect Classification

In 1896 the Supreme Court upheld state actions that segregated the races. In the famous case of *Plessy* v. *Ferguson,* it upheld the right of Louisiana to require racial segregation in railway cars. "Equal protection of the law" was misshaped into the doctrine of "separate but equal": The African American Plessy would travel in a separate railway car, but would reach his destination at the same time and on the same train as a white person. (In practice, segregated facilities for blacks were almost always inferior.) Then in the 1954 landmark case *Brown* v. *Board of Education,* the Supreme Court held that schools segregated by race were inherently unequal and violated the Fourteenth Amendment. After *Brown,* courts struck down almost all laws based on racial categories and made race a suspect classification.

But do racial classifications always violate the Fourteenth Amendment? Are there circumstances in which classification by race is a valid use of governmental power? Courts have upheld racial classifications when used to eliminate prior state-sponsored segregation. In devising plans to desegregate schools, for instance, administrators explicitly took into account the racial characteristics of students attending schools, as well as their teachers. After all, in order to make desegregation work, one would have to put many blacks into schools that had previously been all white. In a 1992 case, *U.S.* v. *Fordice,* the Supreme Court ruled that because of continuing evidence of racial segregation in the state university system, Mississippi would have to intensify efforts to attract blacks to its mostly white campuses and whites to traditionally black colleges.

Affirmative action programs also permit racial classifications. An affirmative action program in schools allows admissions officers to take race and ethnicity into account in awarding places in the entering class. An af-

firmative action program in employment usually requires employers to make efforts to match the racial
and gender composition of their work force with the
pool of qualified workers in their areas. In 1978, in the
University of California Regents v. *Bakke,* the Supreme
Court upheld the principle of affirmative action, holding that it was a "state interest" to provide for diversity
in the entering class of medical students at the University of California at Davis. On the other hand, in that
same case, the Supreme Court held that the use of strict
numerical quotas for minorities was a violation of the
equal protection clause.

The Supreme Court has grown increasingly skepti-
cal of affirmative action programs. In 1986 the court
upheld promotion quotas in *Cleveland Firefighters,* but
only where the quotas were narrowly focused to remedy
employment patterns that caused clearcut racial discrimination. The quotas were considered a remedy for a
specific violation, rather than a general pattern to promote diversity. By 1989, in *City of Richmond* v. *Croson,*
racial classifications by cities and states were thrown
into question. A set-aside program provided that 30
percent of the dollars in city contracts were to go to
minority-controlled firms. The Supreme Court held
that the specific set-aside formula was unconstitutional,
because it gave preference to one race over another.
Adarand v. *Pena* (1995) threw out a federal set-aside
program designed to encourage minority contractors.
While still not declaring all affirmative action programs
unconstitutional, the Court made clear that there had to
be a "compelling interest" to relieve a specific case of
discrimination and that the remedy had to be "narrowly
tailored." Most existing programs were not expected to
survive the Court's "strict scrutiny."

Other branches of the government have increasingly
turned away from affirmative action programs, partly in
response to the Court's actions. The Justice Department, following the Court's ruling, issued guidelines for
federal agencies reminding them that government programs needed to respond to specific discrimination
rather than general racism. While the Clinton administration, with an eye to the 1996 elections, publicly

endorsed affirmative action, it opposed quotas and any actions that led to reverse discrimination. "Mend it, but don't end it," the President said. Meanwhile Republican leaders in Congress announced their intentions to do exactly that—end affirmative action.

Supporters of affirmative action argue that there is a difference between a quota designed to discriminate *against* a minority (such as quotas used by colleges in the 1930s to limit the number of Jews admitted), and a classification designed to *help* a group make up for past discrimination. Others, who are uncomfortable with classifications based on race, no matter how benign, often quote Justice Harlan, a Southerner who cast the only dissenting vote against "separate but equal" in *Plessy* v. *Ferguson*. Harlan wrote, "Our Constitution is color-blind, and neither knows nor tolerates caste among citizens. In respect of civil rights, all citizens are equal before the law."

Is Sex Suspect?

In the nineteenth century, women and children were exploited in factories, where they often worked 14-hour days, seven days a week, for low wages, in unsafe and unsanitary conditions. In the late nineteenth century a coalition of women's rights advocates, labor union organizers, social workers, and public health professionals all advocated that the national and state governments provide special protection for women and children in the form of wage and hour regulations. Some states passed such laws, known as "protective legislation." Many were held unconstitutional by the Supreme Court, which generally opposed state efforts to regulate industry.

But protective legislation did not stop with factory conditions. State legislatures went further in "protecting" women by restricting their opportunities to enter professions. In 1873 the Supreme Court upheld a decision by the Illinois courts that prevented Myra Bradwell from becoming a lawyer. "The natural and proper timidity and delicacy which belongs to the female sex," a justice wrote, "evidently unfits it for many of the occupations of civil life." Under this reasoning, women were denied the right to enter businesses, serve on juries, make contracts, or work at all if they were pregnant. As former Supreme Court Justice William Brennan observed, this "romantic paternalism" put women "not on a pedestal, but in a cage."

The federal courts do retain one part of the protective movement, and that involves sexual harassment. In *Meritor* v. *Vinson,* the Supreme Court ruled that sexual harassment occurs not simply when a man insists on having sex with a female subordinate, but also when a pattern of harassment exists which makes it difficult for women to work in a hostile or abusive environment. In a 1991 civil rights law Congress provided that women who have been sexually harassed on the job may sue in federal court for damages.

In the 1970s women no longer looked for special protections involving working conditions, in large part because laws regarding occupational health and safety applied to all workers. Entering the work force in unprecedented numbers, women sought equality from the government, not protection. The *Equal Pay Act of 1963* and *Civil Rights Act of 1964* provided that women would be hired and paid equally with men. The *Pregnancy Discrimination Act of 1978* forbade discrimination against female workers because they were pregnant. Since wage and employment discrimination remained rampant, many court cases were brought by women under these laws.

Meanwhile, in the 1970s and 1980s, women's groups began attacking the remaining "protective" laws in federal courts. They argued that gender should be considered a suspect classification. The Supreme Court has responded by striking down many laws involving gender, but has not held that gender classifications are suspect. The Court has struck down professional licensing and educational requirements that discriminate against women. It has ruled that men have an equal right to sue for alimony, that the drinking age must be the same for both sexes, and that unwed fathers have rights in deciding whether or not a baby is put up for adoption.

On the other hand, the Court has allowed state laws granting certain tax benefits to widows but not widowers. It upheld a state law permitting men but not women to serve as guards in a maximum security prison. It let stand a lower court decision permitting single-sex schools to continue to receive federal funds. The Court has also upheld gender classifications when used for approved purposes such as an affirmative action plan. No challenges to single-sex bathroom facilities have succeeded.

The Equal Rights Amendment approved by Congress in 1972 would have outlawed gender classifications so that they would be struck down in much the same way as racial categories are under the Fourteenth Amendment. Although not enough states ratified the ERA, it is likely that more sex-based classifications will fall as a result of present standards applied by the courts.

ACTORS IN CIVIL LIBERTIES AND RIGHTS

Many players in the political game act on issues of civil liberties and rights. Within the government, the courts have been the most important players, although Congress may pass laws and the president may issue executive orders that are monitored by the Justice Department. Outside the government a number of organizations champion the rights of particular groups. The politics of civil liberties and rights involves struggles of group against group, as well as group against government, in ongoing attempts to strike a balance among competing claims.

Judges

Many judges have played a leading role in expanding and deepening civil rights and liberties. Activist judges (who along with other supporters of civil liberties are called *civil libertarians*) issue decisions in *class action suits,* in which lawyers bring a case to court not only for their individual clients, but on behalf of everyone in a similar situation—perhaps millions of people. Judges may rely on court-appointed experts and consultants to do the research needed to resolve complicated social and political issues. To decide a case, they may use not only previous cases and laws, but also the equity powers of the judiciary.

Equity is used to prevent permanent damage in situations not covered by existing law. Suppose my neighbor, Jones, decides to cut down a tree in his yard. I see that the tree will crash into my house. My legal remedy is to sue Jones after my house is damaged. My equitable remedy is to obtain a court injunction that prevents Jones from cutting down the tree in the first place. Activist judges use equity powers to shape remedies that overcome the effects of discrimination. Take a school district that has been segregated by race because of state laws and administrative action. Merely requiring that the system act without regard to race may not have any real effect if residential segregation exists so that schools will remain segregated in fact. Some federal judges have applied equitable remedies: They have required that the school districts take into account racial imbalances and come up with plans (some of which involve busing) to overcome these imbalances.

Other judges are more restrained in civil liberties and civil rights cases. They are unsympathetic to class actions and limit their decisions to the individuals before them. They tend to follow past decisions rather than expand the scope of constitutional protections. They are likely to place great weight on the policies of Congress, the president, and state legislatures, even when these weigh against civil rights and liberties. These judges will presume that elected officials are acting rationally and lawfully unless proven otherwise. Because elected officials are directly accountable to the people, these unelected judges hesitate to impose their own views. (See pp. 161–163 for more on activist and restrained judges.)

The Justice Department

Historically the Department of Justice has played a key role in protecting civil rights and liberties. Its lawyers in the U.S. Attorney's offices in each judicial district may prosecute persons, including state or federal officials, accused of violating people's civil rights. After four police officers were acquitted of beating black motorist Rodney King in a state trial, the U.S. Attorney in Los Angeles brought a case against them, alleging that they violated King's civil rights in the course of his arrest. In April 1993 two of the four officers were convicted in a federal court.

Under Presidents Ronald Reagan and George Bush, the Justice Department pulled back from its support of civil rights groups. The department opposed busing plans to overcome segregation of schools, opposed some affirmative action hiring plans, and argued that job discrimination cases should be limited to the individuals involved, and not cover patterns of employment.

President Clinton entered office aggressively backing civil rights enforcement. He appointed the first female attorney general, Janet Reno, as well as liberal judges and U.S. attorneys. The head of Justice's civil rights division was Deval Patrick, an African American lawyer who grew up in the Chicago projects, went to Harvard Law School, and became a strong defender of affirmative action. Yet the Republican takeover of Congress in 1994 and the approach of the 1996 elections put the administration between a rock and a hard place. Black leaders watched for any weakening in the stance toward affirmative action and were rewarded in mid-1995 with a broad administration endorsement of these programs. But Clinton worried about alienating the "angry white male" voter and faced a popular ballot initiative in the must-win state of California which would ban minority preferences. This attempt to steer a middle course led to joking in the Justice Department that the Clinton administration wanted to strongly enforce civil rights laws, as long as no one knew about it.

"Private Attorneys General"

Various organizations have been created to support the rights of individuals and groups. These are called "private attorneys general" because they act, not on behalf of the government, but for groups bringing court cases against the government or against other groups. They are funded in part by foundations and wealthy donors, and in part by dues-paying members.

The largest such group is the *American Civil Liberties Union*. The ACLU has a national staff of about 350

in New York City and has 50 state chapters. Its 5,000 volunteers handle more than 6,000 cases each year. The
ACLU was organized in the 1920s to defend individuals
against the hysteria of "red scares" (a period when social-
ists were persecuted) and has fought against wire-
tapping, surveillance, and "dirty tricks" by government
law enforcement agencies. It is especially active in First
Amendment freedom of speech, press, and religion issues. Most recently it has strongly opposed "civility" codes
on campuses, and has defended the publication rights of
pornographers against attacks by some feminist groups.

Another important organization is the NAACP Legal Defense and Educational Fund, Inc. (LDF). The
LDF was created in 1939, and consisted at first of one
lawyer, Thurgood Marshall, who became the first black
appointed to the Supreme Court. In the past, the LDF
concentrated on school desegregation suits. Today its
dozens of lawyers are focused on discrimination in employment and housing, and on abuses in the judicial sys-
tem.The largest legal organization for women is the National Organization for Women (NOW) Legal Defense
and Education Fund. It works to help women gain
equal employment rights and to strike down legislation
viewed as discriminating.

Legal Strategies

These organizations use a variety of legal tactics. They
conduct research on the problems of their clients, hop-
ing to find a pattern of discrimination for a large class of
people. They then write articles for law journals in order to influence thinking in the legal profession. They
offer their services to individuals whose rights may have
been violated. Such people cannot afford the hundreds
of thousands of dollars it takes to pursue a case all the
way to the Supreme Court, so the assistance of the "private attorneys general," almost always provided free of
charge, is crucial. Civil liberties lawyers can choose
from a large number of complaints to pick one as a *test
case* for their arguments. Such a case offers the group
its best shot because the violation is so obvious, the
damage so great, and the person making the case so appealing to the judges.

The litigating organization hopes that its case eventually will wind up in the Supreme Court as a *landmark* decision, one that involves major changes in the definition of civil rights and liberties. Such a decision creates a new general rule (such as the right to counsel in a state trial), which is then enforced by lower federal and state courts. After the landmark case is announced by the high court, the lawyers from these organizations then must bring dozens of cases in federal district courts to make sure that rights affirmed by the Supreme Court are followed by government officials. (For an example of a landmark decision, see *Brown* v. *Board of Education*, p. 166.)

Obeying the Courts

These private organizations may ask judges to do several things. First, they may ask that a national or state law, executive order, or private action be declared unconstitutional, or that actions of private individuals be found in violation of the law or the Constitution. Second, they may ask that a right be protected by various kinds of judicial action. Of these, the most important are the *injunction,* which prevents someone from taking an action to violate someone else's rights, and the *order,* which requires someone to take a specified action to ensure someone else's rights.

In the event of noncompliance with a judicial injunction or order, the judges may issue a citation for contempt of court. Civil contempt involves the refusal to obey a court order granted to a party in a case, and can lead to imprisonment. The court also may find someone in criminal contempt of court, for taking an action that disrupts the court or shows disrespect for the court's enforcement powers. This too may lead to imprisonment or a stiff fine.

The orders of a federal court are enforced by federal marshals, but if necessary these officers are backed up by the state's National Guard, which may be brought into federal service by proclamation of the president, or by federal troops under the orders of the president as commander-in-chief. In 1957, for example, when Governor Orval Faubus of Arkansas refused to obey a federal court order to desegregate Little Rock Central High School, President Dwight Eisenhower took control of the Arkansas National Guard away from the governor and then used federal troops to protect black students attending the school. In 1961 President John Kennedy used the army to desegregate the University of Mississippi, enforcing a federal court order over the resistance of the governor.

In writing their orders, federal courts can act as administrators over state agencies. At one time in the 1970s federal judges in Alabama were running the state highway patrol, the prison system, and the mental hospitals, because the governor refused to obey various federal court orders guaranteeing equal protection and due process of law in these agencies.

Sometimes state officials do not wish to comply with the spirit or letter of court orders. Consider the landmark decision of *Miranda* v. *Arizona* (1966), in which the Supreme Court held that once an investigation by police focused on an accused, that person had to receive the following warning:

> *You have the right to remain silent.*
> *Anything you say may be used against you in a court of law.*
> *You have the right to be represented by an attorney of your choice.*
> *If you cannot afford an attorney, a public defender will be provided for you if you wish.*

At first, there was only limited acceptance by many police departments of the new rules of the "cops and robbers" game. After all, unless there was a federal judge in every patrol car, voluntary compliance was the only practical way such a rule could be implemented. Some departments ignored the order; others gave only part of the warning. The courts gained compliance through the *exclusionary rule:* They threw out evidence obtained illegally, including confessions where Miranda warnings had not been given. The Supreme Court has narrowed the exclusionary rule recently, sometimes allowing evidence if police officers "acted in good faith," even if they did not follow all due process rules.

Public Opinion and Civil Liberties

Clearly public agreement with a landmark civil rights or civil liberties decision cannot be taken for granted. A majority of the public, for example, does not believe that evidence should be thrown out in state criminal trials on "legal technicalities," which is what the Miranda rule requires. And it is precisely because in many states the majority has discriminated against minorities, or because the rights of politically unpopular groups (like communists) have been violated, that judicial protection has become necessary. (See "Uncle Sam: Enemy of Civil Liberties?") One can assume that the public will oppose the changes and avoid complying with them. Majorities of the public oppose minority preferences and protection for pornography and support prayer in public schools. Where support by local political leaders does not exist and community sentiment runs against the decision, as with the ban on prayer in the public schools, compliance may be spotty. Often a Supreme Court ruling signals the start—not the end—of political debate. In the case of abortion rights, a Supreme Court decision affirming the right to abortion was later followed by congressional and state laws cutting off public funding for abortions and making first trimester abortions more difficult to obtain.

The rightness of judicial action never rests on its popularity with the public. The federal judiciary is not elected and does not directly answer to the people. It is accountable to a Constitution that attempts to secure the rights of the people against governmental action. The judiciary protects the rights of the people against the majority. Low levels of approval for some of its decisions are nothing to be alarmed about. If anything, it is evidence that the system is working.

Of course, for the courts to function in the political game, and for their decisions to be implemented, they must obtain the cooperation of other parts of the government. This is not automatically given, as the following case study of flag burning illustrates.

Uncle Sam: Enemy of Civil Liberties?

Civil liberties in general have received broad support, but few people have come to their defense in unpopular cases. Throughout U.S. history there are uncomfortable reminders of government actions that many would now see as violating the Bill of Rights.

Not many years after the ink had dried on the Constitution, Congress passed the *Alien and Sedition Acts* of 1798. Aimed at the opposition party, these acts promised heavy fines and imprisonment for those guilty of writing or speaking anything false, scandalous, or malicious against any government official. Such a broad prohibition today would put an end to most political campaigns. The slavery issue in 1840 led Congress to pass the "Gag Rule" preventing antislavery petitions from being received by Congress (thus violating a specific First Amendment right).

Violations of civil liberties continued into the twentieth century. Within five months after the United States entered World War I, every leading socialist newspaper had been suspended from the mails at least once, some permanently. The *Smith Act* of 1940, which is still on the books, forbade teaching or advocating the violent overthrow of the government. In 1951, eleven Communist party leaders were convicted under it for activities labeled "preparation for revolution." This "preparation" involved advocating and teaching works like the *Communist Manifesto,* which today can be found in any college library. Ten defendants were sentenced to five years in prison. In more recent times, the FBI infiltrated the anti-Vietnam War movement, spied on civil rights leaders like Martin Luther King Jr., and got into a shoot-out with a right-wing family at Ruby Ridge, Idaho. Down to the present, government respect for the civil liberties of dissenters remains a sometime thing.

Case Study

FLAG BURNING AND FLAG WAVING

Gregory Lee "Joey" Johnson was arrested under a Texas law after he had soaked an American flag in kerosene and burned it during the 1984 Republican National Convention in Dallas. Johnson had been part of a roving demonstration called the "Republican War Chest Tour," aimed against the "policies of the Reagan administration and of certain Dallas corporations." (After he burned the flag, an onlooker gathered the ashes and buried them in his backyard, the proper way for disposing of Old Glory.)

Johnson was the only demonstrator arrested. Charged with the desecration of a venerated object, he was convicted,

fined, and sentenced to one year in prison. At the time all
states except Alaska and Wyoming had flag-desecration laws
on the books. The Texas Court of Criminal Appeals overturned the Texas law on the grounds that it violated the First
Amendment right to freedom of speech. Burning the flag,
the Texas Court ruled, was "protected symbolic speech."
Texas appealed to the Supreme Court.

The Supreme Court Decides

On June 21, 1989, the U.S. Supreme Court in a 5–4 decision
in *Texas* v. *Johnson,* said that Johnson's act was constitutionally protected under the First Amendment. Justice William
Brennan wrote the majority opinion, in which he argued that
freedom of expression could be limited only when there was
a "compelling governmental interest," such as the need to
maintain public order. But since Johnson was not, in Brennan's opinion, engaged in an action likely to bring about a
physical ruckus, the government's interest lay solely in preventing desecration of a venerated object. That, Brennan
ruled, was not a sufficiently compelling government interest
to abridge Johnson's right to free speech. Since the law was
aimed at limiting expression, it would have to pass "the most
exacting scrutiny" of the Court—and it did not. "If there is a
bedrock principle underlying the First Amendment," Brennan wrote, "it is that the Government may not prohibit the
expression of an idea simply because society finds the idea itself offensive or disagreeable."

Brennan's opinion was grounded in several precedents.
In 1969 the Supreme Court had overturned a New York law
under which a demonstrator had been arrested for burning a
flag in protest. In 1974 a man arrested in Massachusetts for
wearing a flag on the seat of his pants was freed (the "flag on
the fanny" decision). In that same year a student who put
peace symbols on the flag and then hung it upside down
(which is the international distress signal) received First
Amendment protection. Because of these precedents, the
"Joey" Johnson decision got support from Reagan appointees
Antonin Scalia and Anthony Kennedy. The latter said in his
concurring opinion that he felt "distaste for the outcome"
even though he felt compelled by the Constitution to uphold
Johnson's freedom of expression.

Brennan asserted for the majority that the Stars and
Stripes was only one symbol among many. It did not have "a
separate juridical category" to insulate it from the vigorous
give and take of public debate. This was a key point on which

Chief Justice Rehnquist, writing for the minority, disagreed. "The flag is not simply another 'idea' or 'point of view' competing for recognition in the marketplace of ideas," Rehnquist wrote. For him it was a "unique" symbol of our nation for which citizens have fought and died. Protecting the physical integrity of this symbol, wrote Rehnquist, was no different than safeguarding grave sites, memorials, and public buildings against vandals.

The Politics of Patriotism

The political reaction was predictable. President Bush called for calm, then went off to the Iwo Jima memorial to declare his support for a constitutional amendment to overturn the Court's decision. Such an amendment would have been the first to limit provisions of the Bill of Rights.

Democrats proposed a law instead of a constitutional amendment. Democrats worried that they would be put on the wrong side of "symbolic politics" that Bush had so effectively used in the 1988 elections when he insisted that teachers be required to salute the flag (gaining public support against Democratic candidate Michael Dukakis, who opposed the idea). Some Democrats hoped that passing the law would provide them with political protection until passions cooled.

Legal scholars backed the Court. The American Bar Association passed a resolution opposing a constitutional amendment or a law. Newspaper editorials raised questions about how such a law or amendment would be enforced. The polls indicated that the public was increasingly reluctant about amending the Constitution for the flag.

Democrats nursed through Congress a law that forbade physically desecrating the flag but without reference to the opinions of the burner or onlookers. Congress passed the law overwhelmingly in October. Such a law would not, however, overturn the court's decision, which was based on the fact that the flagburner was making a political statement—such communication would remain protected. Alas, Johnson and two other demonstrators immediately tested the law on the steps of the Capitol. Johnson's cigarette lighter didn't work, but his three companions started to burn a flag (in full view of the television cameras) and were arrested by Capitol police.

On June 11, 1990, the Supreme Court affirmed two lower federal district courts and found the law unconstitutional. In a 5–4 decision the Court said that the federal law had the same "fundamental flaw" as the Texas law, that of "suppressing expression."

Again President Bush called for a constitutional amendment "to prohibit the physical desecration of the flag." Democrats brought the proposal to a quick vote before Republicans could mobilize public support. On June 21 the House defeated the proposed amendment, 254–177 in favor, falling more than 30 votes short of the needed two-thirds majority. Yet again, in 1995 a new Republican House passed the amendment protecting the flag, but the Senate rejected it by a narrow vote late in the year. After a good deal of political sound and fury a minor incident of flag burning was not allowed to infringe on a major First Amendment right of free speech.

WRAP-UP

Civil rights and liberties are constitutional protections granted to all citizens. They protect people against violations of their rights by other people or by the government. Civil liberties usually refer to rights—such as freedom of speech and religion and guarantees of due process of law—which allow people full participation in a democratic political system. Civil rights guard groups against discrimination by other groups. Historically, both sets of rights have been deepened as to what they cover and widened as to whom they cover.

Using the concepts of "equal protection of the laws" and "due process of law" found in the Fourteenth Amendment, the courts have applied the Bill of Rights to the states as well as the national government. Freedom of speech has been expanded to include freedom of expression. Privacy rights now include protection for consenting adult behavior. Due process rights have been expanded to cover bureaucracies as well as the state criminal justice system. Civil rights have similarly been widened with the use of suspect classifications to deal with racial prejudice. Although the strict scrutiny test does not apply to gender classifications, a large number of statutes containing "protective" gender classifications have been removed from the books. Helping the process along have been activist judges and private attorneys general, whose test cases have served to change the law, sometimes dramatically, and sometimes slowly. The case study of a flag burning illustrates how difficult it is sometimes to grant "freedom for the thoughts that we hate," as Justice Oliver Wendell Holmes put it.

Civil rights and liberties not only protect individuals, they defend our system of government. These well-tested values balance and restrain the drives and ambitions of our leaders. They give us standards by which to judge the actions of these players. They underline the historical truth that majorities can be wrong and that leaders can mislead. These rights and liberties restrain the "tyranny of the majority," and may therefore be considered undemocratic. But by providing us with accepted freedoms and protecting our political communications, they become an essential part of the political game that enables our democracy to work.

Although the Bill of Rights is written in inspiring and absolute language—"Congress shall make no law . . ."—these rights are seldom applied that way. Judges weighing civil liberties and rights (and students considering them as well) are influenced by the political climate of the day and the opinions being expressed. First Amendment freedoms are easier to support when the streets are filled by people we agree with. Liberals may not be quite as upset by violations of free speech when police rough up antiabortion demonstrators. Conservatives may not see an issue of freedom of the press involved when obscene words are used on a radio talk show. But our individual support for these freedoms are their most important defense. As Judge Learned Hand wrote, "Liberty lies in the hearts and minds of men and women; when it dies there, no constitution, no law, no court can save it."

Thought Questions

1. What do you think are the most important civil liberties you have as an American? What are the most important you have as a college student?
2. What accounts for the fact that not all of the Bill of Rights applies against state or other officials? Do you think it

should? How would you determine the due process rights of college students in disciplinary proceedings?

3. Do you think the courts should be allowed to use affirmative action to remedy the effects of discrimination? Should it be used simply to have a more diverse campus, corporation or society? Would you apply such preferences to women as well?

4. Would you have allowed flag burning if you were on the Supreme Court? After Congress passed the law outlawing flag burning, would you have struck it down? Would you have voted for the law if you were in Congress?

Suggested Readings

Alderman, Ellen, and Caroline Kennedy. *In Our Defense— The Bill of Rights in Action.* New York: Avon Books, 1991. Humanizes the Bill of Rights through dramatic cases. (Yes, that's President Kennedy's daughter, now a lawyer.)

Bovard, James. *Lost Rights.* New York: St. Martin's Griffin, 1995. Pb. An alarmist but entertaining critique of how "government officials are tearing the Bill of Rights to pieces."

Hentoff, Nat. *Free Speech for Me—But Not for Thee.* New York: Harper Perennial, 1993.Pb A blunt but good humored attack on the censors of both the Left and the Right.

Lewis, Anthony. *Make No Law.* New York: Vintage Books, 1991. A *New York Times* columnist reviews the *Sullivan* case—a classic challenge to free speech and his newspaper from the civil rights era.

Mezey, Susan. *In Pursuit of Equality: Women, Public Policy, and the Federal Courts.* New York: St. Martin's Press, 1992. A comprehensive review of civil rights laws and court cases involving women.

Sullivan, Andrew. *Virtually Normal: An Argument About Homosexuality.* New York: Alfred A. Knopf, 1995. A discussion by the former editor of *The New Republic* that homosexuals be treated as equal public citizens in matters from marriage to the military.

CHAPTER SEVEN

Voters and Political Parties

The government players and rules we've discussed are not a complete picture of the political game. Next is a look at some important players who were not established by the Constitution. In the following two chapters we will see how voters, political parties, interest groups, and the media influence American politics. A case study of a computerized get-out-the-vote effort will show how political parties can "create" voters to support their candidates. We will first look at voters—who they are, how they vote, and why many others don't. Then we will look at our embattled major political parties, how they link voters and government, and why many think they do it badly. The history, the functions, and the structures of the party system provide the bones of the story. Their political consequences for us provide the meat.

VOTERS

Who Votes?

The answer to "who votes?" may seem obvious. Citizens who are 18 or older (because of the Twenty-sixth Amendment) and who have satisfied the residency requirements of their states can vote, but an increasing number of them do not. In the 1992 presidential election only 54 percent of the voting-age population voted. This was the first significant increase in voting turnout since 1960. (See Figure 7.1.) Voting rates are even lower in nonpresidential elections. In 1994, only an estimated 39 percent of eligible voters turned up at the election booths. These 75 million voters actually were an improvement—a rise from the 35 percent who had voted in 1990.

The questions grow. What influences whether people become voters? What influences how they vote? And what has led to the great numbers of people who don't vote?

Figure 7.1   Voter Participation in Presidential Elections, 1880–1992.

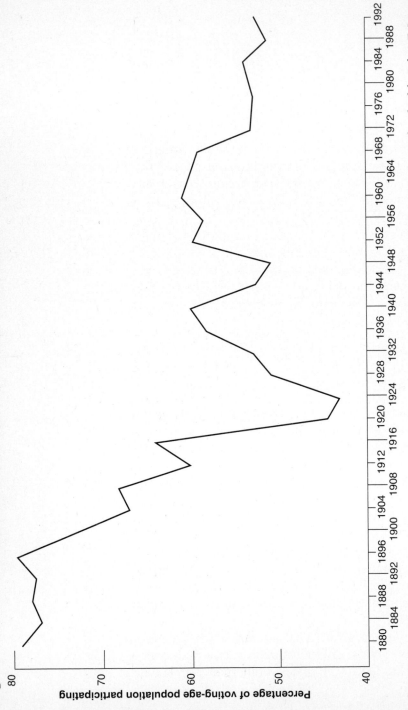

Sources: Figures for 1880 to 1916 reprinted with permission of The Free Press, a division of Macmillan Publishing, Inc., from *Political Life* by Robert E. Lane. Copyright © 1959 by The Free Press. Figures for 1920 to 1948 in U.S. Bureau of the Census, *Statistical Abstract of the United States 1969,* p. 368. Data for 1952 to 1972 in U.S. Bureau of the Census, "Population Estimates and Projections," *Current Population Reports,* Serries P-25, No. 626 (May 1976), p. 11. Later data in *Congressional Quarterly Weekly Report,* April 13, 1985 and *Congressional Quarterly Weekly Report,* November 7, 1992, p. 3553.

Political Socialization

Political socialization provides part of an answer. It helps explain how, or if, people participate in politics. *Political socialization is the process of learning political attitudes and behavior.* The gradual process of socialization takes place as we grow up, in settings like the family and the schools. In the home, children learn about participating in family decisions—for example, the more noise they make, the better chance they have of staying up late. Kids also learn which party their parents favor, how they generally view politics and politicians, and what their basic values and outlook toward their country are. Children, of course, don't always copy their parents' political leanings, but they are influenced by them. Most people stay with the party of their parents. Schools have a similar effect. Students salute the flag, obey their teacher, take civics courses, participate in student politics, and learn that democracy (us) is good and dictatorship (them) is bad.

People's social characteristics also influence their participation in politics. Although it is difficult to weigh how important they are for each individual, whether a person is young or old, black or white, rich or poor, northerner or southerner will affect his or her political opinions and behavior. The views of a person's peer group (friends and neighbors), of political authorities ("The president knows what he's doing"), and of one's political party influence how people vote as well. The influence of religion and ethnic background can be seen in most large cities where parties in the past ran "balanced tickets" with Irish, Italian, and Jewish candidates—and, more recently, blacks, Hispanics, and women as well. Besides the well-known tendency for people to vote for "one of their own," they also share certain political attitudes. Catholics tend to vote Democratic more often than do Protestants. Blacks and Jews are generally supportive of social programs. On specific issues religion may also play a role: Many Catholics back aid to parochial schools, many Jews support arms for Israel, and many fundamentalist Protestants favor prayer in the schools.

Class and Voting

Class may be just as important in shaping people's political opinions and behaviors. The term *social class* refers
to a *group's occupation and income, and the awareness it produces of their relations to other groups or
classes in the society.* In general we can speak of three
broad overlapping categories: a working class, a middle
class, and an upper class. The *working class,* which
almost always includes the majority of people in a
society, receives the lowest incomes and fills "blue-
collar" jobs in factories and farms, as well as "white-
collar" positions like clerical and secretarial jobs in
offices. The *middle class* consists of most professionals
(like teachers and engineers), small businesspeople,
bureaucrats, and some skilled workers (say, those earning more than $30,000 a year). The *upper class* (often
called the elite or ruling class) is composed of those who
run our major economic and political institutions and
receive the highest incomes for doing so.

At least as important as these "objective" categories
that political scientists use is the "subjective" way in
which people in these classes view their own position.
Whether union members or teachers or housewives see
themselves as members of the working class or the middle class will also influence their political attitudes. An
important fact about class in the United States is that
class identification is quite weak. People either don't
know what class they are in or don't think it's important.
Most Americans see themselves as members of the
middle class no matter what "objective" class they may
be put into.

Class as reflected in income and occupation, however, does influence people's attitudes on a variety of issues. Studies have shown that people in the working
class tend to be liberal in wanting greater economic
equality and more social welfare programs. This liberal-
ism on economic issues contrasts strongly with their
ideas on civil liberties. Here, people of lower income
and education tend to be intolerant of dissenters and
not supportive of protection for minority views or new
styles of behavior (such as homosexual rights). Members of the middle class tend to be more conservative in

their economic views and more liberal on issues such as free speech and respect for civil rights. Class attitudes on political questions, then, tend to be both liberal and conservative depending on the type of issue.

Government policies and economic growth may also affect different classes differently. In the prosperous decade of the 1980s under a conservative administration, the average wages earned by those in the under $20,000 income category rose $123—from $8,528 to $8,651. That was an increase of 1.4 percent. The average salaries of people with incomes of more than $1 million rose $255,088—from $515,499 to $770,587—an increase of 49.5 percent. That, it should be stressed, was their increase in wages and salaries alone.

The problem with figuring out how these various characteristics—race, class, religion—influence a person's political behavior is that so many of them overlap. If we say that blacks are more likely not to vote than whites, are we sure that race is the key category? We also know that poorer people, those with less education, and those who feel they have less effect on their government also are less likely to vote. All these categories include the majority of blacks. But we don't yet know which is more important in influencing behavior, and so even the "true" statement that blacks vote less may conceal as much as it reveals. We would also have to examine whether blacks with more income or education also vote less—which they don't. We might then conclude that race is not as important in voter turnout as, say, class.

WHO DOESN'T VOTE?

> *Pollster:* Do you think people don't vote because of ignorance or apathy?
> *Respondent:* I don't know and I don't care.

The difficulty of answering the question of why people don't vote ought to be clear. As the charts indicate turnout varies depending on age, sex, education, and income, and it changes over time. (See Figure 7.2) Studies have shown that nonvoters are most often from the less-educated, nonwhite, rural, southern, poor,

Figure 7.2 Presidential Voting by Education, Income, Race, Gender, Age 1952–92.

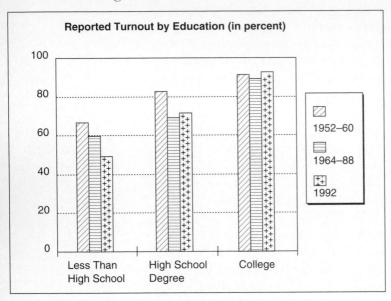

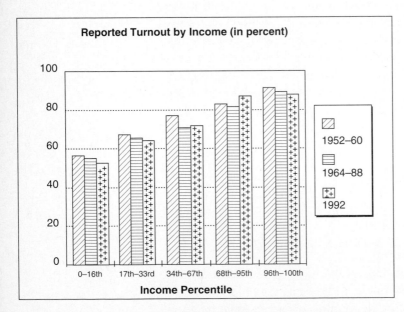

In 1992 dollars: 0–16th: $0–$9,999, 17th–33rd: $10,000–$19,999, 34th–67th: $20,000–$39,999, 68th–95th: $40,000–$89,999, 96th–100th: $90,000+

Source: Sorauf and Beck, *Party Politics in America*, p. 78. Compiled by Mike Toppa.

Figure 7.2 continued

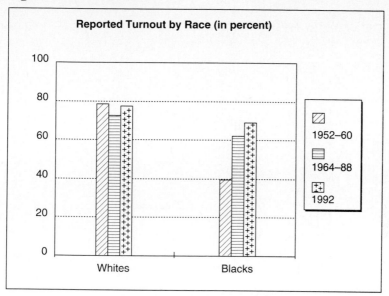

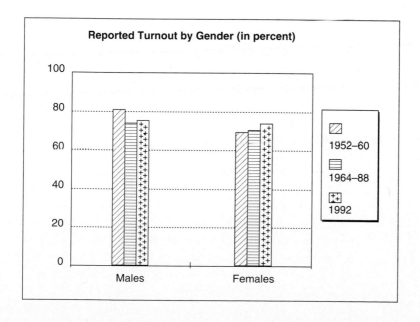

Figure 7.2 continued

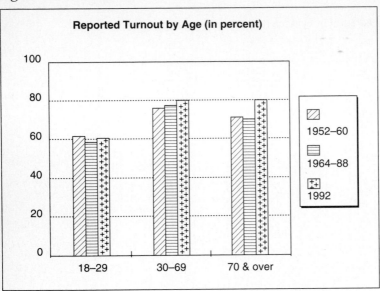

blue-collar, and very old or very young segments of the American population. Voters most often come from the white, middle-aged, college-educated, urban or suburban, affluent, white-collar groups. These are only broad tendencies, with a great many exceptions in each case. One result of these tendencies is that although more Americans are registered Democrats than Republicans, Republicans tend to vote in higher percentages, thus lessening their disadvantage.

There are other things, gathered from various opinion polls, of which we are sure: First, Americans are poorly informed about politics. Surveys show that less than half the voters know the name of their representative in Congress and only about one-fifth know how he or she has voted on any major bills. There is no doubt that the less income you have, the less likely you are to vote or participate in politics. One study found that in a recent presidential election 68 percent of low-income people reported no activity (such as attending a meeting or wearing a campaign button). Only 36 percent of those identifying themselves as "upper middle class" said they had done nothing. Those earning over $75,000 a year accounted for nearly half the number of campaign contributions, while those earning less than $15,000 accounted for less than 3 percent.

Voters are a more elite group than the population as a whole. The 1994 elections, which saw a sharp turn toward conservatives, also showed a drop in voting by low-income Americans with a rise in turnout by wealthier voters. Voting by people who make between $5,000 and $10,000 a year fell from 31 percent to 23 percent, while turnout of those making over $50,000 went from 59 percent to 60 percent. Overall, people in the top income groups made up 23 percent of all voters, up from 18 percent four years earlier. This may have reflected both blue collar indifference toward the Clinton administration as well as anger by wealthier groups at Democratic policies.

Class differences in voting reflect other class differences like economic security. Low-income people who face immediate problems like finding a job or paying bills will likely view politics as a luxury they can't afford. Class differences in political socialization also have an effect. Children of working-class parents, whether because of their more rigidly structured families or because of poor education, are brought up to believe that they can have little influence on politics ("You can't fight City Hall"). At the same time, because of the disadvantaged reality they and their parents face, they tend to have a not-so-favorable image of political leaders. These children, then, end up being both more resentful and more passive toward politics. Middle- and upper-class children have a higher regard for political leaders and are taught in their schools to value participation in politics. They are encouraged to participate and are led to believe that the political system will respond favorably to their participation. Of course, political leaders may in fact be more likely to listen to people with a similar background and education as they have— upper middle class.

Electoral barriers to voting in America also play a role in lower turnout. State registration laws—some requiring 50 days residency and periodic registration— make voting inconvenient. Election day is not a holiday here as it is in many European countries where the law requires that workers have time off to vote.

Until recently the U.S. government stood virtually alone in not taking any responsibility for helping citizens cope with voter registration. The so-called *Motor Voter* legislation made registration easier by allowing voters to register when they got drivers' licenses. It was vetoed by President Bush who believed that Democrats benefit from a large voter turnout. In May 1993 with a new Democratic president urging them on, Congress passed the law over a Republican filibuster. Its first year in operation resulted in an unprecedented large number of new registrants, triple the number as the year before. Over 5 million new voters registered in the first eight months of the law, with some experts predicting that, if this surge kept up, by the turn of the century four of every five adults would be registered, compared with three out of five now. While there is no guarantee that this increase in registration would result in people actually voting in higher numbers, there is a good chance of this happening.

Almost one-third of eligible voters remain unregistered. Two out of three of these unregistered voters live in households with incomes below the median. However, once people are registered, they vote. More than 80 percent of those registered will vote in presidential elections. Consequently, while voter turnout in the United States is practically the worst among the world's democracies, turnout for registered voters in the United States is about the same as in other countries.

Ask any first-year American government class why they think so many Americans do not vote, and their answer will be similar to the following: "They don't think it will make any difference." In this case at least, common sense about nonvoters is backed by political studies. This is a lack of *political efficacy*—a lowered sense that the government will respond to the needs of the voter.

The "makes no difference" reason can also result from the fact that some people have not been socialized to political efficacy. Therefore, they do not consider politics relevant to their lives, or do not identify with a political party, or do not understand how the system works, or do not believe it will respond, or some combination of these. Of course, the belief that government will not respond is not merely a result of faulty socialization. Government may *not* be responsive to people's needs. After scandals, inflation, recession, and huge deficits, newspaper headlines stressing government gone amok reinforce this view. Even the system of voting may hinder government responsiveness. Political parties that assume that poor people will not vote because of a difficult registration system or their own apathy are unlikely to champion their causes. Parties adapt their positions to the narrowed electorate, and then reinforce the barriers to voting by ignoring the needs of the people beyond them.

Ironically, the idea of equality that prevails in the American political game may actually reduce participation by lower-income people. This myth of a "classless society" leads to class being downplayed as a basis for participating in, or even understanding, politics. The United States is the only developed democracy without a Socialist or Labor party to represent and organize the working class. As we will see later in the chapter, the two-party system that does exist tends to push both parties toward moderate policies in seeking support.

The activists and candidates who mobilize people to vote will, for reasons of effectiveness, target the educated, wealthy, or informed groups most likely to respond positively to their appeal. This further encourages middle class participation while overlooking lower class non-voters. The lower class, living in a society not recognizing class differences and not providing organizations to voice its interests, sees its issues ignored and is not encouraged to participate politically. Of course, the less that low-income groups participate, the less they will find the political process responding to their interests, in a vicious circle.

The successful efforts of the Reverend Jesse Jackson to register blacks around his presidential races shows a way out of this dilemma. Reverend Jackson was able to unify and mobilize blacks in Democratic primaries in 1984 and 1988. Although he did not win the Democratic nomination, he could present himself as representing the black electorate and bargain with party leaders on issues of concern to his voters. Because these leaders needed black support, they tended to listen. The new voters Jackson registered helped elect other candidates sympathetic to the needs of low-income people. At a local level, black mayors, labor unions, and Hispanic leaders have all succeeded in bringing increasing numbers of low-income groups to the polls—and thereby winning elections.

These explanations for nonvoting tend to focus on the *individual*—apathetic or uneducated, or the *system*—the difficulties of registering or class biases. But the low political participation that exists may, of course, only be a symptom of a deeper dissatisfaction with the policies and programs provided by elected officials. The problem is that when a widespread distaste for politics leads to apathy little is likely to happen—the status quo is reinforced. But if people do vote, change can be dramatic.

The vote remains a remarkably effective weapon for changing leaders and policies. Take the 1994 elections. Despite a low turnout, these congressional elections drastically changed government's direction. They produced Republican majorities in both houses pledged to specific policy promises. The result, in short order, was a rightward turn in domestic programs including welfare reform, deficit reduction, and Medicare restructuring. Whatever we may think of the results, one thing is clear: Government responded to the vote.

POLITICAL PARTIES

Political parties, more than any other institution, organize voters to shape the government through elections. How have they historically developed? How are they structured? How do they use political power? How well are they presently doing? These are the questions for the rest of the chapter.

The national government, as we have seen, is based on a system of dividing or *decentralizing* power. Political parties, on the other hand, are a method of organizing or *centralizing* power. The framers of the Constitution decentralized power in separate branches and a federal system partly to avoid the development of powerful factions that could take over the government. This decentralization of power, however, created the need for parties that could pull together or centralize that power.

A *political party* is an organization that runs candidates for public office under the party's name. Although the framers seemed more concerned with factions and interests than with parties, they were well aware of the possibility that parties would soon develop. George Washington, in his famous farewell address, warned against "the baneful effects of the spirit of party." Despite his advice, parties began.

Origin of Today's Parties

The *Federalists* and *Anti-Federalists,* the groups that supported and opposed the adoption of the Constitution, were not organized into actual political parties. They did not run candidates for office under party labels, but they were networks of communication and political activity struggling on opposite sides of a great dispute—ratification. Although most of the Founding Fathers preached against political parties, they found them necessary almost as soon as the national government was operating.

After the Constitution was ratified, the Federalist faction grew stronger and more like a political party. Led by Alexander Hamilton, secretary of the treasury under President Washington, the Federalists championed a strong national government that would promote the financial interests of merchants and manufacturers. After Thomas Jefferson left Washington's cabinet in 1793, an opposition party began to form under his leadership. The new *Democratic-Republican* party drew the support of small farmers, debtors, and others who did not benefit from the financial programs of the Federalists. Under the Democratic-Republican label, Jefferson won the presidential election of 1800, and his party continued to control the presidency until 1828. The Federalists, without power or popular support, gradually died out.

At the end of this 28-year period of Democratic-Republican control, the party splintered into many factions. Two of these factions grew into new parties, the *Democrats* and the *Whigs* (first called the National Republicans). Thus the Democratic party, founded in

1828, is the oldest political party in the world. The early Democratic party was led by Andrew Jackson, who was elected president in 1828. It became known as the party of the common people. The Whigs, more like the old Federalists, were supported by the wealthier and more conservative groups in society: bankers, merchants, and big farmers.

In 1854, a *coalition* (a collection of interests that join together for a specific purpose) of Whigs, antislavery Democrats, and minor parties formed the *Republican party.* One of the common goals of the party supporters was to fight slavery. The Republicans nominated a "dark horse" (a political unknown), Abraham Lincoln, on the third ballot for president in 1860. The Democrats were so deeply divided over the slavery issue that the southern and northern wings of the party each nominated a candidate. Against this divided opposition, as well as a fourth candidate, Lincoln won the election in the electoral college with less than a majority of the popular vote, but more than any other candidate.

Maintaining, Deviating, and Realigning Elections

Following many elections it is common to hear predictions of the coming demise of the losing party. Still the Democratic and Republican parties have dominated American politics for the past 135 years. Their relative strength and the nature of their support, however, have shifted back and forth. We can see this shift by looking at three types of presidential elections: maintaining, deviating, and realigning elections. *Maintaining elections* keep party strength and support as they are. *Deviating elections* show a temporary shift in popular support for the parties, usually caused by the exceptional, popular appeal of a candidate of the minority party. *Realigning elections* show a permanent shift in the popular base of support of the parties, and usually a shift in the relative strength of the parties so that the minority party emerges as the majority party. The president who emerges from a realigning election, whether a Lincoln or a Franklin Roosevelt, has a fresh national coalition behind him frequently allowing him to change the course of the nation's history.

Most presidential elections between 1860 and 1932 were maintaining elections. The Republicans (often called the GOP, Grand Old Party) kept the support of a majority of voters, and controlled the executive branch, for all but 16 of those 72 years. When the Democrats did gain control of the presidency, they held office for only short periods. The two Democratic elections of Woodrow Wilson in 1912 and 1916, for example, were caused by temporary voter shifts, or deviations in party support, and splits within the Republican party.

The great social and economic impact of the Great Depression of the 1930s destroyed the Republicans' majority support, and contributed to a realignment in the two-party system. Under Franklin Delano Roosevelt, the Democrats became the majority party and were known as the party of labor, the poor, minorities, the cities, immigrants, eastern liberals, and the white South. This "New Deal Coalition" has existed down to the present and has withstood growing Republican voting strength in the South and West and among the suburban middle class. The question posed by recent elections is whether a Republican realignment similar to the Democratic one of 1932 is now taking place.

Beginning in 1968 and continuing through the two elections of Ronald Reagan in 1980 and 1984, and that of George Bush in 1988, a rolling Republican realignment seemed to be occuring. Prior to the 1992 elections conservative Republicans had been elected president in five of the last six elections, usually with an overwhelming electoral college vote. The southern and western states were consistently voting for Republican presidential nominees, the youth vote shifted to the Republicans, and polls of party identification showed almost as many Republicans as Democrats.

The 1992 election of Bill Clinton complicated things a bit. Not only did Democrats capture the presidency but they also added seats to their majorities in the House and Senate, and picked up strength by controlling a majority of state legislatures and governorships. Analysts in 1992 also had to account for a changeable electorate that

refused to identify with either party. *Dealignment* came
to be a common buzz word, reflecting a decaying loyalty
to both parties among voters. The emergence of Ross
Perot as a nonparty alternative in the presidential race
appeared to expose the weakness of the two major parties. The Texas billionaire used TV and millions of his
own advertising dollars in the closing days of the election
to appeal directly to voters. He avoided the party primary system and for a short time in early summer 1992
outpolled both the Democratic and Republican candidates. By winning nearly one of every five votes in 1992,
Perot may have created a model for other third-party
candidates in future presidential contests.

Predictors of realignment had to scramble again after the 1994 elections. Republican majorities swept into
power in the House and Senate and overnight there was
a newly elected majority of Republican governors. It
seemed clear that the South had changed parties. Since
1980 the South had consistently voted for Republican
presidential nominees. But 1994 marked the first time
in U.S. history that a majority of southerners voted Republican for Congress. More Republicans were elected
than Democrats and it was this shift in the South that
allowed the GOP to control the House. Newt Gingrich
could see this transformation in his own state of Georgia. Four years before he was the lone Republican in
his state's congressional delegation, facing nine House
Democrats and two Democratic senators. Two elections
later (after the census increased Georgia's seats) there
were eight Republicans and three Democrats in the
House delegation. All three Democrats were African
Americans from majority black districts created after
the 1990 census.

Whether this was the long-awaited Republican realignment was less clear. Some analysts saw this as the
end of the ruling New Deal Coalition, completing what
Ronald Reagan had begun. Others pointed to the lack
of strong party loyalties among independent voters
making any realignment between the parties unlikely. It
was also unusual to see this sort of a shift in a nonpresidential election, without a strong leader heading the
ticket. The beachhead that Republicans had made in

the South needed to be expanded nationally to qualify as a realignment. And that would depend on a changing, unpredictable electorate in 1996 and beyond.

Democrats Versus Republicans Versus Independents

What is the difference between the two major parties? The answer lies both in party image and reality. The image of the parties is usually based on a stereotype of people who support the parties. A "typical" Republican is white, middle class, and Protestant; has a college education; and with the rise of the "gender gap" in the 1980s and 90s is less often a woman. He or she supports big business, law and order, limited government intervention in the economy and in our private lives, a hard-line policy in foreign affairs, and refers to him/herself as a conservative. (See Table 7.1.)

The "typical" Democrat is a member of a minority ethnic or racial group, belongs to a labor union, and is a working class, non-Protestant, resident. He or she supports social welfare measures to help the poor

Table 7.1 How to Tell a Liberal from a Conservative

Here are some of the political beliefs likely to be preferred by liberals and conservatives.

	LIBERALS	CONSERVATIVES
On Social Policy:		
Abortion	Support "freedom of choice"	Support "right to life"
School prayer	Are opposed	Are supportive
Affirmative action	Favor	Oppose
On Economic Policy:		
Role of the government	View government as a regulator in the public interest	Favor free-market solutions
Taxes	Want to tax the rich more	Want to keep taxes low
Spending	Want to spend more on the poor	Want to keep spending low
On Crime:		
How to cut crime	Believe we should solve the problems that cause crime	Believe we should stop coddling criminals
Defendants' rights	Believe we should respect them	Believe we should stop letting criminals hide behind the law

at home, government regulation of big business, more equal distribution of wealth, and more liberal foreign policies, except perhaps in favoring trade restrictions to protect jobs.

Of course the reality is much more complex than the image. Leaders of the Democratic and Republican parties do disagree fairly consistently on major issues. In recent years, activists in both parties have gotten more ideological—Republicans more conservative, Democrats more liberal—and therefore the parties have appeared more polarized from each other. But party *followers* who are not actively involved with the party tend to be more moderate (or indifferent) than *leaders* on issues. Democratic and Republican party followers, in fact, often agree more with each other than with their party leaders.

Another complicating factor in party differences is that each party is deeply divided within itself. The Democratic party includes, for example, liberal, black, urban, working-class supporters from the northern industrial cities, and conservative, white, wealthy farmers from the West. The GOP includes moderate business or professional people from the East, and small-town religious fundamentalists or conservative farmers from the South and Midwest. There has been a rise in split-ticket voting where voters favor candidates of another party but retain their party ties. In recent presidential elections many conservative working-class Democrats voted for the Republican nominees on a national level, while supporting their party's candidates for state and local offices. In 1988 more than half of the House Democrats won in districts that were carried by George Bush. And in 1992 Bill Clinton won his three-man race with only 43 percent of the vote, considerably less than a majority.

The decline in partisanship has been reflected in the increase of voters identifying with no political party. By the 1992 presidential election, 38 percent of voters claimed they were political *independents,* as opposed to 21 percent in 1962. Additionally, the number of people who strongly support either party has declined. Political scientists have developed two competing explanations for this change. The first is that voters have simply be-

come less attached to political parties. This has occurred for several reasons: Voters now rely on the media
rather than parties for political information, the rise of
candidate-centered campaigns has decreased the role of
parties in elections, and divisive political events like the
Vietnam War and Watergate turned people off to all political institutions, including parties. Therefore, this decline in partisanship has led to the rise of "issue voting,"
with voters becoming more "volatile." They are more
prone to swing from one party's candidate to the other,
more responsive to personality and issue appeals, and
less predictable.

The second explanation says that there is a "myth of
the independent voter." Since the mid-1960s the increase in independents has been from upper-income
and younger voters, who are as informed and active as
other voters. Further, this rise may be neither real nor
significant. Part of this increase in independents may
come from the attractiveness of labeling oneself an "independent" when pollsters ask for a party identity. Most
significant to this argument is that the majority of today's independents "lean" towards one of the parties.
When it comes time to vote, they act just like people
who identify with a party. An independent who "leans"
Democratic votes Democratic, about as much as someone who claims to be a Democrat. Despite many per-
ceived changes in voting behavior, party identification is
still the single best predictor of how a person votes in a
general election.

Although the debate between these two views has
not ended, the 1992 independent presidential campaign
of Ross Perot indicated that party ties had weakened
and that there existed a substantial bloc of voters who
would support an independent candidate. Perot's 19
percent of the popular vote was the highest third-party
vote since former president Theodore Roosevelt got 27
percent as the Bull Moose candidate in 1912. A majority of voters said that they would like to see an independent run in 1996. Both the election year polls and the
number of candidates from outside the party main-
streams indicated that for a large body of opinion the
two major parties no longer were the only alternatives.

Party Functions

What do political parties do? Political parties throughout the world organize power in order to control the
government. To do so, American political parties (1)
contest elections, (2) organize public opinion, (3) put
together *coalitions* of different interests, and (4) incorporate policy changes proposed by groups and individuals outside the party system and the government.

First, parties *contest elections.* They organize voters
in order to compete with other parties for elected offices. To contest elections, parties—or, more commonly,
their candidates—*recruit* people into the political system to work on campaigns. Parties provide people with
a basis for making political choices. As mentioned, most
people vote for a candidate because of the party he or
she belongs to. (The other major motive behind a
voter's choice is whether to favor or oppose the incumbent.) In addition, when parties contest elections, they
express policy positions on important issues. To some
extent this function of the parties serves to *educate* voters about the political process. Most people are not or-
dinarily involved in politics. They often rely on elections
to keep them informed and active.

Second, parties *organize public opinion.* Despite
the wide variety of opinion within them, parties give the
public a limited channel of communication to express
their desires about how government should operate. At
the least, voters can approve the actions of the party
that has been holding office by voting for it. Or they can
disapprove by voting for the opposition.

Third, the two major parties put together coalitions
or *aggregate various interests.* The Democratic and
Republican parties organize different regions, ethnic
groups, and economic interests into large coalitions for
the purpose of winning elections. Gathering special interests under the broad "umbrella" of a party label is an
important function of American political parties. When
elected, candidates then have the widespread national
support needed to govern.

Finally, the two major parties *incorporate changes*
or reforms proposed by third parties or social protest
movements. If third parties or political movements

show that they have considerable support, their programs are often adopted, though usually in more moderate form, by one of the major parties. President
Clinton's emphasis on deficit reduction reflected Ross
Perot's position and was undoubtedly aimed to appeal
to his supporters.

VIEW FROM THE INSIDE: PARTY ORGANIZATIONS

American parties are weak organizations. Traditionally,
there have been few ties knitting various local party organizations together and fewer still binding them into a
coherent national organization. But powerless parties
have not always been the rule in this country, and it's a
rule that may be changing now.

Machines—Old and Modern

Particularly in the last half of the nineteenth century,
American parties at the local level were so tightly organized that they were often called *political machines.*
Party machines have a party *boss* (leader) who directly
controls the political party workers at lower (usually city
district or ward) levels. Local leaders obey the boss because he controls party nominations, patronage positions (jobs that can be given to loyal supporters), political favors, and party finances. While often an effective
instrument for managing a city government and assuring immigrants a political network to respond to their
needs, machines had a well-deserved reputation for
corruption. Until his death in 1976, Richard Daley,
mayor of Chicago for more than 20 years, kept firm
control of a strong Democratic party machine. Daley's
machine acted as an informal government and social
service agency, meeting the immediate needs of urban
citizens. Chicago's political machine has declined in recent years and this type of party organization, in general, seems to be a leftover from the past. (See "Machine Politics.")

Political machines lost much of their leverage early
in the twentieth century when three things happened:
(1) local, state, and federal agencies took over distribut-

Machine Politics

During Richard Daley Senior's long reign as mayor of Chicago and boss of the "Machine," he was seldom seriously challenged in an election. One who did run against him was a lawyer named Benjamin Adamowski. Mike Royko, a Chicago columnist, illustrates why he and other Daley opponents didn't get very far.

The owner of a small restaurant at Division and Ashland, the heart of the city's Polish neighborhood, put up a big Adamowski sign. The day it went up the precinct captain came around and said, "How come the sign, Harry?" "Ben's a friend of mine," the restaurant owner said. "Ben's a nice guy, Harry, but that's a pretty big sign. I'd appreci-ate it if you'd take it down." "No, it's staying up."

The next day the captain came back. "Look, I'm the precinct captain. Is there anything wrong, any problem, anything I can help you with?" Harry said no. "Then why don't you take it down. You know how this looks in my job." Harry wouldn't budge. The sign stayed up. On the third day, the city building inspectors came. The plumbing improvements alone cost Harry $2,100.

Source: From *Boss: Richard J. Daley of Chicago* by Mike Royko. Copyright © 1971 by Mike Royko. Used by permission of Sutton Signet, an imprint of New American Library, a division of Penguin Books USA Inc.

---

ing benefits to the poor; (2) civil service reforms made most city jobs dependent on results of competitive examinations; and (3) direct primaries made competition for party nomination a contest anyone could enter and win.

Using the new technologies of fundraising and direct mail campaigns, issue-oriented modern machines have appeared. One from the Democratic party is the Los Angeles–based machine named after its founders Congressmen Howard L. Berman and Henry A. Waxman. The *Berman-Waxman machine* differs from the traditional machine in several ways. It is informal, centered on candidates (rather than the party); it uses communications media (rather than local politicians); and it concentrates on influencing national and state issues (rather than solely local politics). The machine uses money from the entertainment industry in Hollywood to elect allies to Congress and to state offices. This modern machine based on ideology and technology, may not have any more of a future than older machines based on ethnicity and patronage. With term limits on a state level in California restraining their allies from running again for state offices, plus disarray within the Democratic party after the 1994 Republican victories, local reporters spoke of the "demise" of Berman-Waxman.

The Clinton White House was frequently accused of using their young campaign staff to form a modern political machine. Often labeled a "permanent campaign" (the same charge was levelled at President Reagan's public relations operatives) many of the media advisers and organizers who shaped his march to the presidency found jobs in the Democratic National Committee. But now they pushed for Clinton's deficit reduction and healthcare reform packages and, later, for his reelection. Direct mail, phone banks, message control, and voter targeting were just some of the techniques transferred from election campaigning to gathering grassroots support for the president.

American Party Structure

Picture the American party structure as a pyramid. Local political organizations or clubs are at the bottom; county committees are above them; and state committees are above the county. (See Figure 7.3.) The national committee of each party is over them all with the national conventions the ultimate elected authority. The strength of the party, which had traditionally been at the bottom, has now gravitated toward the top.

As a result of the welfare, civil service, and primary reforms, most local party organizations have few resources with which to maintain a strong organization. Local parties range from virtual disorganization to still-powerful machines, with most parties falling closer to the pole of disorganization. In much of America, a handful of officials meet occasionally to carry out the essential affairs needed to keep the party going. The party revives only around elections to support a candidate who was generally selected by his or her own efforts.

What do the party's officers do in nonelection years? Their duties primarily depend upon whether

Figure 7.3   Typical State Party Organization

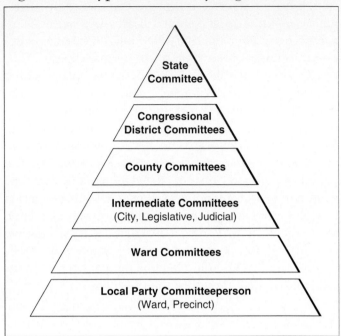

they are the *in-party* or the *out-party*. The basic job of out-party officials is to show that the party is still alive. They may have booths at fairs, issue press releases criticizing public officials of the other party, and conduct voter registration drives. But all political activity takes money, which out-parties have difficulty raising. Systems for collecting regular contributions have been only modestly successful. State parties typically sponsor "Jefferson-Jackson Day" dinners (Democrats) or "Lincoln Day" dinners (Republicans). The success of these dinners is limited without the "clout" of a party member in a powerful public office.

One would guess that the in-party—the party with more of its own members in important government positions—has more power than the out-party. This isn't necessarily so. It is the public official, rather than the party, who actually exercises the power of the office. The government official uses the party organization, rather than vice versa. For example, a governor usually names the state party chairperson, who generally serves as a voice of the governor. The national Democratic party clearly became an instrument for promoting President Clinton's policies after the 1992 election.

State parties are generally stronger than local parties because of their connection to the national party. They usually have a professional staff of several people hired as a result of funds supplied by the national party. Like the national structure, there is a state committee and a chairperson, all chosen by election or state convention. The committee's ability to select party nominees for state or national offices is severely limited by primaries. The state party frequently channels funds from the wealthy campaigns of incumbents to those of new, promising candidates, thus building party loyalty. Patronage, ranging from placing a traffic light to awarding a building contract, helps grease the wheels of state party activities.

National Party Organization

Traditionally the local party was the most effective link to the voter. Volunteers in the community would turn out the vote and deliver needed services (like that traffic light) to the party supporters. However, in recent years, the increased reliance on modern campaign technology (such as direct mail and media ads) has overshadowed the use of local volunteers to reach voters. It has also centralized party functions in professionals in the national organization and in outside consultants.

Each party is officially governed by its *national committee*. The national committee consists of representatives chosen from each state party organization and various other party groups. The committee is led by the *chairperson*, who is often chosen by the party's presidential nominee every four years. Under these authorities are the party's *professional staff*. These professionals have gained power through their understanding of the modern technology of campaigning and the complicated laws that affect how money is raised and spent. The Republican staff is much larger than the Democratic staff because the Democrats contract out much of their work, such as direct mail fundraising, to campaign consultants. The Republicans have also taken the lead in strengthening their national party.

In fundraising and organization the Republicans lead the Democrats, though the gap has narrowed. In the 1993–1994 election cycle, the Republican party raised $245.6 million for its candidates at the national, state and local level, while the Democratic party raised $139.1 million. Republican candidates thus had a five-to-three advantage over Democrats in financial support from their party. This is a decrease from the four-to-one ($255 million–$65 million) bulge the GOP enjoyed in the 1985–1986 election cycle. However, the Republican party remained the single most important source of money in American politics. (See "Al The Pal.")

These funds were used to support the party's candidates and buy expensive campaign technology. The large amounts of money the Republicans have given to their candidates tended to concentrate power in the national organization and produced a great deal of loyalty in party members' votes in Congress. Besides increasing party discipline, the funds were spent on sophisticated media and computerized mail campaigns to reach and register Republican voters. (See Case Study: High-Tech

Al the Pal

Time Magazine described New York Senator Al D'Amato as "the reigning king of Washington's money game." His fundraising clout comes from three positions he holds: chairman of the Senate Banking Committee, head of Senator Dole's presidential steering committee, and chief of the Republican organization that raises money for Senate candidates. Always close to the bankers of Wall Street, D'Amato has used these ties to raise money for Senate candidates and for Bob Dole. His aggressive energy led Dole to call him, "the man who won't take yes for an answer."

D'Amato has been described as the model for a new generation of in-your-face congressional fund raisers. His staff has been accused of requesting contributions from lobbyists with legislation before his committee. Ironically this may at times work against the very interests giving money. For example, the Senator introduced a bill, backed by Wall Street, to deregulate banks allowing them to merge with securities firms. It never came to a vote the year it was introduced. Some lobbyists believed that deregulation was too powerful a motivator for contributing money for D'Amato to allow the bill to pass too soon. Said one, "Al wants to milk it."

Source: Time Magazine, September 11, 1995,

Voting.) Although, until recently, the Democrats have been the majority party, the Republicans have the advantage in money and technology. The power of both national committees is likely to increase as the formerly weak parties strengthen their central organizations.

The National Convention

Most of the public attention the party receives comes at the *national convention.* Held during the summer before the presidential campaign, the national convention is attended by delegates chosen by the state parties in various ways. In 1996 the Republican convention had 2,210 delegates, and the Democratic convention had 4,303. The delegates to the convention adopt a party platform, elect the party's presidential nominee and act as the national party's supreme governing body assembled every four years.

The *party platform* is actually written by a Platform Committee and then approved by the convention. It is generally a long document that states the party's—and its presidential candidate's—views on many issues. If the party is in power, the platform will boast of the party's achievements. If the party is out of power, the platform will criticize the policies of the other party. The platform will emphasize the party's differences with the other major party and minimize the divisions within the party.

Frequently, groups of convention delegates will organize into factions in order to press for statements representing their minority political views to be included in the platform. In 1992 a minority group of women at the Republican national convention pressed unsuccessfully for *planks* (parts of the platform) supporting abortion rights. Platforms are important in reconciling groups within the party before the election. Party platforms are also surprisingly accurate in predicting what a president will actually try to do when in office.

In the early 1970s party reforms, especially among Democrats, led to greater popular participation in the nominating process. Up until these reforms about 40 percent of convention delegates were chosen by *primaries*—elections usually limited to registered voters from that one party; with the rest chosen by *caucuses*—party meetings dominated by party leaders. Since then 70 percent have been chosen directly by voters in primary elections.

But something happened. Critics like Thomas E. Patterson have charged that these reforms made the news media central to election campaigns. The candidates now play to the press. The media coverage emphasizes elections as horse races (who's up, who's down) and stresses disputes that make attractive news headlines (for example, Clinton's womanizing). The media focuses on conflicts and negatives about politics, while neglecting issues. It does not promote coherent choices on how the nation will be governed or help build coalitions of groups the candidates will need once in office. The party has lost its role of making political choices. The results: sensationalized elections and alienated voters.

The names of the candidates for president are placed in nomination toward the end of the convention. A roll-call vote of the delegates is then taken. The final party nominee for the office of president is elected by a simple majority vote. In 1924, the Democratic convention took 103 ballots before it was able to reach a majority decision. In recent decades the presidential nominee has been chosen on the first ballot, reflecting the votes in the state primaries and caucuses. Conventions today can be accurately described as *approving* or *ratifying* the candidate selected by the party voters. The delegates, who are usually pledged to a candidate, don't actually make the choice themselves.

The presidential nominee chooses a vice presidential running mate who is then formally approved by the convention. Usually a main goal is to *"balance the ticket."* Michael Dukakis, a liberal New England governor, in 1988 chose Lloyd Bentsen, a Texas conservative with long Washington experience to be the Democratic vice presidential nominee. At times the vice presidential nominee may be a well-known competitor of the presidential nominee, as was George Bush when Ronald Reagan chose him in 1980. Bush's choice of Dan Quayle, while it befuddled many, was clearly an attempt to calm his party's right wing.

Bill Clinton's 1992 choice of Senator Al Gore from the neighboring state of Tennessee was unusual in putting two southerners on the Democratic ticket, but it reinforced the campaign's message of youth and change.

The national convention is the starting point of the fall presidential campaign. Party workers and supporters, boosted by free prime-time television coverage of at least some of the convention proceedings, set out to make their party's nominee the winner of the presidential election in November. (See "Are Conventions Really TV Miniseries?")

VIEW FROM THE OUTSIDE: THE TWO-PARTY SYSTEM

Despite the current popularity for a third political party, the United States retains a *two-party system,* meaning that two parties dominate national politics. In a *one-party system,* a single party monopolizes the organization of power and the positions of authority. In a *multi-*

Are Conventions Really TV Miniseries?

Don Hewitt, executive producer of CBS's "60 Minutes," made the following remarks about political conventions:

There is no doubt whose convention this really is. The politicians meeting there are now extras in our television show. . . .

In the old days, before the primaries took the steam out of political conventions, you could watch a good credentials fight or a good platform fight—even though a week later no one could remember what they were fighting about. Today, if you want to see a good fight at a political convention, let CBS News's sign be an inch bigger than

NBC's. Now you'll see a fight at a convention. All hell breaks loose.

It's time we gave the politicians back their convention. Tell them it's nothing but a big commercial and that it's not Rather, Brokaw, or Jennings' job to be the emcee of their commercial.

Author's Note: By 1992 audience ratings for the conventions were down almost 20 percent and the networks dropped their weekly coverage from 34 hours in 1988 to 16 hours. So maybe TV is giving the parties their conventions back.

Source: Paul Allen Beck and Frank J. Sorauf *Party Politics in America,* 7th ed. New York: HarperCollins, 1992, p 301.

party system, more than two political parties compete
for power and electoral offices.

From the Civil War until at least the election of
Dwight D. Eisenhower to the presidency in 1952, the
eleven southern states of the Civil War Confederacy
had virtually one-party systems. These states were so
heavily Democratic that the Republicans were a permanent minority. The important electoral contests took
place in the primaries, where blacks were excluded, and
where factions within the party often competed like
separate parties. Multiparty systems have also existed in
the United States. New York State has a four-party system today in which Democrats, Republicans, Liberals,
and Conservatives compete in state and local elections.
Nationally, however, the United States has a two-party
system.

Causes of the Two-Party System

There are four main reasons for the continued dominance of two parties in America. The first is the *historic
dualism* of American political conflict. The first major
political division among Americans was dual, or two-
sided, between Federalists and Anti-Federalists. It is
said that this original two-sided political battle established the tradition of two-party domination in this
country.

The second reason is the *moderate views of the
American voter.* Unlike European democracies, where
radical political parties such as the Communists have legitimacy, American politics tends more toward the center. Americans may be moderate because their political
party system forces them to choose between two moderate parties, or American parties may be moderate because Americans do not want to make more extreme
political choices. As with the chicken and the egg, it's
tough to know which came first.

Third, the *structure of our electoral system* encourages two-party dominance. We elect one representative
at a time from each district to Congress, which is called
election by *single-member districts.* The winning candidate is the one who gets the most votes, or a *plurality.*
(A majority of votes means more than 50 percent of the

votes cast; a plurality simply means more votes than anyone else.) Similarly, in presidential elections, the party with a plurality in a state gets all the electoral votes of that state. This system makes it difficult for minor-party candidates to win elections, and without election victories parties tend to fade fast.

Many countries with multiparty systems elect representatives by *proportional representation.* That is, each district has more than one representative, and each party that receives a certain number of votes gets to send a proportionate number of representatives to the legislature. For example, in a single-member district a minor party that received 10 percent of the vote would not be able to send its candidate to Congress. In a multimember district the size of ten congressional districts, however, that 10 percent of the vote would mean that one out of ten representatives sent from the district would be a minor-party member.

Finally, the Democratic and Republican parties continue to dominate national politics because they are flexible enough to *adopt some of the programs proposed by third parties,* and thus win over third-party supporters. The Socialist party in America, even during its strongest period, always had difficulty achieving national support partly because the Democratic party was able to *co-opt,* or win over, the support of most of organized labor with pro-labor economic programs. The Republican party lured voters away from Alabama Governor George Wallace's American Independent Party (AIP) by emphasizing law and order and de-emphasizing civil rights in its 1968 presidential campaign. Already mentioned is how much like Ross Perot the major parties began to sound after 1992.

The End of the Two-Party System?

For all these historical and structural reasons the odds are against either the emergence of a stable third party or an independent candidate being elected president. Operating as an "umbrella" over the broad moderate center, the two-party system has prevented the country from being *polarized,* or severely divided, by keeping radical factions from winning power. This meant that

dissenting opinions traditionally got little consideration from voters. It kept the parties from taking extreme positions and led them to avoid controversial issues. It also meant that there was little room for third parties, except at the fringe.

And yet. . . . So far the 1990s has reinforced the weakness of the two political parties. Democrats saw a record number of their senators retire after the 1994 elections. Democratic officials in the South became Republican, while new minority-dominated congressional districts helped end the careers of conservative Democrats. Most importantly the party's core ideology—that government could be an effective instrument to improve the lives of working people—was rejected by voters who worried more about government's deficits and failed efforts to eradicate crime and poverty.

While Republicans immediately benefited from Democratic flaws, they too faced similar dilemmas. The growing cynicism of "sound-bite politics," the drift to the right by GOP leadership groups, the gutting of popular social programs like Medicare, and the visible dominance by business lobbyists over the conservative congress led to questions of whether their new majority would hold. The two parties faced the danger of being polarized by their internal wings. From the Republican Right and the Democratic Left both parties were pressured to take stands with little broad popularity and that hindered them from reaching out to voters in the center.

This restless center of middle-class voters appeared increasingly up for grabs. Ross Perot continued to tap into alienated voters. Other potential candidates, like Bill Bradley and Colin Powell, hinted (at times) that they might in the future seek to run as independents for the White House. Their reasons were not hard to find. Polls showed 62 percent of the public supporting a third party and 55 percent wanting an independent in the presidential race. While two-party dominance is reinforced by federal and state election laws, as well as the burden of fundraising, it is no longer a given. In fact, if the electorate remains as unpredictable and distrustful as it is, most anything is possible—including the rise of a third party.

Case Study

█████████████████████████████

HIGH-TECH VOTING

Republican campaigning in Colorado offers a clear example of the type of support a modern party can give its candidates. The skills and resources a party organization retains within its walls can be decisive in elections.

In the spring of a presidential election year voters in several western states were called by a computer. A tape-recorded voice said the following:

> Good evening. This is Reagan-Bush '84 calling you on a special computer that is capable of recording your opinion. Your answers to two short questions are very important and will take less than a minute of your time. Please answer after the tone.
>
> Question No. 1: If the election for president were held today, would you vote for President Reagan or the Democratic candidate? (Tone)
>
> Question No. 2: There are a number of unregistered voters in your neighborhood. Is there anyone in your household who needs to register? (Tone)
>
> Thank you and good night.

In some areas the telephoned person replied to the questions by pressing a button on a push-button phone—5 to indicate support for the president, and 6 to indicate opposition. If 6 was pushed, the computer terminated the interview.

Merging and Purging

The phone calls were a sample of the Republican party's answer to the Democrats' advantages in finding and registering new voters. Since nonvoters were concentrated in lower-income and minority groups that overwhelmingly voted Democratic, Republican efforts to register new voters had to be selective. Money and technology were the core of the Republican strategy to register supporters.

In computer terms this became the "merging and purging" of multiple lists. To find the relatively affluent people who were most likely to support Republican candidates and who had not registered, the party's computers ran through a range of lists: mail-order buyers from upscale stores, licensed drivers, homeowners, new utility hookups, and subscribers to *The Wall Street Journal,* to name just a few. The Colorado party effort was a good example of how well technology could be employed to get votes.

Rocky Mountain High Tech

The state GOP effort to build voting support began with a list of registered Colorado voters, purchased from the state government for $500. Party workers (paid $3.50 an hour) first merged this by computer with a list of all licensed drivers over age 18. They then "purged" all drivers registered to vote, leaving the names of 800,000 unregistered voters who were licensed drivers.

This list was then cut to 120,000 names by removing all unregistered drivers who lived in zip code areas with strong Democratic voting patterns. The list of 120,000 was then matched with names and phone numbers on a list put out by a commercial firm. About half of the names produced a match of a phone number with a name, address, and phone number on the party list.

These 60,000 names were the base from which the phone bank with the computerized message operated. The 60,000 had been screened from the original list of Colorado's 1.2 million registered voters and 2.2 million licensed drivers. The phone survey was designed to further reduce the names to a list of 20,000 solid Republican prospects.

For those 20,000 making the final cut, the computer automatically generated a letter from the Colorado state GOP chairman giving them the address of the nearest county clerk where they could register. In addition, the names were sent to the local county party and the campaign staffs of the president and Republican senator (who was running that year). Someone was then assigned to make sure the person actually registered.

GOP Targeting

The computer operation allowed even greater targeting for purposes other than registering likely Republican voters. Using polling, phone bank, and census information, the party could produce groups of voters most likely to be interested in specific issues.

For example, a Republican candidate for the Senate might find from polls that he or she was running poorly among single women aged 45 and older. The candidate might also discover from polling that this group was particularly concerned about crime. The party lists would then enable this candidate to locate the names and addresses of, say, 25,000 women in this category. A letter focused on crime and what the candidate proposed to do about it could then be generated by computer and sent only to this group.

A similar targeting effort allowed the Republicans to identify potential supporters among ethnic groups that tended to be strongly Democratic. The Republican National Committee developed a list of about 12,000 Hispanic last names. Tapes with those names were run against voter registration lists, then compared with real estate tax lists. This allowed the party to identify unregistered Hispanics who were homeowners. That list could then be run against names of car buyers, the names of subscribers to financial newspapers, and the names of Hispanic business owners, in the search for upper-income Hispanics.

All this took money. In one year the GOP paid an estimated $7 for every new registered voter, with a cost to the party of up to $10 million. The Democratic efforts, on the other hand, depended on generally nonpartisan organizations registering the poor and minorities in grassroot registration drives. These were usually neither controlled nor paid for by the Democratic party. As a result, no one could be sure that the new Democratic registrants actually voted on election day. The Republicans, for their part, had this problem of turnout covered as well. A party official commented: "We are not going to pay $5 for every new Republican and then let that person stay at home on election day. We are going to check those names against our computers all day on November 6, and if some guy hasn't shown up by 6 P.M., we'll carry him to the polls."

WRAP-UP

Voters are the broadest, most representative players in the political game. Elections legitimate how the government is run and voters choose who is to run it. Many factors, like political socialization, party membership, religion, race and class, influence how people vote or even *if* they vote. The continued growth of nonvoting poses serious questions about the representative nature of government and the responsiveness of people to their government.

The political parties provide a major link between voters and their elected officials. Historically the parties have evolved into a two-party system, with the Democrats and Republicans dominating elections for 135 years. Though the parties historically have been weakly organized, recent reforms led by the Republicans have strengthened the national organizations, resulting in high-tech operations like the Colorado voter recruitment drive. Through a process of primaries, nominating conventions, and election campaigns, parties put their labels on candidates who through their own efforts in media-driven primaries reach positions of national leadership.

The traditional two-party system is now threatened by polarizing forces within both parties and by increasing numbers of independent voters who feel little loyalty to either party. However both parties still have a few cards left to play. They have shown great flexibility in adapting to the demands of newly mobilized groups, whether blacks and feminists, or Christian fundamentalists and angry white males. Demonstrating a willingness to grapple with the pressing national issues of the day will allow them to continue as vital links between the people and their government. Not to do so will lead to the questioning of their own role as major players, to the continued indifference of turned-off voters, and to the rise of other parties seeking to replace them in the political game.

Thought Questions

1. If you voted in the last election, what influenced the way you voted? Can you relate your political views to your family, religion, or class background?
2. If you didn't vote, what led you not to vote? What would lead you to vote in the future?
3. How would the development of a third party on the national level change the role and nature of our two political

parties? What would be the advantages and disadvantages of such a multiparty system?

4. "From the Republican Right and the Democratic Left both parties were pressured to take stands with little broad popularity and that hindered them from reaching out to voters in the center." Discuss.

Suggested Readings

Cramer, Richard Ben. *What It Takes, The Way to the White House.* New York: Random House, 1992.
Fascinating if very long insider stories about six of the 1988 contenders for their parties' nomination for president. It answers the questions: Who are these guys? What are they like?

Keith, Bruce E., et al. *The Myth of the Independent Voter.* Berkeley: University of California Press, 1992.
Disputes the rise and importance of independent voters. Pre-Perot.

Matalin, Mary and James Carville. *All's Fair: Love, War, and Running for President.* New York: Random House, 1994.
Two 1992 presidential campaign staffers—she's from Bush, he's from Clinton—give chatty self-serving memoirs of what their hectic work, and romance, was like.

Patterson, Thomas E. *Out of Order.* New York: Alfred E. Knopf, 1993.
A political scientist expertly dissects how the values of journalism and the values of politics conflict when the media try to guide voters in presidential campaigns.

Riordan, William L. *Plunkitt of Tammany Hall.* New York: Dutton, 1963. Pb.
The witty confessions of a New York City political boss covering the politics of his party around the turn of the century.

Rutland, Robert Allen. *The Democrats.* Updated. Columbia: University of Missouri Press. 1995. Pb.
A balanced readable history of the uneven evolution of the Democratic party from Jefferson to Clinton.

Thompson, Dr. Hunter S. *Better Than Sex.* New York: Ballentine Books, 1994. Pb.
A crazed amusing account of the 1992 presidential campaign by an admitted political junkie.

Wayne, Stephen J. *The Road to the White House 1992.* New York: St. Martin's Press, 1992. Pb.
A well-organized "nuts and bolts" description of how the presidential selection system works.

CHAPTER EIGHT

Interest Groups and the Media

Interest groups and media are blamed for much of what is wrong with American politics. "Special interests" are seen as the powers behind the scene manipulating the system to serve their needs. Media, more publicly, are alleged to distort the political process—from sound bites of issues to negative images of leaders. However dark the conclusions we may reach about them, both players are key to understanding the modern game of politics.

The Constitution does not say much about either. Except for the First Amendment's guarantee of freedom of the press, neither is mentioned in the document. The framers of the Constitution recognized various interests in society but not their role in government. Although they made wide use of the press in their efforts to get the Constitution adopted, they could not foresee the influence of today's media on politics. Indeed, what would we want the framers to say about them? Their unforeseen development has filled gaps left by the Constitution in the political process.

Both interest groups and media provide access to the government. Interest groups offer tools for people with common concerns to make their views known to public officials. The media are a communications link (and an actor in their own right) through which people keep informed and understand political issues, actions, and players. In providing instruments of power, the two influence and change the political game they play. Who they are, what they do, and how interest groups and media shape and are shaped by politics in the United States are central to what follows.

INTEREST GROUPS

Alexis de Tocqueville, in his famous book *Democracy in America*, marveled in 1835 that "Americans of all ages, all conditions, and all dispositions constantly form associations."* One type of association is the *interest group,* a group of people who organize to pursue a common interest by applying pressure on the political process. As we have seen, American parties are not organized very well for expressing specific interests or positions. Interest groups partly fill this gap.

Our parties and the electoral system are organized by geography. Senators and representatives represent us on the basis of the state or the district in which we live. But within one district there may be a variety of important group interests. People of different religions, races, income levels, or economic associations may have different political concerns. Interest groups give Americans with common causes a way to express their views to political decision makers. While interest groups may try to influence the outcome of elections, unlike parties they do not compete for public office. A candidate may be sympathetic to a certain group, or even a member of that group, but he or she will not run for election as a candidate of the group.

Interest groups are usually more tightly organized than political parties. They are financed through contributions or dues-paying memberships. Organizers communicate with members through newsletters, mailings, and conferences. Union members, for example, usually receive regular correspondence from their leadership informing them about union activities and positions they are expected to support.

Types of Interest Groups

The largest and probably the most important type of interest group is the economic interest group, including business, professional, labor, and farming groups. James Madison, in *The Federalist Papers,* expressed the fear that if people united on the basis of economic interests, all the have-nots in society would take control of the government. This has obviously not happened. The most influential groups in the political process are generally those with the most money. (See Table 8.1.) *Busi-*

---

*Alexis de Tocqueville, *Democracy in America,* vol. 2 (New York: Schocken Books, 1961), p. 128.

Table 8.1   PAC Top Ten Spenders, 1993–1994 Election Cycle

DRIVE Committee (Teamsters Union)	$8,784,746
Campaign America (Senator Robert Dole)	$8,641,824
Emily's List (Liberal women)	$6,959,427
National Rifle Association Political Victory Fund	$6,831,712
American Federation of State & County Municipal Employees	$5,694,792
Association of Trial Lawyers of America PAC	$4,531,724
National Education Association PAC	$4,500,796
American Medical Association PAC	$4,465,815
United Auto Workers Voluntary Community Action Program	$4,335,563
Realtors PAC	$3,554,354

ness groups have a common interest in making profits, which also involves supporting the economic system that makes profits possible. The Chamber of Commerce, the National Association of Manufacturers, and the National Small Business Association are well-known business groups. Large, powerful companies, like American Telephone and Telegraph (AT&T), United States Steel, and General Motors, often act as interest groups themselves.

Of course, all business groups are seldom united on one side of an issue. Competitors within an industry often extend their rivalries to the political arena. Long distance phone companies bitterly fought local phone companies over the recent telecommunications act. Even when a political conflict is characterized as business opposing, say, environmentalists, a closer look will usually reveal business groups on both sides of the issue. The Superfund cleanup of toxic waste sites saw environmentalists aligned with insurance and chemical companies in opposing oil corporations and other insurance companies. Most contested political issues will demonstrate splits in the business community.

Professional groups include the American Medical Association, the National Association of Realtors, and the American Bar Association, all of which have powerful lobbies in Washington. *Labor unions,* like the International Brotherhood of Teamsters and the unions that make up the American Federation of Labor and the Congress of Industrial Organizations (the AFL-CIO), are among the most influential interest groups in the country. Labor leaders, who tend to stay in power longer than most politicians, are powerful political figures in their own right. However, the influence of organized labor has declined, along with its membership, in recent years.

Agricultural business interests have a long history of influential lobbying activity. The American Farm Bureau Federation, the National Farmers Union, and the National Grange are among the most powerful groups in Washington. Specialized groups, like the Associated Milk Producers, Inc. (AMP), also have a large influence on farm legislation.

Some interest groups are organized around religious, social, or political concerns. Groups like the NAACP, the Urban League, and the Southern Christian Leadership Conference (SCLC) focus on economic and religious constituencies within the black community that they represent in national forums. The Sierra Club lobbies in Washington to protect the environment, but are considered more moderate than Greenpeace, a group of environmental activists who take direct action to stop clearcutting of old growth forests. Some interest groups represent people sharing similar political ideas. These include the liberal Washington-based People for the American Way, which has campaigned against censorship, Common Cause, which promotes bipartisan government reforms, and the conservative Christian Coalition. (See "The Christian Coalition.")

Lobbying

Lobbying is when individuals or interest groups pressure the government to act in their favor. Interest groups today maintain professional staffs of lobbyists or hire professional firms in Washington to protect their interests. These lobbyists include former members of Congress or the executive branch who are knowledgeable in a particular area, are politically experienced, and may be personally connected to decisionmakers. According to the 1995 Lobbying reform bill lobbyists must report who pays them, how much they are paid and

The Christian Coalition

One recent example of a successful religious interest group is the Christian Coalition. Organized in 1989 by religious broadcaster Pat Robertson, its 1.7 million members have been active within the Republican party on issues like abortion, funding for the arts, and school prayer. The conservative Christians they represent are given major credit for Republicans winning control of both houses of Congress for the first time in 40 years.

While not formally endorsing candidates, the Coalition has influenced Republicans seeking the party's presidential nomination to follow its line on policies ranging from taxes to prison reform. Its grassroots organizations distribute voter guides in churches, track local school board activities, recruit volunteer organizers, and contact members of congress and state legislatures. It has become a decisive influence in some state political parties. Nationally, the Coalition claims that its members are "thoroughly integrated and enmeshed into the machinery of the Republican Party." Robertson stated his group's goal was to have 10 organizers in each of the nation's 175,000 political precincts by the 1996 elections.

what issues they work on. The reform measure required most of Washington's 14,000 lobbyists to register while limiting gifts and meals for congressmen to $100 a year from any one person. This followed embarrassing disclosures in former Oregon Senator Bob Packwood's diaries of his close ties with lobbyists. Lobbying scandals have historically produced similar modest gestures toward reform.

Direct lobbying usually takes place in congressional committees and executive bureaucracies. Although lobbying the legislature gets most of the publicity, lobbyists devote as much attention to executive agencies in attempting to influence their regulations. It is sometimes said that the real decisions of government are made among lobbyists, bureaucrats, and congressional committees—the so-called *Iron Triangle*. Lobbyists provide information about their industry or population group to committees and bureaucracies. They argue their position with congressional staffers and they may have their powerful clients speak directly with decisionmakers. Knowledge, personal contacts, and frequent attendance at campaign fundraisers place lobbyists in a position to

The Five Commandments of Lobbying

In meeting with elected officials, lobbyists follow a set of "informal rules" which could be helpful to anyone lobbying Congress:

1. *Demonstrate a constituent interest.* One of the best ways to ensure attention is to show the impact on the representative's voters.
2. *Be well informed.* Officials want information in return for the time and attention they give.
3. *Be well balanced.* Compromise is inevitable in legislation. The lobbyist who presents both sides leaves the official with the impression that he or she has looked at all sides of the question and then arrived at a conclusion.
4. *Keep it short and sweet.* The challenge is to present the relevant information in the shortest time in the most memorable way.
5. *Leave a written summary of the case.* It relieves officials of the necessity of taking notes and ensures that the correct information stays behind.

at least be heard on measures affecting their clients' interests. (See "The Five Commandments of Lobbying.")

Indirect lobbying may involve massive letter-writing campaigns using phone banks to get voters' signatures and computers to make the letters look as if they had been individually written. Modern phone technologies allow lobbying firms to contact sympathetic voters and connect them directly to their member's office. The National Rifle Association has had notable success using mass mailings to fight gun control legislation. More subtle lobbying efforts involve "nonpolitical" public relations campaigns. Oil companies responded to criticism about oil spills with advertising showing their concern for the environment. Lumber companies don't discuss clearcutting of forests but instead show commercials of their employees planting trees. Op-eds, letters to the editor, and even editorials are often the results of lobbying campaigns funded by private interests.

Another form of indirect lobbying is for interest groups to persuade other groups to join them in a *grassroots campaign*. They will form a *coalition* of different groups often using a letter-head name, such as Americans for Free Trade, which is invented for the campaign. Using money from private interests, such as

Japanese businesses opposing trade restrictions, the lobbyists managing the campaign attempt, through some of the tactics mentioned, to give Congress the impression that the public supports their position. Sometimes these campaigns work to influence local opinion leaders, mobilize employees to write their congressman and get allied businesses to join the coalition. At other times these efforts merely produce Washington's famed "smoke and mirrors"—the illusion of broad popular support for what is in fact a narrow interest group spending lots of money. Congress and the press seem to be gaining experience in telling the difference. (See "The Name Game.")

The essence of grassroots lobbying is getting constituents to contact their own elected representative. This demonstrates intensity and breadth of feeling, provides persuasion on the issue's local impact in the member's home district or state, and reminds elected officials of the political pain that awaits a wrong decision. Personal lobbying of this kind is often applied to members of Congress while they are visiting their districts. Organizations with a widespread geographic distribution of members, such as the American Association of Retired Persons (AARP), can make effective use of grassroots pressure just by contacting their own members. Single-issue groups like the National Rifle Association (NRA) and the pro- and anti-abortion groups can often use their members' intense feelings on an issue to influence legislators. These "passionate minorities" are often the only voices

The Name Game

In his satire on Washington's lobbying insanities *Thank You For Smoking*, Chris Buckley makes up some fictional associations, which illustrate the tendency for businesses, guided by public relations consultants, to embellish their origins and goals. For example, there is the Society for the Humane Treatment of Calves, representing the veal industry; the Friends of Dolphins, formerly the Pacific Tuna Fishermen's Association; and the Land Enrichment Foundation, formerly the Coalition for the Responsible Disposal of Radioactive Waste.

members hear on a particular policy, and they are not surprisingly more effective than a less-involved majority. (See "Tip O'Neill's Advice in Grassroots Lobbying.")

Campaign Contributions and PACs

Money has been called the mother's milk of politics. Unlike milk, money in elections is combustible and controversial. By contributing money to a political campaign, interest groups can reward a politician who has supported them in the past and encourage her support in the future. They may contribute money to an opponent to punish politicians for their opposition. Groups may even "hedge their bets" by helping to finance the campaigns of two competing candidates.

One of the most important changes in the role of interest groups in elections has been the rise of *PACs (political action committees)*. PACs are organizations set up by private groups such as businesses or labor unions to influence the political process by raising funds from their members. These organizations are not new in American politics. Their model was created in 1955 when the newly formed AFL-CIO (American Federation of Labor and Congress of Industrial Organizations) started the Committee on Political Education (COPE). Through its national and local units, COPE not only contributed money to pro-union candidates, but also organized get-out-the-vote drives and sought to politically educate its members.

The big expansion in business PACs occurred in the late 1970s as an unexpected result of campaign finance reforms. These laws, backed by labor, put strict limits on individual donations and provided for public disclosure. Before this legislation, money could legally go into campaigns in large amounts as individual donations from wealthy corporate leaders. There was thus little need for business PACs.

The reforms backfired. Instead of reducing the influence of large contributors, the reforms increased them. Corporations and trade associations organized PACs that more effectively channeled their money and influence into campaigns than individuals had been

Tip O'Neill's Advice on Grassroots Lobbying

When a few years ago Lee Iacocca, chairman of Chrysler, found his company in deep financial trouble, he appealed to the government for loan guarantees. One of his first visits was to House Speaker Thomas P. "Tip" O'Neill who offered Iacocca the following advice:

"Tell me, how many people in my district work for Chrysler or one of its suppliers?"

"I have no idea," [Iacocca] replied.

"Find out," I told him. "That's the key to this thing, and do the same for every district in the country. Make up a list and have your employees and dealers in each district call and write letters to their own member of Congress.

You've heard my famous phrase that all politics is local. A lot of jobs will be lost if Chrysler goes under and believe me, no member wants to see something like that happen in his district."

Source: Tip O'Neill, *Man of the House* (New York: Random House, 1987), p. 388.

able to do. The number of PACs mushroomed from 608 in 1975 to 4,618 by 1994. There were over seven times as many corporate and trade association PACs, compared with labor PACs.

Spending also skyrocketed. In 1974 interest group donations to congressional candidates totaled $12.5 million. By the 1994 elections, PAC contributions reached $189.4 million for the two-year election cycle. Incumbents, who were mostly Democrats, got 73 percent of the PAC money. However, after the Republicans won majorities in Congress, money from PACs started to flow towards them, and away from the Democrats. For example, prior to the 1994 elections AT&T gave only 39 percent of its $1.3 million in PAC money to Republican candidates. After the Republican victory, 80 percent of its contributions went to Republicans. By 1995 Republicans received 58 percent of PAC contributions compared with 30 percent in 1993. The Democrats' revival and a large inflow of union money evened things out in 1996.

The 1994 congressional elections were the most expensive in history. Candidates for the House and Senate raised a record $724 million, up from $659 million in 1992. To win a seat in the Senate cost about $5 million, and getting to the House cost over $500,000. However, this doesn't mean that spending more money than an opponent always led to victory. In 1994 the 34 successful Republican challengers in the House spent an average of $650,000 each, while the 34 defeated Democrats spent about $1 million each. Similarly in the California Senate race, Republican Michael Huffington spent a record-breaking $29.4 million in his attempt to beat incumbent Democrat Dianne Feinstein, who spent $14 million. He lost.

What does this money buy? At the least—*access*, the right to talk to the elected official. Former Representative Michael Barnes of Maryland offered a congressman's perspective:

> *You have to make a choice. Who are you going to let in the door first? You get back from lunch. You've got fourteen phone messages on your desk. Thirteen of them are from constituents you've never heard of, and one of them is from a guy who just came to your fundraiser two weeks earlier and gave you $2,000. Which phone call are you going to return first?*

The implicit threat of using money against an incumbent can also have a strong negative influence. When a wealthy interest group supports one side of an issue, money may affect how members vote, even if no money actually changes hands. If a member votes "wrong," the interest group might finance a serious opponent in an upcoming election. Thus the implied *threat* of money being used against an incumbent and the implied *offer* of a financial contribution to the incumbent may both affect decision making.

Clearly this increasing spending has affected Congress. One representative remarked, "It is a simple fact of life that when big money enters the political arena, big obligations are entertained." There also may be relatively little that can be done to block the impact of money and the creative ways campaigning politicians use to get it. As one lobbyist skeptically concluded: "Trying to cleanse the political system from the evils of money is like writing a law ordering teenagers not to think about sex. . . . You don't need a law, you need a lobotomy." (See "Lobbyists.")

There is another side to the Washington money game. Not all the money contributed to politicians' campaigns is done at the initiative of the contributor. Most money is donated after some pressure by an elected official. With this comes the implicit, and sometimes explicit, threat that without the contribution the donor will not get much help from the member of Congress. As one senator bluntly put it: "I've had people who contribute to my campaign, and they get access; the others get good government." Of course, giving money doesn't guarantee that the representative will vote the right way. A lobbyist who had just seen his bill voted down and was shortly thereafter approached for another contribution said, "It's almost like blackmail. They ask for money from you as they're screwing you to the wall."

Attempts have been made to restrain PAC influence and reform campaign spending. The efforts, usually unsuccessful, have tended to favor the party introducing the bill. However the 104th Congress, prompted by voters angry with a congress that seemed out of touch with ordinary voters and under the thumb of wealthy interests, moved towards campaign finance reform. Speaker Newt Gingrich agreed with President

---

Lobbyists

The term *lobbying* originally came from the "lobby-agents" who waited in the lobbies of the legislature to pressure legislators for favorable treatment. Sometimes they cause scandals.

The questionable ethics of the "Keating Five" emerged a few years ago. Five senators had attempted to intervene with the Federal Home Loan Bank Board to protect Lincoln Savings and Loan from regulatory penalties. The bank's owner, Charles H. Keating Jr., had contributed over $1.3 million to

the five senators' campaigns, each of whom claimed the intervention amounted to constituent service because Lincoln S&L had assets in their states. The S&L failed anyway, costing taxpayers some $2 billion in deposit insurance costs. Afterward Keating himself raised and answered the question of "whether my financial support in any way influenced several political figures to take up my cause. I want to say in the most forceful way I can, I certainly hope so."

Clinton to try to come up with bipartisan lobbying and campaign spending reforms. A bipartisan bill proposed in the Senate would ban all contributions from PACs. It required candidates to raise at least 60 percent of their funds in their home state, and provided free television air-time and reduced postal rates for candidates who limited their spending. Another less bipartisan effort was undertaken by House Republicans to limit non-profit organizations from lobbying the government if they got money from the government. In 1996, against intense opposition within his own party, speaker Gingrich backed a ban on PACs. None of these restraints on lobbying has become law.

Do Group Interests Overwhelm the Public Interest?

When Ross Perot announced plans to form a third political party he stressed how it would be different: "It will not be owned by the special interests." The idea that interest groups and their lobbyists dominate politics is widely accepted today. What the framers of the Constitution saw as a plurality of voices harmonized by the institutions of government has become for the liberal critic William Greider a "Grand Bazaar" of deal making. In his opinion, modern lobbying has changed the art of governing into a haggling marketplace where special interests negotiate laws, regulations, and the use of public assets. Political power, especially that of corporations, has become a tool for avoiding laws you don't like and passing laws you do like. Whatever the public purposes proclaimed in the laws, just below the surface lies the real spirit of lobbying—"universalized ticket fixing."

There is little argument that the sheer amount of lobbying has vastly increased. Between 1961 and 1982 the number of corporations with Washington offices increased tenfold. The number of lobbyists at least doubled. Already mentioned in the chapter is the steep rise in the number of PACs and the amount of money contributed to campaigns.

These factors have produced a huge rise in the demands on government. Not only corporations, but veterans, farmers, realtors, doctors, universities, retirees, and students, among others, push their claims for the resources of government. As the subsidies and benefits of government increase, more groups organize to protect what they have or to get more. The results are what Jonathan Rauch, calls *hyperpluralism,* too many groups making too many demands on government. Groups demand benefits, but these benefits encourage new groups, until at last government begins to choke. Government loses its flexibility to change. There are too many intense narrow interests—and their lobbyists/ lawyers/public relations experts—to overcome. Programs serving a general interest get less support, while those helping special interests keep their hold on public resources—almost forever.

These criticisms are hard to argue with. Reforms to reduce the influence of wealthy interest groups have failed. Their lobbying, through modern technologies and campaign contributions, has increased. Government often appears to be held hostage by narrow groups resisting all changes that don't benefit them. Average Washington deal making is not available to average American citizens. Nonetheless, as Ross Perot's actions (rather than words) indicate, these "special interests" don't control everything. Politicians still get elected on platforms that call for broad changes in government and these officials have to explain to voters what they've accomplished when they run for reelection. The press investigates cozy deals by lobbyists, the civil service is generally competent and committed to their agencies' programs, and grassroots public interest groups can often elbow their issues onto the country's agenda. As we will see in the next section, new forms of communications from radio talk shows to e-mail are constantly upsetting policy-making expectations.

The outcomes of the political game remain unpredictable. No set of lobbyists dominate. Nor is any explanation of the game based on such domination able to understand the surprising directions American politics has already taken, and is likely to take in the future. Some of these surprises will probably come from our last political player—the media.

MEDIA

The month following the 1992 presidential election brought another demonstration of the"power of the press." U.S. Marines landed in Somalia to protect food relief shipments. Without American television beaming a steady stream of pictures of starving Somali children, such an action was unimaginable. President Bush would have been unlikely to intervene in Somalia or to win the support of the American public when he did. Then, when troops were withdrawn in early 1994, it was largely attributed to public revulsion at televised pictures of a dead American soldier being dragged through the streets of Mogadishu following a disastrous army raid.

How we see politics and politicians and what we think are important national issues are heavily influenced by the press and television. Politicians recognize those facts and act accordingly, often influencing the media at least as often as they are influenced by them.

The media have often been labeled "the fourth branch of government," rivaling the three official branches in political power. Although the press can't actually *do* what the other three branches can, the way the media shape political attitudes makes them vital to the game. In this part of the chapter, we will attempt to come to grips with these questions: What are the media? What do the media do? Who controls media? How are they influenced by the other players and how do media influence politics?

What Are the Media?

Media are those means of communication that permit messages to be made public. Media such as television, radio, newspapers and, recently, computers provide important links connecting people to one another. But these are links with an important quality: They have the ability to communicate messages from a single source to a great many people at roughly the same time. The major forms of media we will concentrate on are television and newspapers. (See Figure 8.1.) With more than 125 million television sets in the United States, television dominates the mass media (and dominates American

Figure 8.1   Audiences Reached by Leading Media, 1995.

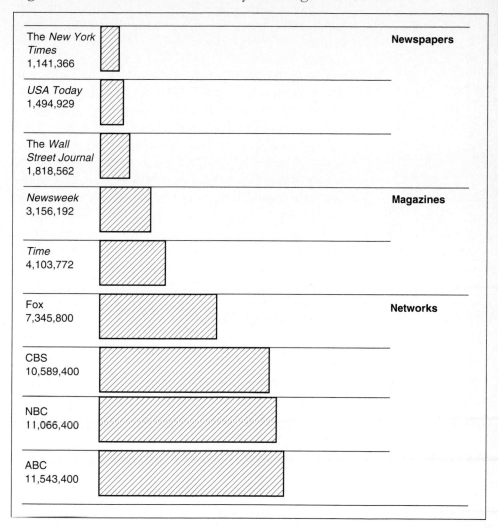

Sources: Newspapers and Magazines: *World Almanac* and *Book of Facts 1995.* Circulation figures for newspapers are average daily circulation for morning editions as of September 30, 1993. Circulation figures for magazines are based on total average paid circulation during the six months prior to December 31, 1993. Networks: *Rocky Mountain News* 4/19/95; figures are estimates based on the Nielsen ratings for each networks' daily prime time hours for the 1994–95 television season.

children who watch an average of 22 hours of TV a week). Its political influence is illustrated not only by an exceptional event, such as the presidential debates watched by more than 100 million Americans, but also by the networks' evening news programs, which reach some 45 million people each night.

Although weakening, television continues to be led by the traditional major *TV networks:* CBS, NBC, and ABC, and a fourth one, Fox Broadcasting. In the past government regulations have barred the networks from owning more than 12 television stations each. Under the sweeping 1996 telecommunications bill, the networks will be allowed to reach up to 35 percent of the television audience with their stations, and are allowed to own cable systems.

The networks sell programs with advertising to local broadcast stations called *affiliates.* In 1995 each of the three major networks had over 200 affiliates and Fox had 158. The networks contract with their affiliates to allow the networks to buy or produce programs and sell time to advertisers for what will be nationally broadcast programs. Then they offer these programs with ads to the af-

---

Mediating the 1992 Presidential Election

1992 was a very different presidential election for TV coverage. Usually the critical events of an election unfold on the network news shows. But in this election the call-in shows, morning and late-night talk shows, and cable news provided critical formats for reaching the public. Memories of the election include: Ross Perot declaring his candidacy on Larry King's show, Gennifer Flowers making her accusations live on CNN, and Bill Clinton playing the sax for Arsenio Hall.

Candidates liked these formats because they provided greater opportunity to reach voters without interruption or analysis by news reporters. Others worried that these settings allowed candidates to speak in generalities and prevented reporters from pointing out inconsistencies.

An example of the value of good re-

porters pinning down candidates was shown in June 1992 when CBS anchor Dan Rather interviewed Ross Perot.

Rather asked: "Would you consider raising taxes or not?"

"That's like giving narcotics to an addict," Perot replied.

After another exchange between them, Rather said: "Is it fair to say that you're opposed to raising taxes but you don't rule it out. . . ?"

"The thing we have to do is bring our fiscal house in order," Perot said.

"So, no new taxes?"

"I have said it as clearly as I can."

"Well, I want to hear it from you, though, not from me."

"I would only consider raising taxes if all else fails."

Source: The Washington Post, June 21, 1992, © 1992 The Washington Post. Reprinted with permission.

filiates, who can sell time locally to advertisers—"and now a word from our local stations." The affiliates get the shows, and the networks get the national coverage which allows them to sell time at $1 million for six minutes of advertising during prime evening viewing hours.

In recent years, the three major television networks have been challenged not only by new networks such as Fox, but also by technologies that are widening the choices available to media consumers. Now 63 percent of the nation's 95 million television households get their signals not over the air but through cables. Over half of America's households have access to more than 30 channels. This has led to the rise of cable-only channels, such as CNN (Cable News Network), C-SPAN (Cable-Satellite Public Affairs Network), The Discovery Channel, Nickelodeon, and MTV (Music Television), which are available to 60 million subscribers. As a result, the audience share of the three major networks has been declining, from 85 percent of all viewers in 1980 to 53 percent in the 1992–1993 television season. (See "Mediating the 1992 Presidential Election.")

New technologies are causing the distinctions between television, computers, and telephones to become increasingly blurred. A stunning example is the vast computer network known as the *Internet*. Started as an experiment by the U.S. military in 1969, it grew slowly into a network of 213 computers in 1981. Now it is a global network of 2.2 million computers, with an estimated 30 million users worldwide. Over 10 million of them are in the United States, and 6 million more Americans are expected to go "on-line" by the end of 1996. The number of Internet users is growing at an astonishing rate of 10 percent every month. It provides access to countless sources of information and entertainment, as well as nearly instantaneous communication by electronic mail—"e-mail"—to anyone, anywhere on the Internet. The graphic part of the Internet, known as the World Wide Web, followed by a simple software tool called a Web browser, made the Internet easier to use. The Web has prompted many businesses, media, and political organizations to make themselves available on-line. Thus, people are now using the Inter-

net to respond to opinion polls, write to newspapers, and find out about political candidates and government agencies. However, before this medium takes its place with other mass media, it needs to produce the profitable business that American capitalism demands from its instruments of communication. This forum of democratic anarchy hasn't yet done this. (See Chapter 6, "Freedom in Cyberspace," p. 180.)

Despite these new technologies, the oldest form of mass media in the United States—newspapers—is still around. More than 100 million Americans (80 percent of the adult population) read a daily newspaper on a regular basis. There are a wide variety of papers, which range in quality from the utterly respectable *The New York Times,* which carries national and international news collected by its own reporters, to small-town dailies that relay crop reports and local fires, but provide sketchy coverage of national events reprinted from the wire services. (*Wire services* are specialized agencies like the Associated Press [AP] and United Press International [UPI] that gather, write, and sell news to the media that subscribe to them.)

However, newspapers are becoming less numerous and less competitive. In 1900, there were 2,226 daily papers in the United States. By 1994, though the population had more than tripled, there were only 1,556. The same period has seen a decline in the number of cities with competing newspapers. In 1920, there were 700 cities with competing daily papers. Currently, there are 13 cities left with competing newspaper ownerships. Of major American cities, only New York has three separately owned daily papers—its fourth, *Newsday,* closed in 1995. We'll get to the reasons for this trend shortly.

What Do the Media Do?

The media provide three major types of messages. Through their *news reports, entertainment programs,* and *advertising,* the media help shape public opinion on many things—including politics.

In news reports, the media supply up-to-date accounts of what journalists believe to be the most important, interesting, and newsworthy events, issues, and developments in the nation and the world. But the influence of news reports goes well beyond relaying facts. The key to this power is *selectivity*. By reporting certain things (President Clinton's jogging) and ignoring others (President Roosevelt's wheelchair), the media suggest to us what's important. Media coverage gives status to people and events—a national television interview or a *Time* magazine cover creates a "national figure." (See "Is No News Good News?")

There are limits. Few people pay much attention to most political news. Except for the special political event—a presidential address on prime time, or election night coverage—continuing attention to politics on television is uncommon. Even the rare event, like a presidential debate, generally reinforces whatever views people have brought to the news.

The most important political function the media perform has been called *agenda setting:* putting together an agenda of national priorities—what should be taken seriously, what lightly, and what ignored altogether. "The media can't tell people what to think," as one expert put it, "but they can tell people what to think *about*." The attention the media give to education in the inner cities, environmental pollution, or the budget deficit will affect how important most people think these issues are. How the problems are presented will influence which explanations of them are

Is No News Good News?

Television network news shows are in trouble. In Chicago, only half the viewers watch network news. In San Francisco, more people watch *Wheel of Fortune* than watch the two competing CBS and ABC nightly news programs *combined.* Just as bad is that the game show attracts younger people, especially women, that advertisers want to reach, while people 50 and older watch the news. In addition, local stations' news programs are muscling out network news with earlier headlines and larger audiences. The networks also have a problem attracting an audience that seems to prefer "soft" news shows like *A Current Affair* and *Hard Copy,* stressing crime and scandals.

more acceptable than others, and which policies are appropriate as responses. Whether inner-city crime is tied to the need for more police or with inadequate drug programs will help shape public debate. Likewise, if unemployment in California is tied to illegal immigration rather than the lack of vocational training, the solution may be frontier barriers rather than aid to education.

Entertainment programs offer amusement while giving people images of "normal" behavior. Certain standards are upheld by heroes, who are rewarded, and violated by outlaws, who are punished. Whether this television behavior offers socially acceptable models is another question. Soap characters (such as Amanda of *Melrose Place*) engage in immoral business practices that bring wealth and power (and the occasional hunk). These television experiences may substitute for learning from life's more complex experiences, but they may be just as important as other realities. As one analyst of television observed: "If you can write a nation's stories, you needn't worry about who makes its laws. Today, television tells most of the stories to most of the people most of the time."

Finally, the programs and news that media present are built around a constant flow of *advertisements*. Television programs are constructed to reach emotional high points just before the commercials so that the audience will stay put during the advertisement. Newspapers devote almost two-thirds of their space to ads rather than to news, leading one English author to define a journalist as "someone who writes on the back of advertisements." Ads, especially television commercials, present images of what the audience finds pleasing and soothing about themselves. Presented in 30-second compelling symbols—"Reach Out and Touch Someone"— commercials offer viewers charm, good looks, and amusement. They may also change what we expect in other arenas including politics. Media critic Neil Postman has charged that TV's emphasis on entertaining visuals has altered how we look at our political leaders, and how they present themselves: Instead of a public discussion of issues, we find a competition between reassuring televised images. In this case, the medium has changed the message of politics.

MEDIA AND THE MARKETPLACE OF IDEAS

The framers of the Constitution believed that a free flow of information from a great many sources was basic to maintaining their system of government. Ideas would compete with one another without restraint in a "marketplace of ideas." Fearing that the greatest enemy of free speech was the government, the framers added the First Amendment forbidding government officials from "abridging the freedom of speech, or of the press." The phrase has since been interpreted to include radio and television. The principle, however, remains the same, as Judge Learned Hand wrote:

> *Right conclusions are more likely to be gathered out of a multitude of tongues than through any kind of authoritative selection. To many this is, and always will be folly; but we have staked upon it our all.*

The ability of media to fulfill this goal of presenting a variety of opinion, representing the widest range of political ideas has, to no one's surprise, been limited in practice. It is limited by the media, by the government and by the public.

Media, such as television stations and newspapers, are privately owned economic assets bought and sold to make money for their owners. Profitability, not public service, has led to the increasing concentration of media ownership. The decrease in competition among newspapers mentioned earlier has been a reflection of the increase in *chains,* which are companies that combine different media in different cities under one owner. More than 80 percent of the nation's newspapers are owned by chains, and only three corporations own most of the nation's 11,000 magazines.

Market calculations in the mid-1990s caused a number of U.S. television and media companies to merge, leaving ownership of almost all major media outlets concentrated in a few corporate hands. In 1995, Disney purchased ABC for $19 billion, Westinghouse paid $5.4 billion for CBS, and Time Warner bought Turner Broadcasting for $7.5 billion. Time Warner is now the largest media giant, owning about half the cable systems in the United States—CNN, *Time* magazine, HBO, *Sports Illustrated,* Atlantic Records, Looney Toons cartoons, and much more. These mergers are the continuation of a trend of shrinking ownership within the expanding media marketplace. Ten years earlier ABC had been purchased by Capital Cities Communication, and NBC had been bought by General Electric.

These recent mergers were unprecedented in that they allowed television producers, broadcasters, and distributors to combine into single companies. In the past, federal regulators prevented such mergers, arguing that monopolies over information didn't serve the public interest. Organizations like the Consumers Union have opposed these mergers, believing that the results will be soaring cable rates, shrinking entertainment options, and news coverage declining into sensationalism. Critics pointed to the late-1995 incident where CBS lawyers prevented "60 Minutes" from airing an interview with a former tobacco executive on health issues in the industry. They feared a law suit. This more cautious attitude toward the news may have been connected to CBS pending merger with Westinghouse, and concerns that a lawsuit would mess up the multibillion dollar deal. Arguably this symbolized changing values in the news business and the increasing financial pressures coming from these mergers. *The Christian Science Monitor* accurately concluded: "The bulk of what we see, hear, learn, sing, play, rent and consume will shortly be controlled by a dozen corporate entities. . . ."

Beyond the arguments concerning the *quality* or variety of views heard on televsion, there is no question that the *quantity* of information has increased. The first of the new sources of information was the Cable News Network (CNN), which provides news coverage 24 hours a day. Started in 1980 by Ted Turner, few people believed there would be enough demand for such a station, and it was jokingly called "Chicken Noodle News." CNN went on to become a success, and in times of crisis or news events it has become the channel of choice for the general public, political leaders, and news junkies. During the O.J. Simpson trial CNN and Court TV's gavel-to-gavel coverage helped elevate a celebrity murder case into a national spectacle. Less popular C-SPAN provides continuous coverage of both houses of Congress, and many community cable stations provide similar coverage of state and local governments.

Other media provide opportunities for communication from the audience as well. With the increasing availability of the Internet to the general public, citizens are learning about politicians by exploring political candidates' "pages" on the World Wide Web, and they are flooding many newspapers and magazines with "letters to the editor" in the form of e-mail. The popularity of radio talk shows and call-in shows has made that medium into a new force in politics. Jovial conservative talk-show host, Rush Limbaugh, was publicly, if overexuberantly, thanked by newly elected Republican members of Congress in 1994 for their victory.

Profits have also increased in the media industry. Network advertising revenues have climbed over $11 billion, and network programs have regained audience shares from cable in recent years. Newspapers, though not as profitable, earn even more than the television industry—bringing in annual advertising revenues of some $30 billion. Although customers purchase newspapers, most of the papers' expenses are covered by advertising.

Advertisers approach media with certain expectations. They want their ads to be seen or read by as many people as possible; they want the people seeing the ads to be potential customers; and they don't want the surrounding programs or articles to detract from the ads. As a result, advertising encourages media content— whether news or entertainment—to be conventional and inoffensive in order to keep the customer satisfied. Tobacco companies have contracts that keep their ads away from articles linking cigarette smoking to cancer. Airlines have standard arrangements with most newspapers that provide for their ads to be pulled from editions that carry news of airline disasters. Ownership may bring "advertising" privileges. "NBC Nightly News" ran three segments, totaling 14 minutes, about a new device to detect breast cancer without mentioning that its parent corporation—GE—manufactured the machine.

Newscasts also affect the political information available. To get the largest possible audience, TV news packages itself as entertainment. This means bite-sized, novel, action-oriented news with emphasis on stimulating visuals. The credibility of the news is largely dependent on the attractiveness of likeable broadcasters—or talking hairdos—who appear sincere to the audience. Television news is also divided up by commercials which may make the news seem less serious, less complex and, perhaps less worth being concerned about. One critic noted how strange it was to see a newscaster who, having just presented a report on the inevitability of nuclear war, goes on to say he will be right back after this word from Burger King. *(Think as you're reading this book if I was to pause here, tell you that I will return to this discussion in a moment, and then write a few words about, say, Ben & Jerry's Ice Cream. If this happened several times in a chapter you might think the text was not worth your further attention.)*

Media and Government

Politicians and government officials have a number of formal and informal means for influencing the media. Their formal powers include the requirement that radio and television stations renew their broadcast licenses with a regulatory commission, the Federal Communications Commission, every six years. Although usually a formality, the threat of losing a license can be an effective means of pressuring broadcasters that are hostile to a particular administration or policy. Until 1987, the FCC tried to enforce a *fairness doctrine*, which required that contrasting views on controversial issues be presented. If the stations did not give a balanced presentation, they would have to provide air time to correct the imbalance. It was sometimes used against political opponents. President Johnson used it in 1964 to intimi-

date radio stations favorable to his Republican chal-
lenger, Senator Barry Goldwater. The Reagan administration's FCC abolished this standard because it interfered with an unregulated marketplace; broadcast
journalism was to be treated like print journalism—with
no "fairness doctrine."

For campaigning politicians, the media are both opportunity and adversary. Sixty percent of the money in
presidential races goes to advertising. Politicians—as
noted in the case study at the end of this chapter—live
and die by media coverage. While the availability of
coverage has been increased by the rise in media outlets
such as cable, the quality and depth of political news
has not necessarily improved. For example one study
showed that the average *sound bite*—a video clip of a
candidate speaking—had declined from 42 seconds in
1968 to just over 7 seconds in 1992. Newscasts were
emphasizing the quick and the dramatic in covering
politics. (See "Granddaughters and Elections.")

Considerable effort also goes into engineering
"newsworthy" events that will capture free media
time. Some of these activities have been called *pseudoevents*—not real events at all, but staged in order to be
reported. Candidates Bill Clinton and Al Gore took a

Granddaughters and Elections

Using children is a favorite technique
in political ads on TV. Children play to
viewers' feelings of hope, innocence,
and vulnerability.

George Bush had a TV ad in 1988
called "The Future." It began with a
close-up of one of Bush's granddaughters running across a field. Cut to the
Republican convention; cut to family
scenes; cut to a Bush close-up. "I want
a kinder and gentler nation. . . " Bush
says. Cut to the granddaughter as she
reaches her grandfather and is swept
high in his arms. The frame freezes and
the words read: "EXPERIENCED
LEADERSHIP FOR AMERICA'S
FUTURE."

This emotional appeal, run early
in the campaign when Bush was not
well liked, was designed to show
the human side of a candidate
often viewed as remote and elitist.
It illustrated his concern for the
future in a very personal way through
his grandchild. It also offered the
viewer a warm emotional bond
with George Bush as a caring
grandfather.

series of bus tours through rural areas of crucial states during their 1992 campaign. The trips were designed to bring the candidates "closer" to the people, gain local media coverage, and present a TV visual of campaigning in old-fashioned rural America. The bus tours also put distance between the candidates and the image of the Democrats as the party of liberals, minorities, and big cities.

The examples of government leaders informally pressuring media are numerous. Presidents try to get on the good side of the media by giving favored reporters exclusive "leaks" of information and by controlling information going to the public. Often the president delivers the good news in person to the TV cameras, like the Bosnia peace agreement, while leaving it to others to communicate bad news, like renewed fighting. Putting the right "spin" on an issue means presenting it in a way that makes the elected official look the best. When the president opposes cuts in Medicare he is defending impoverished grandparents against heartless Republicans rather than trying to win votes for reelection in the crucial state of Florida. All of this is called *news management.*

Press conferences have been used by presidents since Theodore Roosevelt to give the media direct contact with the chief executive. With radio, and then television, such conferences have allowed presidents to bypass journalists and present their views directly to the public. Franklin Roosevelt's radio "fireside chats" were a skillful use of direct communication during the Great Depression. Television and politicians can also make uneasy partners. In 1960, presidential candidate Richard Nixon's streaky makeup, dull suit, and heavy beard made a poor impression—and may have cost him the election—in the first-ever televised debate with his opponent, John F. Kennedy.

Presidents now have large staffs of media experts and speech writers to perfect their images. As a former movie actor and television personality, Ronald Reagan understood the importance of television news to his image—and the importance of "visuals" to television news. (See "Mixed Media Messages.") Reagan spent up to ten

Mixed Media Messages

During the 1984 presidential campaign, Lesley Stahl, a CBS reporter, prepared a critical commentary on how President Reagan used television. Her blunt report charged the president with manipulation, if not hypocrisy. She reported that he will appear at the Special Olympics or the opening of a senior housing facility, but no hint is given that he cut the budgets for subsidized housing for the elderly. He also distanced himself from bad news, Stahl reported. After he pulled marines out of Lebanon, he flew off to his California ranch, allowing others to make the announcement.

To illustrate her piece, Stahl put together Reagan's video clips: Reagan greeting handicapped athletes, cutting the ribbon at a home for the elderly, and relaxing on his ranch in jeans.

"I thought it was the single toughest piece I had ever done on Reagan," Stahl said. She worried about White House reaction.

After the piece aired, the phone rang. It was a senior White House official.

"And the voice said, 'Great piece.'"
"I said, 'What?'"
"And he said, 'Great piece!'"
"I said, 'Did you listen to what I said?'"

"He said, 'Lesley, when you're showing four and a half minutes of great pictures of Ronald Reagan, no one listens to what you say. Don't you know that the pictures are overriding your message because they conflict with your message? The public sees those pictures and they block your message . . . it was a four-and-a-half-minute free ad for the Ronald Reagan campaign for reelection.'"

"I sat here numb. . . . None of us had figured that out." She broke into laughter. "They loved it. They really did love it."

Source: Hedrick Smith, *The Power Game* (New York: Random House, 1988), pp. 413–414.

hours a week rehearsing speeches. (Jimmy Carter, by contrast, averaged three hours or less.) The result of Reagan's skill as "The Great Communicator" was an ability, unrivaled before or since, to look and sound absolutely honest and forthright.

George Bush understood that journalists, among others, cozy up to those in power. Before becoming president, he was portrayed as a spineless preppy who stood for nothing. Sixteen months before he entered the White House, *Newsweek* pictured Mr. Bush in his powerboat to illustrate its cover story, "Fighting the 'Wimp Factor.'" With his 1988 victory came his transformation into a tough sportsman and regular guy. Two weeks before his inauguration, *Newsweek* showed Bush fishing from the back of a motorboat illustrating "The 'Liberation' of George Bush." As newscaster Barbara Walters said, "It's as if Clark Kent became Superman." Alas, by the time of his unsuccessful 1992 reelection campaign, Bush was again being "bashed" by the media.

President Clinton came to the White House somewhat wary of journalists. He had endured a campaign full of stories about womanizing and draft controversies. He initially pursued an *alternative-media* strategy, avoiding White House correspondents while granting interviews to local news anchors and holding televised town meetings. The hope that this would avoid negative confrontations with the traditional press proved fruitless. His early press relations were poor, with his staff viewed as inexperienced and the president seen as not entirely candid. On major issues like health care or the government shutdown a campaign-style "War Room" would be set up at the White House to manage and co-ordinate messages, media responses, spokesmen and congressional relations, often with mixed results.

Things improved after the midterm elections with Leon Panetta becoming Chief of Staff and the appointment of a new White House press secretary, Mike Mc-Curry. The president was more likely to be "on message"—which meant deciding on a single issue to communicate for the day and being disciplined enough to stay on it. The president was also helped by the widespread opinion after the Republican takeover of Congress that someone else was responsible for "the mess in Washington." (See "Clinton and the Media.")

Media and the Public

The "definition of alternatives is the supreme instrument of power" wrote political scientist E. E. Schattschneider. By "definition of alternatives" he meant the ability to set limits on political debates, to define what is politically important and what is not, and to make certain solutions reasonable and acceptable and others not. Media, to a great extent, have this power. Who influences the exercise of this power is another question.

Certainly the media managers (editors, newscasters, producers, reporters) have a vital role in shaping

President Clinton and the Media

Presidents usually rank at the top of the media food chain. But sometimes it's hard to get the press to take a bite.

After the Republicans took over Congress, attention focused on the new victors, especially Speaker Newt Gingrich. President Clinton seemed to disappear from the press. For example, in the spring of 1995 President Clinton called his first prime-time news conference since the Republican triumph. It was only the fourth of his presidency. The media's lack of enthusiasm showed itself when two of the three major television networks declined to broadcast the news conference.

The perception of a presidential disappearance from the media wasn't necessarily the reality. A study by the nonpartisan Center for Media and Public Affairs found that during the first three months of 1995 the networks' evening news spent 12 minutes on the administration and 10.5 minutes on Congress each night. They had broadcast 309 stories about President Clinton compared with 114 on Speaker Gingrich. This did represent a drastic change in coverage compared with the three months after the President's inauguration in 1993. Then the administration got 14.5 minutes a night and Congress only 4.8 minutes.

Of course, press coverage can be a mixed blessing. The Center noted that of the comments broadcast, 61 percent about Mr. Gingrich were negative while 62 percent about Mr. Clinton were negative. Since two-thirds of all Americans get their news from television and find it the most believable media, this may have something (not everything) to do with both leaders showing up badly in public opinion polls.

political views. The owners of media, whether television networks, cable operators or newspaper chains, play a part in selecting who will handle the day-to-day running of the press and what the general "slant" of the media they own will be. Advertisers, by buying space in some programs or papers and not in others, affect the messages sent out to the public.

Government leaders have a whole range of laws and tactics to pressure media into conforming to their political priorities. By dramatizing certain policies, by withholding information on other issues, and by favoring some reporters over others, experienced politicians can manipulate the press. They may be able to successfully confront the media on issues important to their constituents. For example, in his race for the presidency Senator Robert Dole attacked media owners for "putting profit ahead of common decency." In condemning the casual violence and sex in Hollywood movies and records aimed at children, the Senator said, "One of the greatest threats to American family values is the way our popular culture ridicules them." Several months later the corporation (Time Warner) named by Senator Dole sold the entertainment unit that produced the rap music records he had singled out for attack.

And where does this leave the public? People have a right to expect that the press will fulfill its two major political functions of (1) informing the public of what its leaders are doing and (2) acting as a watchdog monitoring government actions. The emphasis on profitability which has led to shaping newscasts into entertainment has limited the media's ability to fulfill either political function. The results are that the public is bombarded by more news from more outlets, but the news they get is less informative and, perhaps, less relevant. The O.J. Simpson trial receives saturation coverage, while the depletion of the ozone layer of the atmosphere is simply not news. Yet which "news" does an informed public need in order to make decisions about public policies?

The public need not be passive about the quality of mass communications. By watching or not watching certain programs, by buying or not buying publications, by demanding or not demanding that dissenting voices be heard, the public can help "manage" the output of the media. The rise of talk-radio, of the Internet, of community-based programs on cable and public access channels, show the flexibility and diversity available in the media today.

Yet, in the main, the messages that the media provide reflect the power of those in the political game. The official players, through press conferences, paid public relations advisors, and news management, can be fairly sure of reaching the public through the media. Using paid advertising, corporations can claim media time to persuade the public to act in certain ways—usually by buying the goods they produce, but sometimes (like oil or tobacco companies) simply by thinking well of them. The ability of members of the general public to address each other, as well as their political representa-

tives, is far more limited. Free speech without broader
access to the modern medium of free speech remains a
limited right for most people.

Case Study

THE CANDIDATE: A DAY IN THE LIFE . . .

Elections allow interest groups and media to influence who
will gain power in the political game. In this fictional account
of a day in the life of a candidate we see, through her eyes,
the importance of these players.

Morning

The phone jars her awake. It is still dark outside. But months
ago, she started leaving the light on in the bathroom of each
motel she stayed in so that she could quickly get her bearings
when, like this morning, she woke up disoriented.

"Yes?" she asks rasping into the mouthpiece, her voice
slightly hoarse from too many speeches.

"Time to get moving, boss," an aide's voice says. There is
an important breakfast meeting this morning with the state
teachers' union. They have already given her the maximum
allowable contribution, but she hopes they will get their national PAC to contribute and that they will encourage their
members to volunteer for her campaign.

She has learned to travel light and dress quickly. Her
short functional haircut is ready as soon as it dries. As she
settles into the backseat of her midsize American-made car,
she tries to recall what brought her to the southeast part of
the state for two days of campaigning.

Her schedule is done by regions. To save travel time and
money she does events in neighboring communities. The two
good-sized towns she will be in today offer her enough voters
to make her stay worthwhile and, more important, offer opportunities for money and media. Every day must include a
money event in the community being visited. And, of course,
if you don't get media on a trip, you weren't there.

She works the crowd, prodded by an aide's earlier reminders of the key names, spouses, and previous times she
has met them. As she eases into her seat at the head table,
she turns to the aide for her purse, which reminds her of an
argument at the beginning of the campaign.

Should she carry a purse? Her campaign manager said
no. Why should a candidate for the U.S. Senate carry a
purse? That wasn't even the worst of the special problems
facing women running for office. How feminine should she
look? Does she wear dresses or suits? Jewelry? Lipstick? Do
heels make her look too tall or do people want to look up at
their next senator?

At the breakfast, she tries to eat the by-now-cold eggs
because she has been losing weight and her face is looking
haggard on television. Her major campaign promise is a cut
in income taxes for the middle class, but she assures the
teachers that savings in management will still allow for a
cost-of-living increase in educational salaries. She thanks
them for their contribution and makes a pitch that teachers
are the best volunteers—bright but used to scrub work.

There is a ten-o'clock news conference at the local press
club. A reporter rides with her. He is doing a story about her
family life. "But don't you feel bad about having to be away
from your children so much?" he asks. It is a question she
has fielded a hundred times before. "My husband is very
good with them," she says, "and then Betsy, who's eleven,
and Henry, who's fourteen, are very much involved in the
campaign themselves, and they feel that what we are all doing together is very important."

The press conference goes smoothly. She reads the prepared statement, which explains how much the proposed income tax cut will mean for an average family. During the last
two weeks of the campaign, she will issue two such statements each day, one for the morning newspapers and one for
the afternoon papers. But the main hope is that one of them
will get a segment on the nightly news. Television news is the
key to a successful statewide campaign, and she has planned
her campaign accordingly. In this case she is well under the
2:00 P.M. deadline for the 6:00 local news.

Afternoon

At noon, she visits a senior citizen's center where hot lunches
are served to about 60 retirees each day. Unfortunately the
local college student serving as her driver gets lost. She is
late. This happens once a week.

After lunch, she goes back to her motel room for some
urgent fundraising. She learns that she could lose some vital
last-week TV advertising spots unless she can come up with
$30,000 before the day ends. At the motel, two wealthy sup-
porters are waiting. She has another cup of coffee, pours

them a beer, and makes the pitch. "I know you've given more than you should be asked to give, but we've got to raise the money for these spots." She always finds this a little demeaning. One of the men heads the state Bankers' Association. The other is a homebuilder. She wonders, What will they want when she becomes senator?

Since they've already contributed the maximum $1,000, the two commit to raising from friends another $5,000 and leave. She talks to more prospective contributors on the telephone, as each is dialed in turn by an aide. A number of these are directors of PACs in Washington, D.C. "Did you see the *Tribune* poll?" she asks. "We're really coming up, but these spots are crucial." With all but $4,000 of the needed money raised (which will probably be picked up through an aide's follow-up calls), she changes clothes and heads for a low-budget cafe to film a TV spot.

The cafe is crammed with television lights, reflectors, cameras, technicians, and spectators anxious to get into the picture. The candidate briefly studies a script, which will take 45 seconds to recite. With the cafe and its customers as backdrops, she looks into the camera on cue and begins. "In the closing days of this campaign, ordinary people have increasingly been joining with me in demanding a cut in income taxes. . . ."

"Hold it!" the producer says. "We're getting a buzzing on the sound track from the ice machine."

She starts again. "In the closing days of this campaign . . ."

"Wait a minute," the producer interrupts. "We're getting some kind of funny shadow on her face."

The lights are adjusted, and she begins again—and again and again. A minute spot takes two hours to film.

After filming the TV spot she hurries to two "coffees," one at the home of a wealthy supporter active in environmental groups, the other sponsored by the sisterhood of a local synagogue. She makes a brief opening statement at each coffee, and then answers questions. At the end of each session, she asks those who are willing to help with telephoning, canvassing, stuffing envelopes, or other campaign chores to sign a pledge sheet. After she leaves, her hosts make a pitch for money. Almost $1,200 is promised at the two coffees.

Evening

Back at the motel, she takes the phone from an aide and responds to a prearranged, live radio interview for 15 minutes.

She spends 20 minutes with her campaign manager going over the latest poll results. "We're cutting down the general, but I'm worried about the increase in your 'negatives'; maybe we should soften our attack a little," the manager says. She knows that her attacks on an opponent will also increase voters' negative feelings toward her. She agrees.

"Then there's the soft-money contribution by Sleazer. We've really got the state party steamed at us for telling them to wait on this one." She nods. "Soft-money" is given to the party for its activities that indirectly help candidates, in this case, her. The money isn't subject to campaign limitations or disclosure. Now, Ben A. Sleazer, the owner of Jefferson S&L, wants to give $100,000 to the state party for get-out-the-vote activities aimed at supporting her campaign. She knows that the S&L has some regulatory problems and clearly Sleazer is going to expect help from her if she wins.

Besides the fact that her campaign desperately needs the money, the party also wants the funds to build up their voter contact program. The party chairman, who says he's amazed Sleazer would even offer help to a nonincumbent, is leaning on her to OK the money. It's all perfectly legal. Yet she worries about the bad press when it leaks out, and she doesn't trust or like Sleazer, who is rumored to have Mob ties. But as her manager said, "It's only a press problem. You need the money now; you can deal with the media later, when you're Senator." She wonders. She decides to talk with her husband about it and tells her manager she'll let him know her decision in the morning.

Her stomach tightens as she begins to think ahead to the last of the day's activities, a televised "debate" with the other senatorial candidates before a League of Women Voters' audience. Too tense to eat, she turns down a sandwich and goes over her notes. "Should I be rough with the general or not?" she asks nobody in particular.

Riding back to the motel after the debate, she feels good. She is sure that the local news tomorrow evening will make a "sound bite" out of her statement "The general may want to be a senator as an honor to cap off his career, but I want to be a senator because I feel deeply about what we ought to be doing for our people."

She talks to her husband and one of the children by telephone; the younger child is already asleep. Her husband is enthusiastic about the debate, and that is a good note to end the day on. Maybe that's why she doesn't raise the issue of the soft-money contribution, or maybe she's too

tired to remember. Just before she gets into bed, she calls
the motel desk. "Would you ring me in the morning at
five o'clock?"*

---

*With thanks to Fred R. Harris

WRAP-UP

Both interest groups and media are bridges over which
people and players can reach the political game. Interest groups provide the means for business, labor, professional, or citizens' organizations to make their views
known to government officials. They unify people with
common concerns to bring pressure on decision makers through grassroots campaigns, fundraising, lobbying, or publicity. Interest groups with the most resources tend to be the most effective. Reforms to limit
the influence of wealthy interests have been notably
unsuccessful.

 Media seem to be everywhere. Besides being both a
communications tool and a profitable economic asset,
media also influence politics. Through news reports,
entertainment, and advertisements, media directly and
indirectly shape political attitudes. What is and is not
broadcast and printed establishes political figures, sets
priorities, focuses attention on issues, and largely makes
politics understandable to most people. The media in
turn are affected by the corporations that own them,
the advertisers that pay for their messages, the managers who run them, and the public that looks, reads
and listens to what they offer. Technology has increased
the variety of media outlets and led to the merger of
many of them under giant corporate banners. Political
leaders grant them licenses (if they're television or radio), stage pseudoevents, and distribute or withhold information as it serves their interests. And campaigning
candidates spend much of their days seeking free access
to media or raising the money for ads on it. As both a
political player and a communications link, the media
are among the game's most powerful, complex, and controversial forces.

Interest groups and media offer the potential for wide public access to the political game. The huge rise in the number of interest groups and the vast expansion of media outlets show the possibilities of these linkages being used by a broader public. But at present it is the public that is more likely to be used by these players to enhance their own political positions. Interest groups through lobbying campaigns mobilize parts of the public only to support their own policies. Media offer the public news-as-entertainment for the commercial and political benefits that come from claiming a larger share of a popular audience. The public is the object, not the subject. These instruments of power remain in the hands of the powerful.

Thought Questions

1. Which interests are represented best by American interest groups? How would you remedy the limits of interest groups so that groups that are now poorly represented would be guaranteed a greater voice?
2. Does the need for an informed public conflict with the commercial need to make a buck by making news entertaining? Are public discussions and media entertainment contradictory to each other?
3. What are the arguments for and against changing the media to make them more available for differing political viewpoints? Must this change mean more government control and regulation?
4. Do you think our candidate for the Senate will accept the "soft-money" contribution? If you were her aide, what would you recommend? How would you suggest that she "spin" her responses to press questions about the contribution?

Suggested Readings

Interest Groups

Buckley, Christopher. *Thank You for Smoking.* New York: Random House, 1994. Pb.
     A very funny, insightful novel of a tobacco lobbyist and his uphill struggle to preserve truth, justice, and the American smoker.
Choate, Pat. *Agents of Influence.* New York: Alfred A. Knopf, 1990.

A stinging indictment of the influence of Japan and its American lobbyists over Washington politics.

Jackson, Brooks. *Honest Graft.* Washington: Farragut Press, 1990. Pb.

An excellent case study of PACs and their power, or lack of power, in dealings with House Democrats.

Rauch, Jonathan. *Demosclerosis: The Silent Killer of American Government.* New York: Times Books, 1995.Pb

Argues that what ails the body politic is too many interest groups clogging the arteries of government. Hyperpluralism is the disease, government paralysis is the result.

Media

Bagdikian, Ben H. *The Media Monopoly,* 4th ed. Boston: Beacon Press, 1992. Pb.

Blasts the concentration of media power in the hands of fewer and fewer giant corporations.

Diamond, Edwin, and Robert Silverman. *White House to Your House.* Cambridge, Mass.: MIT Press, 1995.

An intelligent talk about current media politics in an age of electronic populism.

Jamieson, Kathleen Hall. *Packaging the Presidency,* 3rd ed. New York: Oxford University Press, 1996. Pb.

Critically discusses the history of presidential campaign advertising through 1992.

Postman, Neil. Amusing Ourselves To Death. New York: Penguin Books, 1985. Pb.

Powerfully attacks TV's domination of our thinking and how TV has turned political debate into another form of entertainment.

Sabato, Larry J. *Feeding Frenzy.* New York: The Free Press, 1993. Pb.

An argument against journalism's shark-like attacks on politicians for their personal scandals.

CHAPTER NINE

Who Wins, Who Loses: Pluralism Versus Elitism

Has American politics come into a clearer focus? Or have we, in describing the players and rules, the terms, institutions and case studies lost sight of the game? This chapter will give us a chance to step back a bit and ask some basic questions: Who (if anyone) is running the game? Who wins, who loses? Who plays and who doesn't?

It should not be a surprise that there is no accepted answer to these basic questions. Rather, there are two major competing approaches to an answer. The dominant one, supported in some form by most political scientists and most of the players in the political game, is *pluralism*. Its competitor, the *power elite* school of thought, has attracted supporters on both the Right and Left critical of the American political game. More recent views have attempted to bridge the gap between the two approaches.

PLURALISM

Pluralism is a *group theory of democracy.* Pluralism states that society contains many conflicting groups with access to government officials, and that these groups compete with one another to influence policy decisions. Although people as individuals don't usually have much leverage in politics, they can get influence through their membership in various groups. These groups bargain both among themselves and with government institutions. The compromises that result become public policy.

Several key concepts make up the pluralist argument: fragmentation of power, bargaining, compromise, and consensus.

Fragmentation of power is the pluralists' way of saying that no one group dominates the political game. Power is divided, though not equally, among a large number of groups—labor unions, corporations, ethnic groups, and many others. To gain their goals, the groups must *bargain* with each other. Within this bargaining process, the government, though it may have its own interests, acts essentially as a referee. The government will make sure the rules of the game are followed and may intervene to help groups that consistently have less power than their opponents. It is also to the advantage of all the groups to follow the "rules of the game," for the bargaining-compromise method is the most effective way to win changes.

The result of this many-sided bargaining process is inevitably a series of *compromises*. Because no group has dominant power, each must take a little less than it wants in order to gain the support of the others. This accommodation is made easier because both the interests and the membership of the groups overlap. Groups disagreeing on one issue must keep in mind that they may need each others' support in the future on another issue on which they agree. An individual may even be a member of two groups with different views on an issue. His membership in both will tend to reduce the conflict between them. A black doctor may be a member of the American Medical Association (AMA), which opposes most expanded programs of government-sponsored health care, and also a member of the National Association for the Advancement of Colored People (NAACP), which supports these programs. As a member of both, she may influence the groups to reach a compromise with each other.

Underlying this bargaining-compromise process is a *consensus*—an agreement on basic political questions that most of the groups are reasonably satisfied with. This agreement on the rules of the game, and also on most of its results, is the basic cooperative cement that holds society together. Aspects of this consensus in American society are things like the general agreement on the importance of civil liberties, on the goal of equal opportunity for all citizens, on the necessity for compromise, and on the duty of citizens to participate in politics. The pluralists maintain not only that there is widespread participation (open to all who wish to organize) in political decisions but also that the decisions themselves, and the procedures by which they are reached, have a consensus in society behind them. Government, in the pluralist universe, essentially reflects the compromises reached by the groups.

What we have then in pluralism is a process of bargaining among organized groups, and also between these groups and various parts of the government. The bargaining results in a series of compromises that become public policy and determine who gets what, when, and how. A widespread consensus on the rules and results of this process keeps the political game from degenerating into unmanageable conflict.

Examples of Pluralism

Examples of the whole bargaining-compromise process, pluralists claim, are easy to find. When major environmental groups decided that a new law regulating air pollution was needed, they formed a Clean Air Coalition to lead the fight. Helped by environmental lobbyists, the Coalition raised funds from members of wealthy groups like the Environmental Defense Fund and the Sierra Club. Chemical and oil companies, tired of fighting lawsuits brought under what they considered unrealistic regulations, reluctantly supported compromise proposals. They also worried about public opinion which strongly supported the environmentalists' safety arguments over the corporations' cost objections. The press weighed in with editorials and generally favorable coverage. The Environmental Protection Agency (EPA) supported the bill with studies and testimony. The appropriate committees of the House and Senate, reacting to competing arguments and pressures, approved a bill that became the Clean Air Act of 1990. Pluralists would say the law reflected the relative power of the various groups as well as the compromises they reached among themselves.

One well-known study attempting to support the pluralist model is Robert Dahl's book on politics in New Haven, Connecticut, *Who Governs?* Dahl tried to find out who actually has influence over political decisions in an American city. He examined several important issues, such as urban development and public education, to see who made the key decisions in these areas. He concluded that different groups influenced decisions in the different areas. The people who had the most influence over education policy were not the same as those influencing urban development or political nominations. There was, Dahl concluded, no one economic and social elite wielding political power in New Haven. (See "The Pluralist View.")

Criticisms of Pluralist Theory

Who Governs? and other studies supporting pluralist ideas have run into numerous criticisms. One major argument condemns pluralism for emphasizing *how* the political game is played rather than *why* people play it. Critics say that pluralism does not give enough importance to how benefits really are distributed. A consensus supporting equal opportunity is not the same as actually having equality. A system of democratic procedures may simply conceal the powerful getting their way. The argument often goes on to say that there can be no political democracy without social and economic conditions also being equal for all. Critics of pluralism ask: What good are the rules of the game to the majority of people who never get a chance to play?

The Pluralist View

"The fact is that the Economic Notables operate within that vague political consensus, the prevailing system of beliefs, to which all the major groups in the community subscribe. . . . Within limits, they can influence the content of that belief system; but they cannot determine it wholly. . . ." (p. 84)

"In the United States the political stratum does not constitute a homogeneous class with well-defined class interests." (p. 91)

"Thus the distribution of resources and the ways in which they are or are not used in a pluralistic political system like New Haven's constitute an important source of both political change and political stability. If the distribution and use of resources gives aspiring leaders great opportunities for gaining influences, these very features also provide a built-in throttle that makes it difficult for any leader, no matter how skillful, to run away with the system." (p. 310)

Source: Robert A. Dahl, *Who Governs?* (New Haven: Yale University Press, 1961).

Other critics point out that pluralists seem to believe that groups will balance off each other, producing a stable system. But what if everyone sees the value in forming a group to gain more benefits from the government. Political inflation leads to so many competing groups making so many demands that the government begins to choke on deficits caused by trying to please all the groups. This *hyperpluralism* is for some observers a more accurate, if more pessimistic, picture of current American politics than is traditional pluralism.

POWER ELITE

Many dissenters from pluralism believe a *power elite* approach more realistically describes the American political game. Supporters of this approach see society as dominated by a unified and nonrepresentative elite. This elite secures the important decision-making positions for its members while encouraging powerlessness below. Those in power do not represent the varied interests in society. Instead they look after their own interests and prevent differing views from surfacing. American politics is not a collection of pluralist groups maintaining a balance of power among themselves, but an elite of economic, political, and military leaders in unchallenged and unresponsive control of the political game.

This elite rules the country through the positions its members occupy. Power does not come from individuals but from *institutions*. Thus, to have power you need a role of leadership in a key institution of the society—you have to be the chief executive of a large corporation or a cabinet secretary, or a full admiral in the navy. These leadership roles are not open to everyone. They are open only to the rich and the powerful, the *ruling class* of the country, whose names can be found in major newspapers' society columns and whose children go to the "right" schools. This influential class controls the country's economy and is in basic agreement that political power should be used to preserve the economic status quo.

The results of this elite control, needless to say, are different from the pluralist outcome. Political decisions, rather than representing a consensus in society, merely represent the *conflict* within it. Society is held together not by widespread agreement but by force and control: the control the elite has over the majority. The only consensus that exists is everyone's agreement that some have power and others do not. From this pessimistic viewpoint, politics is a constant conflict between those with power, who seek to keep it, and those without power, who seek to gain it. The policies that result from the political game reflect the conflict between elite and majority, and the domination of the latter by the former.

Examples of the Power Elite

One of the largest, best-known and frequently denounced, elite policy organizations is *The Council on Foreign Relations*. It was founded after World War I by what would loosely be called the Eastern Establishment—socially connected, New York–based bankers, lawyers, and academics. One study found that 23 of the country's largest banks and corporations had four or more directors who were members of the Council. Its members were especially important in foreign affairs after World War II, influencing the creation of the International Monetary Fund, the World Bank, and the United Nations. Its journal, *Foreign Affairs,* is must-reading by decision makers in the field, most of whom are members of the Council. Its discussion groups bring together leaders from business, government, universities, and the military for detailed consideration of specific topics. To those within the Council, it is a policy-oriented group analyzing issues and producing broad leadership agreements on American foreign policies. To power elite critics it looks more like an Old Boy Network dividing up jobs and deciding issues among themselves.

A well-known study of elite control in America, *The Power Elite* was written by a sociologist, C. Wright Mills. Mills maintained that American politics is dominated by a unified group of leaders from corporations, the military, and politics. They make most of the important policy decisions, and cooperate among themselves because they need each other. Mills pointed to the frequent movement among the three areas, with business leaders taking jobs at high levels of government, military leaders getting positions in corporations, and so forth. He also discussed the similarity in background, education, and social class of the leaders in these different arenas. Supporters of Mills's ideas often point to President Eisenhower's farewell address, in which he warned of a vast "military-industrial complex" whose influence "is felt in every city, every state house, every office of the federal government." (See "The Power Elite View.")

Criticisms of the Power Elite View

Critics have been quick to do battle with the power elite view. Although they may agree that only a few people

The Power Elite View

"The power elite is composed of men whose positions enable them to transcend the ordinary environments of ordinary men and women; they are in positions to make decisions having major consequences. . . . They rule the big corporations. They run the machinery of the state and claim its prerogatives. They direct the military establishment. They occupy the strategic command posts of the social structure, in which are now centered the effective means of the power and the wealth and the celebrity which they enjoy." (pp. 3–4)

"Within American society, major national power now resides in the eco-

nomic, the political, and the military domains." (p. 6)

"The men of the higher circles are not representative men; their high position is not a result of moral virtue; their fabulous success is not firmly connected with meritorious ability. . . . They are not men held in responsible check by a plurality of voluntary associations which connect debating publics with the pinnacles of decision. Commanders of power unequaled in human history, they have succeeded within the American system of organized irresponsibility." (p. 361)

Source: C. Wright Mills, *The Power Elite* (New York: Oxford University Press, 1959).

participate in politics, they argue that this minority of activists is much less unified than Mills maintains. They point to political conflicts over taxes or the environment, or any presidential election, as examples of how elites check each other. These elites compete, and democracy consists of people choosing between them through the vote. Besides, some critics argue, the political ideals of democracy are probably in better hands than they would be with an uninformed majority. Public surveys have shown a lack of tolerance for dissent among members of the lower classes. Hence greater participation by people might, curiously enough, mean less liberty and justice, not more.

Another criticism aimed at some careless power elite supporters is that they are *conspiracy theorists.* The reasoning of these theorists of both the Right and Left, which may veer close to blaming specific racial, religious, or ethnic groups, becomes circular: American politics is governed by a secret conspiracy "covered up" by certain famous people. Such conspiracies are responsible for everything from President Kennedy's assassination, to slavery, the AIDS epidemic, and a coming UN invasion. This unified, frequently evil, elite is, of course, secret and thus unprovable. Conspiracies remove politics from analysis and allow fruitcake demagogues to manipulate naive people, often for purposes of raising money.

THE DEBATE

The debate between supporters of the pluralist and elite theories does not usually come down to *whether* a small number of people dominate the political game. Even in the pluralist model, the bargaining among the groups is carried on by a relatively few leaders representing their groups. Clearly only a minority of people directly participate in politics, and this small group has more influence than the majority of people. The central questions are how *competitive* and *representative* these elites are.

To what degree do elites compete rather than cooperate with one another over who gets what, when, and how? How much conflict is there between, say, heads of government agencies and corporations over regulation and taxes? Or how much do they share views on major questions of policy and cooperate among themselves regardless of the "public good"? Certainly anyone reading the daily newspaper can point to numerous examples of conflicts over policy among groups in the political arena. Are these conflicts to be dismissed as mere bickering among a small unified group on the top? Or are vital issues being resolved in fairly open free-for-all contests?

Then there is the question of how *representative* these elites are of the broader public. Do powerful groups reflect, however imperfectly, the wishes of the majority? In recent years, elite circles of our society have opened their doors, not always voluntarily, to minorities and women. Has this made these institutions more representative or at least more aware of the wishes of formerly excluded groups in our country? Is this just tokenism, or can the leaders of these associations, businesses, or parties claim to represent their public's opinion?

Is there, in fact, a "public opinion," or has that been manipulated beyond recognition? Take, for example, the question of what we see on TV. During the 1996 presidential campaign it was charged that television was presenting a wasteland of programs undermining traditional family values. But do we know why? Some say it's because an elite seeking its own profits controls what we see. Others argue that abundant violence, casual sex, and silly commercials reflect what the majority wants, as shown by countless opinion polls. But do these polls reflect what people actually want or what they are conditioned to want? Is there a real public opinion, or just one produced by an elite to further its own interests?

A glance back at the book's case studies is a reminder of how difficult it is to put the political game under a single umbrella of ideas. The first case study, the war with Iraq, shows an elite of presidential decision makers meeting in secret and then shaping congressional and public reactions. On the other side, the case study of the decline and fall of racial segregation reflects a widespread political conflict with an emerging pluralistic participation forcing its resolution.

But most of the other cases are not as clear. In Colorado's get-out-the-vote study, a party looks for wider public support but in a selective and manipulative way. The congressional case shows a newly elected Republican majority trying unsuccessfully to overcome institutional obstacles and a rival party to enact a controversial balanced budget amendment to the Constitution. In a candidate's day, a woman running for the senate aims to win a popular vote, but her immediate targets are narrowed to special interest groups and media. Both in results and process the pluralist and elite frameworks highlight certain parts of America's politics while ignoring others.

Newer Views

The pluralist and elite approaches can also be seen as two ends of a range of theories about American politics.

Recent modifications have discussed a *plural elitism*. This stresses that politics is divided into different policy arenas where narrow elites dominate, usually at the expense of the public interest. So, for example, when it comes to deciding on public spending for the military, a trio of military leaders, defense businesses, and congressional leaders of key committees dominate the decision making. The general public is confused by ideology and patriotic symbols from clearly seeing the elite dominance that is occurring in these issue arenas.

There is then, according to this view, no "right" answer to the argument between pluralists and the power elite school. It may depend on which political conflict we are talking about. Sometimes, as in town meetings held in many New England towns, we can see a number of views being expressed and a democratic decision being reached by the community. In other areas, such as the making of foreign policy, a small number of high officials meeting behind closed doors decides policies that will affect the lives of millions. We might conclude that the issue being decided is likely to affect how decisions will be made. Pluralism may be most appropriate in describing a small community's politics, but the power elite approach may help us understand how foreign policy is made.

Other students of American politics have emphasized how the *government* itself acts. In both pluralism and elitism, government actions are basically viewed as the result of outside forces: in one case, compromises by different groups; in the other, the wishes of a unified elite. But clearly government—its major branches and agencies—is more than a passive mirror of dominant private groups. Government has interests of its own and may even act to represent a national interest.

The concepts we adopt as most accurately reflecting political reality are bound also to reflect our own ideals. The pluralists and elitists (and those in between) are asking and answering not only what *is* but what *should be*. The pluralists state that politics in America is democratic, with widespread participation in decisions to which most people agree. The elitists say that politics is dominated by an elite that controls and manipulates the rest of us in its own interest. The elitists contend that basic changes in the American system are needed to create a pluralist democracy, whereas the pluralists argue that we have one and that the means for change are available within it.

What do you think? The position you take will reflect not only your understanding and study of politics, but also your ideals and experience. Further, the position you take will guide your political choices.

WRAP-UP

We have written about American politics as a game. We have discussed the nature of the game and how the competition takes place. We talked about the rules of the conflict, many of them in the Constitution, and how they have changed. Most of the book has been devoted to the governmental and nongovernmental players, their history, organization, and powers. And in this last chapter we have looked at two schools of thought that try to analyze how the game is really played and sum up who wins and loses. But we're not quite finished.

We said in the beginning that most of us are spectators of the game—nonparticipants. But just as politics is a special kind of game, so too are we a special kind of audience. We *can* participate in the game and, by participating, change the way the game is played and, perhaps, its outcome. As a respected scholar of politics once wrote:

> *Political conflict is not like a football game, played on a measured field by a fixed number of players in the presence of an audience scrupulously excluded from the playing field. Politics is much more like the original primitive game of football in which everybody was free to join, a game in which the whole population of one town might play the entire population of another town moving freely back and forth across the countryside.*
>
> *Many conflicts are narrowly confined by a variety of devices, but the distinctive quality of political conflicts is that the relations between the players*

*and the audience have not been well defined and
there is usually nothing to keep the audience from
getting into the game.* [*]

In whatever way you think best, get in the game.
American politics has become too important to leave to
the players.

Thought Questions

1. Give examples from throughout the book which support
   the pluralist approach. What are other examples that lean
   toward the power elite?
2. Pluralism has been described as essentially "liberal,"
   whereas elitism can be either "radical" or "conservative."
   Do you agree?
3. Which approach, pluralism or elitism, do you feel best describes the political game in your own community? Give
   examples.
4. Do you think participation in politics is growing among
   students? Why? How is it encouraged or discouraged?

Suggested Readings

Dahl, Robert A. *Who Governs?* New Haven: Yale University
   Press, 1961. Pb.
   A case study showing pluralism operating in New Haven's city
   government.
Greider, William. *Who Will Tell the People.* New York: Simon
   & Schuster, 1992.
   This *Rolling Stone* editor gives us a good muckraking view at
   how issues are wheeled and dealed in Washington with little re-
   gard for the American people.
Mills, C. Wright. *The Power Elite.* New York: Oxford Univer-
   sity Press, 1959. Pb.
   The well-known attempt to show that an elite governs America
   in its own interest.
Schattschneider, E. E. *The Semisovereign People.* New York:
   Holt, Rinehart & Winston, 1961. Pb.
   This landmark work presents a basic explanation of how and why
   some people get into politics and some stay out.
Smith, Hedrick. *The Power Game: How Washington Works.*
   New York: Random House, 1988. Pb.
   A long but revealing look at how the modern power game is
   played.

---

[*]E. E. Schattschneider, *The Semisovereign People* (New York: Holt, Rinehart & Winston, 1961), p. 18.

GLOSSARY

CHAPTER ONE: INTRODUCTION

politics—the process of who gets what, when, and how; actions among a number of people involving influence.

power—the ability to influence another's behavior.

elites—those who get most of society's values, especially wealth and power.

authority—legitimate power.

legitimacy—a publically recognized quality of an institution like a family or government that make the actions of people connected to that institution both legal and right.

anarchy—a society without government.

political conflict—a widespread dispute over society's values, for example, wealth.

democracy—a form of government in which the people effectively participate.

representative democracy—government in which the people rule indirectly through elected representatives.

government—a political association that makes rules determining the distribution of values of a society and is the ultimate regulator of legitimate force.

social sciences—the academic disciplines, like history, economics, or political science, that study the relationships among people.

political science—the study of those social relations involving power and authority, especially those including government.

CHAPTER TWO: CONSTITUTION

Mayflower compact—early example (1620) of American settlers' (Pilgrims) desire to be governed by a publically accepted rule of law.

Articles of Confederation—a document that in 1781 loosely unified the newly independent American states; its shortcomings led to the U.S. Constitution.

Federalists—supporters of the Constitution in the struggle to adopt it; wanted strong conservative federal government.

Anti-Federalists—opposed adopting the Constitution; preferred stronger state governments and more popular participation.

Bill of Rights—first ten amendments to the Constitution including freedoms of speech, press, religion, due process, and jury trial.

separation of powers—constitutional principle that the powers of government should be separated into three branches of government, legislative, executive, and judicial.

checks and balances—the principle that mixes together these separate powers to give each branch some powers of the others; protects and balances the functions of the agencies of government.

federalism—the distribution of political authority between the federal government and the governments of the states.

reserved powers—those powers not delegated to the federal government are reserved to the states or people by the Tenth Amendment.

New Federalism—a modern attempt, first announced by President Reagan, to shift federal government programs and responsibilities to state and local governments.

limited government—the constitutional principle by which the powers of government are limited by the rights and liberties of the people.

judicial review—the courts' authority to decide on the contitutionality of the acts of state, local, and federal governments.

exclusive powers—those powers only exercised by the federal government, such as the right to coin money.

concurrent powers—those powers shared by the states and federal government such as the power to tax.

CHAPTER THREE: THE EXECUTIVE BRANCH

lame duck—negative description of a president weakened because he is in the last months of his final term.

electoral college—antiquated constitutional provision whereby voters on election day select electors to reflect their state's choice for president.

residual powers—those powers not spelled out in the Constitution but necessary for the president to carry out his other responsibilities; used to expand powers of the president.

Chief of State—role of the president as a head of the nation as well as of the government.

executive agreements—international agreements only needing approval by the president because they are usually less important than treaties.

Commander-in-Chief—president's authority over the military; principle behind civilian supremacy.

Chief Executive—president's role as head of the executive branch and its federal bureaucracy.

State of the Union address—presidential speech before Congress at the beginning of the year outlining his legislative program

veto—president's constitutional power to refuse to sign legislation thus preventing it from becoming law unless overridden by a two-thirds vote of both houses of Congress.

bureaucrat—an administrator in a large organization, often government; often refers to someone who slows things down by enforcing too many rules and red tape.

cabinet—the major departments of the federal government such as State and Defense; there are now 14.

executive agencies—major parts of the government that are not in the cabinet, for example, National Aeronautics and Space Administration (NASA).

regulatory commissions—agencies semi-independent from the rest of government charged with regulating parts of the economy, for example, the Federal Communications Commission (FCC).

spoils system—process of filling government positions with supporters of the winning politicians; largely replaced by the civil service.

CHAPTER FOUR: CONGRESS

bicameral—a legislature with two houses, such as the U.S. Congress with the House of Representatives and Senate.

104th Congress—the Congress elected in 1994 with the first Republican majority in both houses since the 1950s.

incumbent—an elected official currently in office with all the advantages that confers.

term limits—popular effort to limit the number of times that members of congress can run for re-election.

gerrymandering—designing legislative districts to favor one party's candidates over another.

Speaker of the House—the head of the House of Representatives and the leader of the majority party, currently Newt Gingrich.

caucus—a gathering of all the members of a political party serving in either house of Congress.

Senate majority leader—leader of the Senate majority party and the Senate equivalent to the Speaker, currently Trent Lott.

CHAPTER FIVE: COURTS

U.S. District Courts—the federal courts where most cases involving federal law are tried first.

original jurisdiction—authority of the court to initially try cases.

appellate jurisdiction—authority of some courts to hear appeals from lower courts.

U.S. Court of Appeals—thirteen federal courts above the district courts which mainly hear appeals from those courts.

senatorial courtesy—practice of the senate to only approve judicial nominees who are acceptable to the senator from that state.

exclusive and concurrent jurisdiction—refers to whether federal courts have sole authority over a case (exclusive) or whether they share that authority with state courts (concurrent).

U.S. Supreme Court—composed of a chief justice and eight associate justices, it is the head of the federal court system.

writ of certiorari—order of a higher court to a lower court to send the record of a case for review.

memorandum orders—method by which the Supreme Court decides most cases without the need for oral arguments.

Rehnquist court—the current Supreme Court named after William Rehnquist, Chief Justice since 1986.

political questions—controversial issues that the courts refuse to deal with because they feel they lack the capacity and that other branches are most suited to resolve it.

precedent or stare decisis—the judicial practice by which the courts generally follow previous court decisions involving the same issue.

judicial restraint—the concept that the courts should not impose their views on other branches of the government except in extreme instances; a passive role for the courts.

whips—floor leaders who work to coordinate votes and assist the party leaders.

calendars—the agendas or schedules for legislation in Congress.

filibuster—the right under Senate rules to delay action by speaking for an unlimited amount of time; only stopped by a cloture vote.

Standing Committees—the permanent specialized units of both houses that draft legislation in subject areas like taxes and agriculture.

Conference Committees—a temporary body of members from the two houses set up to resolve different versions of legislation passed by both houses.

Joint Committees—permanent bodies including both senators and representatives, eg. the Joint Economic Committee.

seniority—an informal rule by which the chairman of a committee is automatically the member from the majority party who has served the longest on the committee.

specialization—an expectation that members will remain on the same committee and become experts in its issues.

reciprocity—the practice of members to look for guidance on legislation to members of their party on committees specializing in that area.

oversight—a nonlegislative power of congress to investigate and examine the activities of executive branch agencies.

impeachment—the right of Congress to remove high officials of the executive or judicial branches from office for misconduct.

judicial restraint—the concept that the courts should not impose their views on other branches of the government except in extreme instances; a passive role for the courts.

judicial activism—the concept that the courts should be an active partner with the other branches of government in shaping policy.

affirmative action—effort to remove affects of discrimination by promoting and expanding minority job and promotion opportunities.

CHAPTER SIX: CIVIL LIBERTIES

civil liberties—legal protections against government restrictions on freedoms of speech, press, and religion.

civil rights—legal protections against discrimination because of race, religion, ethnicity, or gender.

Fourteenth Amendment—post–Civil War amendment that has been used to extend the protections in the Bill of Rights to actions by state and local governments and private individuals and groups.

equal protection—clause in the Fourteenth Amendment used to prevent state officials and others from engaging in racial or sex discrimination.

due process—phrase in the Fourteenth Amendment used to incorporate freedoms of the Bill of Rights to cover states' actions, including the rights to procedural fairness and impartiality by government officials.

partial incorporationists—judicial position that believes only *preferred freedoms* such as the First Amendment freedoms should be included in the Fourteenth Amendment and applied to the states.

complete incorporationists—judicial position that the entire Bill of Rights was incorporated into the Fourteenth Amendment.

First Amendment freedoms—freedoms of religion, speech, press and assembly.

suspect classifications—a judicial doctrine that states that laws with classifications involving race, religion, or ethnicity will be subject to close scrutiny by the courts because they are "suspect."

class action suits—cases representing a whole class of people whose rights may have been violated.

equity—a flexible judicial doctrine that allows judges to resolve a case based on a sense of fairness.

test case—brought by lawyers to a court as the best example of a major violation affecting a group of people.

landmark decision—a judicial decision involving major changes in the law.

injunction—a court order preventing someone from violating someone else's rights.

exclusionary rule—a judicial rule that excludes any evidence obtained by illegal means.

Chapter Seven: Voters and Parties

political socialization—the process of learning political attitudes and behavior.

social class—a major social division based on occupation and income and the awareness this produces of relations towards other classes.

electoral barriers—legal obstacles to voting, such as residency and registration requirements.

political efficacy—the sense of political effectiveness; that efforts like voting will produce results like a change in government policies.

political party—an organization that runs candidates for public office under the party's name.

maintaining elections—elections that continue the parties' popular support at the same level.

deviating elections—elections that show a temporary shift in popular support for the parties.

realigning elections—elections that show a long-term shift in the popular base of support of the parties.

dealignment—current term referring to the growing lack of support for either major party.

independents—voters publically identifying with neither major political party.

political machine—a traditional locally based political organization led by a *boss* which controlled government jobs and services through loyalty and corruption.

national convention—an assembly of party delegates usually selected by primaries who meet every four years to nominate their party's candidates for president and vice president.

party platform—a document stating the party's and the nominee's positions on issues.

presidential primaries—elections held by states to determine which nominee's delegates will be sent to the national convention.

"balance the ticket"—the effort by parties to represent different groups and regions in their candidates for office.

single-member district—electoral system of electing one member of Congress from each district; considered an obstacle to the rise of minor parties.

Chapter Eight: Interest Groups and Media

interest group—an association organized to pursue a common interest by bringing pressure on the political process.

lobbying—the process of influencing government officials by private interests.

Iron Triangle—refers to public policy being shaped by a trio of lobbyists, bureaucrats, and congressional committees.

grassroots campaigns—the effort to bring pressure on Washington officials by mobilizing voters in their own districts and states using mail, phones, or visits.

coalition—a political grouping representing diverse interests organized to represent popular opinion on a particular issue.

PACs (political action committees)—legally sanctioned organizations set up by private groups to raise campaign funds.

media—those means of communications, such as television, radio, and newspapers, that permit messages to be made public.

TV networks—corporations owning nationwide television outlets to whom they produce and sell programs.

agenda setting—a listing of national priorities; a major media function.

Internet—a global computer network allowing near instant communication by electronic mail.

chain—companies that combine different media in different cities under one ownership.

sound bite—a brief video clip of a candidate or political official talking.

news management—techniques used by public officials to control information going to the media.

CHAPTER NINE: WHO WINS, WHO LOSES

pluralism—a group theory of democracy; positively views the competition between many different groups resulting in compromises that produce public policies.

fragmentation of power—a key pluralist perspective that no one group dominates American politics.

consensus—a general agreement among the groups on basic political questions and "rules of the game."

hyperpluralism—the view that participation by too many groups demanding too many resources from the government leads to political paralysis.

power elite—theory that American politics is dominated by a unified nonrepresentative elite.

ruling class—the economically privileged group that controls the major institutions of society according to the power elite view.

conspiracy theory—usually unprovable argument that America and specific activities are dominated by a unified, secret elite.

plural elitism—views American politics as divided into different policy arenas where various special interest elites dominate.

The Declaration of Independence

THE UNANIMOUS DECLARATION OF THE THIRTEEN UNITED STATES OF AMERICA

When in the Course of human events, it becomes necessary for one people to dissolve the political bands, which have connected them with another, and to assume among the powers of the earth, the separate and equal station to which the Laws of Nature and of Nature's God entitle them, a decent respect to the opinions of mankind requires that they should declare the causes which impel them to the separation.—We hold these truths to be self-evident, that all men are created equal, that they are endowed by their Creator with certain unalienable Rights, that among these are Life, Liberty and the pursuit of Happiness.—That to secure these rights, Governments are instituted among Men, deriving their just powers from the consent of the governed,—That whenever any Form of Government becomes destructive of these ends, it is the Right of the People to alter or to abolish it, and to institute new Government, laying its foundation on such principles and organizing its powers in such form, as to them shall seem most likely to effect their Safety and Happiness. Prudence, indeed, will dictate that Governments long established should not be changed for light and transient causes; and accordingly all experience hath shown, that mankind are more disposed to suffer, while evils are sufferable, than to right themselves by abolishing the forms to which they are accustomed. But when a long train of abuses and usurpations, pursuing invariably the same Object evinces a design to reduce them under absolute Despotism, it is their right, it is their duty, to throw off such Government, and to provide new Guards for their future security.—Such has been the patient sufferance of these Colonies; and such is now the necessity which constrains them to alter their former Systems of Government. The history of the present King of Great Britain is a history of repeated injuries and usurpations, all having in direct object the establishment of an absolute Tyranny over these States. To prove this, let Facts be submitted to a candid world.—He has refused his Assent to Laws, the most wholesome and necessary for the public good.—He has forbidden his Governors to pass Laws of immediate and pressing importance, unless suspended in their operation till his Assent should be obtained; and when so suspended, he has utterly neglected to attend to them.—He has refused to pass other Laws for the accommodation of large districts of people, unless those people would relinquish the right of Representation in the Legislature, a right inestimable to them and formidable to tyrants only.—He has called together legislative bodies at places unusual, uncomfortable, and distant from the depository of their public Records, for the sole purpose of fatiguing them into compliance with his measures.—He has dissolved Representative Houses repeatedly, for opposing with manly firmness his invasions on the rights of the people.—He has refused for a long time, after such dissolutions, to cause others to be elected; whereby the Legislative powers, incapable of Annihilation, have returned to the People at large for their exercise; the State remaining in the meantime exposed to all the dangers of invasion from without, and convulsions within.—He has endeavored to prevent the population of these States; for that purpose obstructing the Laws for Naturalization of Foreigners; refusing to pass others to encourage their migrations hither, and raising the conditions of new Appropriations of Lands.—He has obstructed the Administration of Justice, by refusing his Assent to Laws for establishing Judiciary powers.—He has made Judges dependent on his Will alone, for the tenure of their offices, and the amount and payment of their salaries.—He has erected a multitude of New Offices, and sent hither swarms of Officers to harass our people, and eat out their substance.—He has kept among us, in times of peace, Standing Armies without the Consent of our legislatures.—He has affected to render the Military independent of and superior to the Civil power.—He has combined with others to subject us to a jurisdiction foreign to our constitution, and unacknowledged by our laws; giving his Assent to their Acts of pretended Legislation.—For quartering large bodies of armed troops among us:—For protecting them, by a mock Trial, from punishment for any Murders which they should commit on the Inhabitants of these States:—For cutting off our Trade with all parts of the world:—For imposing Taxes on us without our Consent:—For depriving us in many cases, of the benefits of Trial by Jury:—For transporting us beyond Seas to be tried for pretended offenses:—For abolishing the free System of English Laws in a neighboring Province, establishing therein an Arbitrary government, and enlarging its Boundaries so as to render it at once an example and fit instrument for introducing the same absolute rule into these Colonies:—For taking away our Charters, abolishing our most valuable Laws, and altering fundamentally the Forms of our Governments:—For suspending our own Legislatures, and declaring themselves invested with power to legislate for us in all cases whatsoever.—He has abdicated Government here, by declaring us out of his Protection and waging War against us.—He has plundered our seas, ravaged our Coasts, burnt our towns, and destroyed the lives of our people.—He is at this time transporting large armies of foreign Mercenaries to complete the works of death, desolation and tyranny, already begun with circumstances of Cruelty & perfidy, scarcely paralleled in the most barbarous ages, and totally unworthy the Head of a civilized nation.—He has constrained our fellow Citizens taken Captive on the High Seas to bear Arms against their Country, to become the executioners of their friends and Brethren, or to fall themselves by their hands.—He has excited domestic insurrections amongst us, and has endeavored to bring on the inhabitants of our frontiers, the merciless Indian Savages, whose known rule of warfare, is an undistinguished destruction of all ages, sexes and conditions. In every stage of these Oppressions We have Petitioned for Redress in the most humble terms: Our repeated Petitions have been answered only by repeated injury. A Prince whose character is thus marked by every act which may define a Tyrant, is unfit to be the ruler of a free people. Nor have We been wanting in attentions to our British brethren. We have warned them from time to time of attempts by their legislature to extend an unwarrantable jurisdiction over us. We have reminded them of the circumstances of our emigration and settlement here. We have appealed to their native justice and magnanimity, and we have conjured them by the ties of our common kindred to disavow these usurpations, which would inevitably interrupt our connections and correspondence. They too have been deaf to the voice of justice and of consanguinity. We must, therefore, acquiesce in the necessity, which denounces our Separation, and hold them, as we hold the rest of mankind, Enemies in War, in Peace Friends.—

We, therefore, the Representatives of the United States of America, in General Congress, Assembled, appealing to the Supreme Judge of the world for the rectitude of our intentions do, in the Name, and by the Authority of the good People of these Colonies, solemnly publish and declare, That these United Colonies are, and of Right ought to be Free and Independent States, that they are Absolved from all Allegiance to the British Crown, and that all political connection between them and the State of Great Britain, is and ought to be totally dissolved; and that as Free and Independent States, they have full Power to levy War, conclude Peace, contract Alliances, establish Commerce, and to do all other Acts and Things which Independent States may of right do.—And for the support of this Declaration, with a firm reliance on the protection of divine Providence, we mutually pledge to each other our Lives, our Fortunes and our sacred Honor.

The Constitution of the United States

We the People of the United States, in Order to form a more perfect Union, establish Justice, insure domestic Tranquility, provide for the common defence, promote the general Welfare, and secure the Blessings of Liberty to ourselves and our Posterity, do ordain and establish this CONSTITUTION for the United States of America.

ARTICLE I

Section 1. All legislative Powers herein granted shall be vested in a Congress of the United States, which shall consist of a Senate and House of Representatives.

Section 2. (1) The House of Representatives shall be composed of Members chosen every second Year by the People of the several States, and the Electors in each State shall have the Qualifications requisite for Electors of the most numerous Branch of the State Legislature.

(2) No Person shall be a Representative who shall not have attained to the Age of twenty-five Years, and been seven Years a Citizen of the United States, and who shall not, when elected, be an Inhabitant of that State in which he shall be chosen.

(3) [Representatives and direct Taxes[1] shall be apportioned among the several States which may be included within this Union, according to their respective Numbers, which shall be determined by adding to the whole Number of free Persons, including those bound to Service for a Term of Years, and excluding Indians not taxed, three fifths of all other Persons.][2] The actual Enumeration shall be made within three Years after the first Meeting of the Congress of the United States, and within every subsequent Term of ten Years, in such Manner as they shall by Law direct. The Number of Representatives shall not exceed one for every thirty Thousand, but each State shall have at Least one Representative; and until such enumeration shall be made, the State of New Hampshire shall be entitled to choose three, Massachusetts eight, Rhode-Island and Providence Plantations one, Connecticut five, New York six, New Jersey four, Pennsylvania eight, Delaware one, Maryland six, Virginia ten, North Carolina five, South Carolina five, and Georgia three.

[1]The Sixteenth Amendment replaced this with respect to income taxes.
[2]Repealed by the Fourteenth Amendment.

(4) When vacancies happen in the Representation from any State, the Executive Authority thereof shall issue Writs of Election to fill such Vacancies.

(5) The House of Representatives shall choose their Speaker and other Officers; and shall have the sole Power of Impeachment.

Section 3. (1) The Senate of the United States shall be composed of two Senators from each State, [chosen by the Legislature][3] thereof, for six Years; and each Senator shall have one Vote.

(2) Immediately after they shall be assembled in Consequence of the first Election, they shall be divided as equally as may be into three Classes. The Seats of the Senators of the first Class shall be vacated at the Expiration of the second Year, of the second Class at the Expiration of the fourth Year, and of the third Class at the Expiration of the sixth Year, so that one-third may be chosen every second year; [and if Vacancies happen by Resignation, or otherwise, during the Recess of the Legislature of any State, the Executive thereof may make temporary Appointments until the next Meeting of the Legislature, which shall then fill such Vacancies].[4]

(3) No person shall be a Senator who shall not have attained to the Age of thirty Years, and been nine Years a Citizen of the United States, and who shall not, when elected, be an Inhabitant of that State for which he shall be chosen.

(4) The Vice President of the United States shall be President of the Senate, but shall have no Vote, unless they be equally divided.

(5) The Senate shall choose their other Officers, and also a President pro tempore, in the Absence of the Vice President, or when he shall exercise the Office of President of the United States.

(6) The Senate shall have the sole Power to try all Impeachments. When sitting for that Purpose, they shall be on Oath or Affirmation. When the President of the United States is tried, the Chief Justice shall preside: And no Person shall be convicted without the Concurrence of two thirds of the Members present.

(7) Judgment in Cases of Impeachment shall not extend further than to removal from Office, and disqualification to hold and enjoy any Office of honor, Trust or Profit under the United States: but the Party convicted shall nevertheless be liable and subject to Indictment, Trial, Judgment and Punishment according to Law.

Section 4. (1) The Times, Places and Manner of holding Elections for Senators and Representatives, shall be prescribed in each State by the Legisla-

[3]Repealed by the Seventeenth Amendment.
[4]Changed by the Seventeenth Amendment.

ture thereof; but the Congress may at any time by Law make or alter such Regulations, except as to the Places of choosing Senators.

(2) The Congress shall assemble at least once in every Year, and such Meeting shall [be on the first Monday in December,][5] unless they shall by Law appoint a different Day.

Section 5. (1) Each House shall be the Judge of the Elections, Returns and Qualifications of its own Members, and a Majority of each shall constitute a Quorum to do Business; but a smaller Number may adjourn from day to day, and may be authorized to compel the Attendance of absent Members, in such Manner, and under such Penalties as each House may provide.

(2) Each House may determine the Rules of its Proceedings, punish its Members for disorderly Behavior, and, with the Concurrence of two thirds, expel a Member.

(3) Each House shall keep a Journal of its Proceedings, and from time to time publish the same, excepting such Parts as may in their Judgment require Secrecy; and the Yeas and Nays of the Members of either House on any question shall, at the Desire of one fifth of those Present, be entered on the Journal.

(4) Neither House, during the Session of Congress, shall, without the Consent of the other, adjourn for more than three days, nor to any other Place than that in which the two Houses shall be sitting.

Section 6. (1) The Senators and Representatives shall receive a Compensation for their Services, to be ascertained by Law, and paid out of the Treasury of the United States. They shall in all Cases, except Treason, Felony and Breach of the Peace, be privileged from Arrest during their Attendance at the Session of their respective Houses, and in going to and returning from the same; and for any Speech or Debate in either House, they shall not be questioned in any other Place.

(2) No Senator or Representative shall, during the Time for which he was elected, be appointed to any civil Office under the Authority of the United States, which shall have been created, or the Emoluments whereof have been increased during such time; and no Person holding any Office under the United States, shall be a Member of either House during his Continuance in Office.

Section 7. (1) All Bills for raising Revenue shall originate in the House of Representatives; but the Senate may propose or concur with Amendments as on other Bills.

(2) Every Bill which shall have passed the House of Representatives and the Senate, shall, before it becomes a Law, be presented to the Pres-

[5]Changed by the Twentieth Amendment, Section 2.

ident of the United States; If he approve he shall sign it, but if not he shall return it, with his Objections to that House in which it shall have originated, who shall enter the Objections at large on their Journal, and proceed to reconsider it. If after such Reconsideration two thirds of that House shall agree to pass the Bill, it shall be sent, together with the Objections, to the other House, by which it shall likewise be reconsidered, and if approved by two thirds of that House, it shall become a Law. But in all such Cases the Votes of both Houses shall be determined by Yeas and Nays, and the Names of the Persons voting for and against the Bill shall be entered on the Journal of each House respectively. If any Bill shall not be returned by the President within ten Days (Sundays excepted) after it shall have been presented to him, the Same shall be a Law, in like Manner as if he had signed it, unless the Congress by their Adjournment prevent its Return, in which Case it shall not be a Law.

(3) Every Order, Resolution, or Vote to which the Concurrence of the Senate and House of Representatives may be necessary (except on a question of Adjournment) shall be presented to the President of the United States; and before the Same shall take Effect, shall be approved by him, or being disapproved by him, shall be repassed by two thirds of the Senate and House of Representatives, according to the Rules and Limitations prescribed in the Case of a Bill.

Section 8. (1) The Congress shall have Power To lay and collect Taxes, Duties, Imposts and Excises, to pay the Debts and provide for the common Defense and general Welfare of the United States; but all Duties, Imposts and Excises shall be uniform throughout the United States;

(2) To borrow money on the credit of the United States;

(3) To regulate Commerce with foreign Nations, and among the several States, and with the Indian Tribes;

(4) To establish an uniform Rule of Naturalization, and uniform Laws on the subject of Bankruptcies throughout the United States;

(5) To coin Money, regulate the Value thereof, and of foreign Coin, and fix the Standard of Weights and Measures;

(6) To provide for the Punishment of counterfeiting the Securities and current Coin of the United States;

(7) To establish Post Offices and post Roads;

(8) To promote the Progress of Science and useful Arts, by securing for limited Times to Authors and Inventors the exclusive Right to their respective Writings and Discoveries;

(9) To constitute Tribunals inferior to the supreme Court;

(10) To define and punish Piracies and Felonies committed on the high Seas, and Offenses against the Law of Nations;

(11) To declare War, grant Letters of Marque and Reprisal, and make Rules concerning Captures on Land and Water;

(12) To raise and support Armies, but no Appropriation of Money to that Use shall be for a longer Term than two Years;

(13) To provide and maintain a Navy;

(14) To make Rules for the Government and Regulation of the land and naval Forces;

(15) To provide for calling forth the Militia to execute the Laws of the Union, suppress Insurrections and repel Invasions;

(16) To provide for organizing, arming, and disciplining the Militia, and for governing such Part of them as may be employed in the Service of the United States, reserving to the States respectively, the Appointment of the Officers, and the Authority of training the Militia according to the discipline prescribed by Congress;

(17) To exercise exclusive Legislation in all Cases whatsoever, over such District (not exceeding ten Miles square) as may, by Cession of particular States, and the Acceptance of Congress, become the Seat of the Government of the United States, and to exercise like Authority over all Places purchased by the Consent of the Legislature of the State in which the Same shall be, for the Erection of Forts, Magazines, Arsenals, dock-Yards, and other needful Buildings;—And

(18) To make all Laws which shall be necessary and proper for carrying into Execution the foregoing Powers, and all other Powers vested by this Constitution in the Government of the United States, or in any Department or Officer thereof.

Section 9. (1) The Migration or Importation of such Persons as any of the States now existing shall think proper to admit, shall not be prohibited by the Congress prior to the Year one thousand eight hundred and eight, but a tax or duty may be imposed on such Importation, not exceeding ten dollars for each Person.

(2) The Privilege of the Writ of Habeas Corpus shall not be suspended, unless when in Cases of Rebellion or Invasion the public Safety may require it.

(3) No Bill of Attainder or ex post facto Law shall be passed.

(4) No Capitation, or other direct, Tax shall be laid, unless in Proportion to the Census or Enumeration herein before directed to be taken.[6]

(5) No Tax or Duty shall be laid on Articles exported from any State.

(6) No Preference shall be given by any Regulation of Commerce or Revenue to the Ports of one State over those of another; nor shall Vessels bound to, or from, one State, be obliged to enter, clear, or pay Duties in another.

[6]Changed by the Sixteenth Amendment.

(7) No Money shall be drawn from the Treasury, but in Consequence of Appropriations made by Law; and a regular Statement and Account of the Receipts and Expenditures of all public Money shall be published from time to time.

(8) No Title of Nobility shall be granted by the United States: And no Person holding any Office of Profit or Trust under them, shall, without the Consent of the Congress, accept of any present, Emolument, Office, or Title, of any kind whatever, from any King, Prince, or foreign State.

Section 10. (1) No State shall enter into any Treaty, Alliance, or Confederation; grant Letters of Marque and Reprisal; coin Money; emit Bills of Credit; make any Thing but gold and silver Coin a Tender in Payment of Debts; pass any Bill of Attainder, ex post facto Law, or Law impairing the Obligation of Contracts, or grant any Title of Nobility.

(2) No State shall, without the Consent of the Congress, lay any Imposts or Duties on Imports or Exports, except what may be absolutely necessary for executing its inspection Laws: and the net Produce of all Duties and Imposts, laid by any State on Imports or Exports, shall be for the Use of the Treasury of the United States; and all such laws shall be subject to the Revision and Control of the Congress.

(3) No State shall, without the Consent of Congress, lay any duty of Tonnage, keep Troops, or Ships of War in time of Peace, enter into any Agreement or Compact with another State, or with a foreign Power, or engage in War, unless actually invaded, or in such imminent Danger as will not admit of delay.

ARTICLE II

Section 1. (1) The executive Power shall be vested in a President of the United States of America. He shall hold his Office during the Term of four Years, and, together with the Vice-President, chosen for the same Term, be elected, as follows:

(2) Each State shall appoint, in such Manner as the Legislature thereof may direct, a Number of Electors, equal to the whole Number of Senators and Representatives to which the State may be entitled in the Congress; but no Senator or Representative, or Person holding an Office of Trust or Profit under the United States, shall be appointed an Elector.

[The Electors shall meet in their respective States, and vote by Ballot for two persons, of whom one at least shall not be an Inhabitant of the same State with themselves. And they shall make a List of all the Persons voted for, and of the Number of Votes for each; which List they shall sign and certify, and transmit sealed to the Seat of the Government of the United States, directed to the President of the Senate. The President of the Senate shall, in the Presence of the Senate and House of Representatives, open all the Certificates, and the Votes shall then be counted. The Person having the greatest Number of Votes shall be the President, if such Number be a Majority of the whole Number of Electors appointed; and if there be more than one who have such Majority, and have an equal Number of Votes, then the House of Representatives shall immediately choose by Ballot one of them for President; and if no Person have a Majority, then from the five highest on the List the said House shall in like Manner choose the President. But in choosing the President, the Votes shall be taken by States, the Representation from each State having one Vote; A quorum for this purpose shall consist of a Member or Members from two-thirds of the States, and a Majority of all the States shall be necessary to a Choice. In every Case, after the Choice of the President, the Person having the greatest Number of Votes of the Electors shall be the Vice-President. But if there should remain two or more who have equal Votes, the Senate shall choose from them by Ballot the Vice-President.][7]

(3) The Congress may determine the Time of choosing the Electors, and the Day on which they shall give their Votes; which Day shall be the same throughout the United States.

(4) No person except a natural born Citizen, or a Citizen of the United States, at the time of the Adoption of this Constitution, shall be eligible to the Office of President; neither shall any Person be eligible to that Office who shall not have attained to the Age of thirty-five Years, and been fourteen Years a Resident within the United States.

(5) In case of the Removal of the President from Office, or of his Death, Resignation, or Inability to discharge the Powers and Duties of the said Office, the same shall devolve on the Vice-President, and the Congress may by Law provide for the Case of Removal, Death, Resignation or Inability, both of the President and Vice-President, declaring what Officer shall then act as President, and such Officer shall act accordingly, until the Disability be removed, or a President shall be elected.[8]

(6) The President shall, at stated Times, receive for his Services, a Compensation, which shall neither be increased nor diminished during the Period for which he shall have been elected, and he shall not receive within that Period any other Emolument from the United States, or any of them.

(7) Before he enter on the Execution of his Office, he shall take the following Oath or Affirmation:—"I do solemnly swear (or affirm) that I will

[7]This paragraph was superseded in 1804 by the Twelfth Amendment.
[8]Changed by the Twenty-fifth Amendment.

faithfully execute the Office of President of the United States, and will to the best of my Ability, preserve, protect and defend the Constitution of the United States."

Section 2. (1) The President shall be Commander in Chief of the Army and Navy of the United States, and of the Militia of the several States, when called into the actual Service of the United States; he may require the Opinion in writing, of the principal Officer in each of the executive Departments, upon any subject relating to the Duties of their respective Offices, and he shall have Power to Grant Reprieves and Pardons for Offenses against the United States, except in Cases of Impeachment.

(2) He shall have Power, by and with the Advice and Consent of the Senate, to make Treaties, provided two-thirds of the Senators present concur; and he shall nominate, and by and with the Advice and Consent of the Senate, shall appoint Ambassadors, other public Ministers and Consuls, Judges of the supreme Court, and all other Officers of the United States, whose Appointments are not herein otherwise provided for, and which shall be established by Law: but the Congress may by Law vest the Appointment of such inferior Officers, as they think proper, in the President alone, in the Court of Law, or in the Heads of Departments.

(3) The President shall have Power to fill up all Vacancies that may happen during the Recess of the Senate, by granting Commissions which shall expire at the End of their next Session.

Section 3. He shall from time to time give to the Congress Information of the State of the Union, and recommend to their Consideration such Measures as he shall judge necessary and expedient; he may, on extraordinary Occasions, convene both Houses, or either of them, and in Case of Disagreement between them, with Respect to the Time of Adjournment, he may adjourn them to such Time as he shall think proper; he shall receive Ambassadors and other public Ministers; he shall take Care that the Laws be faithfully executed, and shall Commission all the Officers of the United States.

Section 4. The President, Vice President and all civil Officers of the United States, shall be removed from Office on Impeachment for, and Conviction of, Treason, Bribery, or other high Crimes and Misdemeanors.

ARTICLE III

Section 1. The judicial Power of the United States, shall be vested in one supreme Court, and in such inferior Courts as the Congress may from time to time ordain and establish. The Judges, both of the supreme and inferior Courts, shall hold their Offices during good Behavior, and shall, at stated Times, receive for their Services a Compensation which shall not be diminished during their Continuance in Office.

Section 2. (1) The judicial Power shall extend to all Cases, in Law and Equity, arising under this Constitution, the Laws of the United States, and Treaties made, or which shall be made, under their Authority;—to all Cases affecting Ambassadors, other public Ministers and Consuls;—to all Cases of admiralty and maritime Jurisdiction;—to Controversies to which the United States shall be a Party;—to Controversies between two or more states;—[between a State and Citizens of another State];[9]—between Citizens of different States;—between Citizens of the same State claiming Lands under Grants of different States, and [between a State, or the Citizens thereof, and foreign States, Citizens or Subjects].[10]

(2) In all Cases affecting Ambassadors, other public Ministers and Consuls, and those in which a State shall be Party, the supreme Court shall have original Jurisdiction. In all the other Cases before mentioned, the supreme Court shall have appellate Jurisdiction, both as to Law and Fact, with such Exceptions, and under such Regulations as the Congress shall make.

(3) The trial of all Crimes, except in Cases of Impeachment, shall be by Jury; and such Trial shall be held in the State where the said Crimes shall have been committed: but when not committed within any State, the Trial shall be at such Place or Places as the Congress may by Law have directed.

Section 3. (1) Treason against the United States, shall consist only in levying War against them, or in adhering to their Enemies, giving them Aid and Comfort. No Person shall be convicted of Treason unless on the Testimony of two Witnesses to the same overt Act, or on Confession in open Court.

(2) The Congress shall have Power to declare the Punishment of Treason, but no Attainder of Treason shall work Corruption of Blood, or Forfeiture except during the Life of the Person attained.

ARTICLE IV

Section 1. Full Faith and Credit shall be given in each State to the public Acts, Records, and judicial Proceedings of every other State. And the Congress may by general Laws prescribe the Manner in which such Acts, Records and Proceedings shall be proved, and the Effect thereof.

---

[9]Restricted by the Eleventh Amendment.
[10]Restricted by the Eleventh Amendment.

Section 2. (1) The Citizens of each State shall be entitled to all Privileges and Immunities of Citizens in the several States.

(2) A Person charged in any State with Treason, Felony, or other Crime, who shall flee from Justice, and be found in another State, shall on demand of the executive Authority of the State from which he fled, be delivered up, to be removed to the State having Jurisdiction of the Crime.

(3) [No Person held to Service or Labor in one State, under the Laws thereof, escaping into another, shall, in Consequence of any Law or Regulation therein, be discharged from such Service or Labor, but shall be delivered up on Claim of the Party to whom such Service or Labor may be due.][11]

Section 3. (1) New States may be admitted by the Congress into this Union; but no new State shall be formed or erected within the Jurisdiction of any other State; nor any State be formed by the Junction of two or more States, or Parts of States, without the Consent of the Legislatures of the States concerned as well as of the Congress.

(2) The Congress shall have Power to dispose of and make all needful Rules and Regulations respecting the Territory or other Property belonging to the United States; and nothing in this Constitution shall be so construed as to Prejudice any Claims of the United States, or of any particular State.

Section 4. The United States shall guarantee to every State in this Union a Republican Form of Government, and shall protect each of them against Invasion; and on Application of the Legislature, or of the Executive (when the Legislature cannot be convened) against domestic Violence.

ARTICLE V

The Congress, whenever two-thirds of both Houses shall deem it necessary, shall propose Amendments to this Constitution, or, on the Application of the Legislatures of two-thirds of the several States, shall call a Convention for proposing Amendments, which, in either Case, shall be valid to all Intents and Purposes, as part of this Constitution, when ratified by the Legislature of three-fourths of the several States, or by Conventions in three-fourths thereof, as the one or the other Mode of Ratification may be proposed by the Congress; Provided that no Amendment which may be made prior to the Year One thousand eight hundred and eight shall in any Manner affect the first and fourth Clauses in the Ninth Section of the first Article; and that no State, without its Consent, shall be deprived of its equal Suffrage in the Senate.

[11]This paragraph was superseded by the Thirteenth Amendment.

ARTICLE VI

(1) All Debts contracted and Engagements entered into, before the Adoption of this Constitution, shall be as valid against the United States under this Constitution, as under the Confederation.

(2) This Constitution, and the Laws of the United States which shall be made in Pursuance thereof; and all Treaties made, or which shall be made, under the Authority of the United States, shall be the supreme Law of the Land; and the Judges in every State shall be bound thereby, any Thing in the Constitution or Laws of any State to the Contrary notwithstanding.

(3) The Senators and Representatives before mentioned, and the Members of the several State Legislatures, and all executive and judicial Officers, both of the United States and of the several States, shall be bound by Oath or Affirmation, to support this Constitution; but no religious Test shall ever be required as a Qualification to any Office or public Trust under the United States.

ARTICLE VII

The Ratification of the Conventions of nine States, shall be sufficient for the Establishment of this Constitution between the States so ratifying the Same.

DONE in Convention by the Unanimous Consent of the States present the Seventeenth Day of September in the Year of our Lord one thousand seven hundred and Eighty seven and the Independence of the United States of America the Twelfth. In Witness whereof We have hereunto subscribed our Names.

Go. WASHINGTON
President and deputy from Virginia

ARTICLES IN ADDITION TO, AND AMENDMENT OF, THE CONSTITUTION OF THE UNITED STATES OF AMERICA, PROPOSED BY CONGRESS, AND RATIFIED BY THE LEGISLATURES OF THE SEVERAL STATES, PURSUANT TO THE FIFTH ARTICLE OF THE ORIGINAL CONSTITUTION.

AMENDMENT I[12]

Congress shall make no law respecting an establishment of religion, or prohibiting the free exercise thereof; or abridging the freedom of speech, or of the press; or the right of the people peaceably to assemble, and to petition the Government for a redress of grievances.

[12] The first ten amendments were adopted in 1791.

AMENDMENT II

A well regulated Militia, being necessary to the security of a free State, the right of the people to keep and bear Arms, shall not be infringed.

AMENDMENT III

No Soldier shall, in time of peace be quartered in any house, without the consent of the Owner, nor in time of war, but in a manner to be prescribed by law.

AMENDMENT IV

The right of the people to be secure in their persons, houses, papers, and effects, against unreasonable searches and seizures, shall not be violated, and no Warrants shall issue, but upon probable cause, supported by Oath or affirmation, and particularly describing the place to be searched, and the persons or things to be seized.

AMENDMENT V

No person shall be held to answer for a capital, or otherwise infamous crime, unless on a presentment or indictment of a Grand Jury, except in cases arising in the land or naval forces, or in the Militia, when in actual service in time of War or public danger; nor shall any person be subject for the same offense to be twice put in jeopardy of life or limb; nor shall be compelled in any criminal case to be witness against himself, nor be deprived of life, liberty, or property, without due process of law; nor shall private property be taken for public use without just compensation.

AMENDMENT VI

In all criminal prosecutions, the accused shall enjoy the right to a speedy and public trial, by an impartial jury of the State and district wherein the crime shall have been committed, which district shall have been previously ascertained by law, and to be informed of the nature and cause of the accusation, to be confronted with the witnesses against him; to have compulsory process for obtaining witnesses in his favor, and to have the Assistance of Counsel for his defense.

AMENDMENT VII

In Suits at common law, where the value in controversy shall exceed twenty dollars, the right of trial by jury shall be preserved, and no fact tried by a jury, shall be otherwise reexamined in any Court of the United States, than according to the rules of the common law.

AMENDMENT VIII

Excessive bail shall not be required, nor excessive fines imposed, nor cruel and unusual punishments inflicted.

AMENDMENT IX

The enumeration in the Constitution, of certain rights, shall not be construed to deny or disparage others retained by the people.

AMENDMENT X

The powers not delegated to the United States by the Constitution, nor prohibited by it to the States, are reserved to the States respectively, or to the people.

AMENDMENT XI[13]

The Judicial power of the United States shall not be construed to extend to any suit in law or equity, commenced or prosecuted against one of the United States by Citizens of another State, or by Citizens or Subjects of any Foreign State.

AMENDMENT XII[14]

The Electors shall meet in their respective states and vote by ballot for President and Vice-President, one of whom, at least, shall not be an inhabitant of the same state with themselves; they shall name in their ballots the person voted for as President, and in distinct ballots the person voted for as

[13]Adopted in 1798.
[14]Adopted in 1804.

Vice-President, and they shall make distinct lists of all persons voted for as President, and of all persons voted for as Vice-President, and of the number of votes for each, which lists they shall sign and certify, and transmit sealed to the seat of the government of the United States, directed to the President of the Senate;—The President of the Senate shall, in presence of the Senate and House of Representatives, open all the certificates and the votes shall then be counted;—The person having the greatest number of votes for President, shall be the President, if such number be a majority of the whole number of Electors appointed; and if no person have such majority, then from the persons having the highest numbers not exceeding three on the list of those voted for as President, the House of Representatives shall choose immediately, by ballot, the President. But in choosing the President, the votes shall be taken by states, the representation from each state having one vote; a quorum for this purpose shall consist of a member or members from two-thirds of the states, and a majority of all the states shall be necessary to a choice. [And if the House of Representatives shall not choose a President whenever the right of choice shall devolve upon them, before the fourth day of March next following, then the Vice-President shall act as President, as in the case of the death or other constitutional disability of the President.][15]— The person having the greatest number of votes as Vice-President, shall be the Vice-President, if such number be a majority of the whole number of Electors appointed, and if no person have a majority, then from the two highest numbers on the list, the Senate shall choose the Vice-President; a quorum for the purpose shall consist of two-thirds of the whole number of Senators, and a majority of the whole number shall be necessary to a choice. But no person constitutionally ineligible to the office of President shall be eligible to that of Vice-President of the United States.

AMENDMENT XIII[16]

Section 1. Neither slavery nor involuntary servitude, except as a punishment for crime whereof the party shall have been duly convicted, shall exist within the United States, or any place subject to their jurisdiction.

Section 2. Congress shall have power to enforce this article by appropriate legislation.

[15]Superseded by the Twentieth Amendment, Section 3.
[16]Adopted in 1865.

AMENDMENT XIV[17]

Section 1. All persons born or naturalized in the United States, and subject to the jurisdiction thereof, are citizens of the United States and of the State wherein they reside. No state shall make or enforce any law which shall abridge the privileges or immunities of citizens of the United States; nor shall any State deprive any person of life, liberty, or property, without due process of law; nor deny to any person within its jurisdiction the equal protection of the laws.

Section 2. Representatives shall be apportioned among the several States according to their respective numbers, counting the whole number of persons in each State, excluding Indians not taxed. But when the right to vote at any election for the choice of electors for President and Vice-President of the United States, Representatives in Congress, the Executive and Judicial officers of a State, or the members of the Legislature thereof, is denied to any of the male inhabitants of such State, being twenty-one years of age, and citizens of the United States, or in any way abridged, except for participation in rebellion, or other crime, the basis of representation therein shall be reduced in the proportion which the number of such male citizens shall bear to the whole number of male citizens twenty-one years of age in such State.

Section 3. No person shall be a Senator or Representative in Congress, or elector of President and Vice-President, or hold any office, civil or military, under the United States, or under any State, who, having previously taken an oath, as a member of Congress, or as an officer of the United States, or as a member of any State legislature, or as an executive or judicial officer of any State, to support the Constitution of the United States, shall have engaged in insurrection or rebellion against the same, or given aid or comfort to the enemies thereof. But Congress may by a vote of two-thirds of each House, remove such disability.

Section 4. The validity of the public debt of the United States, authorized by law, including debts incurred for payment of pensions and bounties for services in suppressing insurrection or rebellion, shall not be questioned. But neither the United States nor any State shall assume or pay any debt or obligation incurred in aid of insurrection or rebellion against the United States, or any claim for the loss or emancipation of any slave; but all such debts, obligations and claims shall be held illegal and void.

[17]Adopted in 1868.

Section 5. The Congress shall have power to enforce, by appropriate legislation, the provisions of this article.

AMENDMENT XV[18]

Section 1. The right of citizens of the United States to vote shall not be denied or abridged by the United States or by any State on account of race, color, or previous condition of servitude.

Section 2. The Congress shall have power to enforce this article by appropriate legislation.

AMENDMENT XVI[19]

The Congress shall have power to lay and collect taxes on incomes, from whatever source derived, without apportionment among the several States, and without regard to any census or enumeration.

AMENDMENT XVII[20]

The Senate of the United States shall be composed of two Senators from each State, elected by the people thereof, for six years; and each Senator shall have one vote. The electors in each State shall have the qualifications requisite for electors of the most numerous branch of the State legislatures.

When vacancies happen in the representation of any State in the Senate, the executive authority of such State shall issue writs of election to fill such vacancies: *Provided,* That the legislature of any State may empower the executive thereof to make temporary appointments until the people fill the vacancies by election as the legislature may direct.

This amendment shall not be so construed as to affect the election or term of any Senator chosen before it becomes valid as part of the Constitution.

AMENDMENT XVIII[21]

Section 1. After one year from the ratification of this article the manufacture, sale, or transportation of intoxicating liquors within, the importation

[18]Adopted in 1870.
[19]Adopted in 1913.
[20]Adopted in 1913.
[21]Adopted in 1919. Repealed by Section 1 of the Twenty-first Amendment.

thereof into, or the exportation thereof from the United States and all territory subject to the jurisdiction thereof for beverage purposes is hereby prohibited.

Section 2. The Congress and the several States shall have concurrent power to enforce this article by appropriate legislation.

Section 3. This article shall be inoperative unless it shall have been ratified as an amendment to the Constitution by the legislatures of the several States, as provided in the Constitution, within seven years from the date of the submission hereof to the States by the Congress.

AMENDMENT XIX[22]

The right of citizens of the United States to vote shall not be denied or abridged by the United States or by any State on account of sex.

Congress shall have power to enforce this article by appropriate legislation.

AMENDMENT XX[23]

Section 1. The terms of the President and Vice-President shall end at noon on the 20th day of January, and the terms of Senators and Representatives at noon on the 3rd day of January, of the years in which such terms would have ended if this article had not been ratified; and the terms of their successors shall then begin.

Section 2. The Congress shall assemble at least once in every year, and such meeting shall begin at noon on the 3rd day of January, unless they shall by law appoint a different day.

Section 3. If, at the time fixed for the beginning of the term of the President, the President elect shall have died, the Vice-President elect shall become President. If a President shall not have been chosen before the time fixed for the beginning of his term, or if the President elect shall have failed to qualify, then the Vice-President elect shall act as President until a President shall have qualified; and the Congress may by law provide for the case wherein neither a President elect nor a Vice-President elect shall have quali-

[22]Adopted in 1920.
[23]Adopted in 1933.

fied, declaring who shall then act as President, or the manner in which one who is to act shall be selected, and such person shall act accordingly until a President or Vice-President shall have qualified.

Section 4. The Congress may by law provide for the case of the death of any of the persons from whom the House of Representatives may choose a President whenever the right of choice shall have devolved upon them, and for the case of the death of any of the persons from whom the Senate may choose a Vice-President whenever the right of choice shall have devolved upon them.

Section 5. Sections 1 and 2 shall take effect on the 15th day of October following the ratification of this article.

Section 6. This article shall be inoperative unless it shall have been ratified as an amendment to the Constitution by the legislatures of three-fourths of the several States within seven years from the date of its submission.

AMENDMENT XXI[24]

Section 1. The eighteenth article of amendment to the Constitution of the United States is hereby repealed.

Section 2. The transportation or importation into any State, Territory, or possession of the United States for delivery or use therein of intoxicating liquors, in violation of the laws thereof, is hereby prohibited.

Section 3. This article shall be inoperative unless it shall have been ratified as an amendment to the Constitution by conventions in the several States, as provided in the Constitution, within seven years from the date of the submission hereof to the States by the Congress.

AMENDMENT XXII[25]

Section 1. No person shall be elected to the office of the President more than twice, and no person who has held the office of President, or acted as President, for more than two years of a term to which some other person was elected President shall be elected to the office of the President more than once. But this Article shall not apply to any person holding the of-

---

[24]Adopted in 1933.
[25]Adopted in 1951.

fice of President when this Article was proposed by the Congress, and shall not prevent any person who may be holding the office of President, or acting as President, during the term within which this Article becomes operative from holding the office of President or acting as President during the remainder of such term.

Section 2. This article shall be inoperative unless it shall have been ratified as an amendment to the Constitution by the legislatures of three-fourths of the several States within seven years from the date of its submission to the States by the Congress.

AMENDMENT XXIII[26]

Section 1. The District constituting the seat of Government of the United States shall appoint in such manner as the Congress may direct:

A number of electors of President and Vice-President equal to the whole number of Senators and Representatives in Congress to which the District would be entitled if it were a State, but in no event more than the least populous State; they shall be in addition to those appointed by the States, but they shall be considered, for the purposes of the election of President and Vice-President, to be electors appointed by a State, and they shall meet in the District and perform such duties as provided by the twelfth article of amendment.

Section 2. The Congress shall have power to enforce this article by appropriate legislation.

AMENDMENT XXIV[27]

Section 1. The right of citizens of the United States to vote in any primary or other election for President or Vice-President, for electors for President or Vice-President, or for Senator or Representative in Congress, shall not be denied or abridged by the United States or any state by reasons of failure to pay any poll tax or other tax.

Section 2. The Congress shall have power to enforce this article by appropriate legislation.

[26]Adopted in 1961.
[27]Adopted in 1964.

AMENDMENT XXV[28]

Section 1. In case of the removal of the President from office or of his death or resignation, the Vice-President shall become President.

Section 2. Whenever there is a vacancy in the office of the Vice-President, the President shall nominate a Vice-President who shall take office upon confirmation by a majority vote of both Houses of Congress.

Section 3. Whenever the President transmits to the President pro tempore of the Senate and the Speaker of the House of Representatives his written declaration that he is unable to discharge the powers and duties of his office, and until he transmits to them a written declaration to the contrary, such powers and duties shall be discharged by the Vice-President as Acting President.

Section 4. Whenever the Vice-President and a majority of either the principal officers of the Executive departments or of such other body as Congress may by law provide, transmit to the President pro tempore of the Senate and the Speaker of the House of Representatives their written declaration that the President is unable to discharge the powers and duties of his office, The Vice-President shall immediately assume the powers and duties of the office as Acting President.

Thereafter, when the President transmits to the President pro tempore of the Senate and the Speaker of the House of Representatives his written declaration that no inability exists, he shall resume the powers and duties of his office unless the Vice-President and a majority of either the principal officers of the executive departments or of such other body as Congress may by law provide, transmit within four days to the President pro tempore of the Senate and the Speaker of the House of Representatives their written declaration that the President is unable to discharge the powers and duties of his office. Thereupon Congress shall decide the issue, assembling within forty-eight hours for that purpose if not in session. If the Congress, within twenty-one days after receipt of the latter written declaration, or, if Congress is not in session, within twenty-one days after Congress is required to assemble, determines by two-thirds vote of both houses that the President is unable to discharge the powers and duties of his office, the Vice-President shall continue to discharge the same as Acting President; otherwise, the President shall resume the powers and duties of his office.

[28]Adopted in 1967.

AMENDMENT XXVI[29]

Section 1. The right of citizens of the United States, who are 18 years of age or older, to vote shall not be denied or abridged by the United States or any state on account of age.

Section 2. The Congress shall have power to enforce this article by appropriate legislation.

AMENDMENT XXVII[30]

Article the Second . . . No law, varying the compensation for the services of the Senators and Representatives, shall take effect, until an election of Representatives shall have intervened.

[29]Adopted in 1971.
[30]See "The Long and Winding Road of the Twenty-seventh Amendment," p. 42.

INDEX